Extraordinary Ornamental Edibles

MIKE LASCELLE

Extraordinary Ornamental Edibles

100 Perennials, Trees, Shrubs and Vines for Canadian Gardens

Douglas & McIntyre

1 2 3 4 5 — 22 21 20 19 18

Douglas and McIntyre (2013) Ltd.
P.O. Box 219, Madeira Park, BC, V0N 2H0
www.douglas-mcintyre.com

All cover and interior photos by Mike Lascelle except where otherwise noted

Edited by Carol Pope
Indexed by Emma Skagen
Text and cover design by Diane Robertson
Printed and bound in China

Douglas and McIntyre (2013) Ltd. acknowledges the support of the Canada Council for the Arts, which last year invested $153 million to bring the arts to Canadians throughout the country. We also gratefully acknowledge financial support from the Government of Canada and from the Province of British Columbia through the BC Arts Council and the Book Publishing Tax Credit.

Canada

Canada Council for the Arts · Conseil des Arts du Canada

British Columbia Arts Council
An agency of the Province of British Columbia

For my daughters—
Nicole, Rochelle and
Madeleine—in hopes
that one day they
better understand
what makes the
"old man" tick.

PAGES II–III: Ripening lemon fruits. *Photo © Maksim Shebeko / Adobe Stock*

OPPOSITE, LEFT TO RIGHT. TOP ROW: 'Romeo' dwarf sour cherry tree; salad burnet. MIDDLE: 'Albion' strawberries. BOTTOM ROW: English daisy; 'Variegated Pink' lemon.

THIS PAGE, LEFT TO RIGHT. TOP ROW: Maturing apple; 'Whitney' crabapples. MIDDLE: Training hops; Nicole, Rochelle and Madeleine; oso berries. BOTTOM ROW: Strawberry spinach; 'Frisia' black locust.

Table of Contents

Meet the Plants • (continued)

PAGE VI, CLOCKWISE FROM TOP LEFT: 'Fall Gold' raspberries; Saskatoon berries; lilac flower syrup; electric daisy flowers; fruit salad featuring fish mint.

Acknowledgements

THE PEOPLE BEHIND THE PLANTS

Far too often, it is the talking heads of horticulture (like me) that get all the credit for new plant introductions, while the individuals who really deserve this praise and our gratitude remain in obscurity . . . people like Doug De Jong, who spent years evaluating columnar apple seedlings, and John Schroeder, who invests heavily in new edibles, and Ray Mattei of Tropic to Tropic Plants, who promotes rare fruit trees. This point really came into sharp focus as I was researching this book, running to nurseries and demonstration gardens to interview the people who know their edible plants from years of growing experience. *Extraordinary Ornamental Edibles* is a reflection of their hard work and the often-dogged persistence that goes into any success story—such as George Petkov's acres of kiwi in Abbotsford or Bob Duncan's fruiting citrus on Vancouver Island.

I would also like to thank the people who have provided me with quality fruit trees and berries for the past 20 years, including Misty Meadow Nursery, Kato's Nursery, Van Noort Bulb Co., Cannor Nurseries, Valleybrook Gardens, Linnaea Nurseries, Dasmesh Nursery, TG Nursery and Sons, JRT Nurseries, Erica Enterprises, KS Nurseries, Maple Leaf Nursery and, last but not least, Amsterdam Greenhouses & Garden Centre, who has allowed me to purchase these plants on their behalf.

Then there are those who helped out with photography, including Klaus and Betty von Hardenberg, Bob and Verna Duncan of Fruit Trees and More, Michael Bostock, Zdena Novy of Novi Organics, Jim and Mary Ann Rahe of Annie's Orchard, Specimen Trees, Hawaiian Botanicals, Sonja and Raymond Barker of the Silverhill Apple Orchard, Heimat Farm, Ken and Elke Knechtel of Red Barn Plants and Produce, and Pierre Piroche of Piroche Plants. A special thank you goes to Peter Janes and

OPPOSITE, CLOCKWISE FROM TOP LEFT: Espalier 'Rainier' cherries; secateurs; 'Golden Prolific' nectarine tree in container; wisteria spring rolls; goji berries.

A selection of edible flowers.

Magdalene Joly of Tree Eater Nursery, who shared their images and provided valuable insight on the rare shipova.

Credit should also go to Carol Pope and Douglas & McIntyre for having the vision to print this guide to edible ornamental plants for gardeners across Canada.

Finally, I would like to acknowledge my wife of 35 years, Pauline, for putting up with me and becoming a book widow while I stole the time to research and write this tome.

Foreword

Did you know there are 100 extraordinary perennial plants, trees, shrubs and vines that look great year after year in front or back yards and patio containers while filling your kitchen with exciting new flavours?

With this ground-breaking new book by Mike Lascelle, garden pioneers across Canada can plant gorgeous, long-lasting landscapes loaded with food—from sumptuous seasonings to fruits, drupes, hips and berries, edible leaves, fronds, pads, pods, shoots, stems, cones, buds and flowers, *and* tasty seeds, nuts, tubers, roots and rhizomes! There is no need to replant every year, as these permanent plantings deliver the goods again and again with every harvest season.

As an innovative nursery manager in constant pursuit of new ideas for reliable edibles to grow in Canadian gardens, Lascelle—the highly respected author of several plant and landscaping books and a long-time horticultural columnist, certified arborist, estate gardener and landscape designer who has lived and worked across the country—brings decades of hands-on grow-your-own know-how to his newest book.

Along with plant-specific landscaping expertise, Lascelle includes tips on hardiness, plant type, size, bloom, and what is required for successful pollination, pruning and irrigation. Plus, most importantly, what to pick *and when*—with simple and delicious suggestions for how to best enjoy the many exciting foods and flavours gathered from your own ornamental garden.

Imagine an exotic akebia or "chocolate vine" twisting over your arbour with colossal clusters of purple-skinned seed pods full of translucent fruity pulp that tastes of lychee nuts. Or a compact evergreen yuzu tree yielding 100 to 200 yellow fruits fragrantly suggestive of lemon-lime and grapefruit. Or, perfect for a patio container, a sansho with peppery citrus leaves, flowers and berries that are wonderful in miso soup or a truly aromatic pesto.

Picture buckets of blossoms from your cold-hardy deciduous black locust, with hints of garden peas and honey, unforgettable when folded into crepes drizzled with homemade blackcurrant syrup. Or pungent fruit from the shipova, another cold-resistant stalwart, with the essence of European pear but more dense and chewy. Or a jujube with a date-like harvest with the zing of green apple.

LEFT: 'Dolgo' crabapple jelly. RIGHT: Cardoon in a mixed border

And, below these trees and shrubs, elegant ostrich ferns evocative of asparagus, rare herbs like fish mint, and bulb edibles such as saffron, with its three stigmas that were coveted by the ancient Greeks, Romans and Phoenicians. Or give a nod to Japanese cuisine with your own wasabi or zingiber, for a robust statement both in the garden and on your plate.

Over and above Lascelle's 100 selections for the top ornamental edibles to plant in Canadian gardens, you'll find sections on Growing Edibles (pollination to pests to propagation, simple pruning and planting in pots), Design Essentials (vines with food value, appetizing ornamental annual vegetables and flowers, edible native plants, crops with fall colour) and The Food Guide (weeds to eat, how to make green tea, summer cordials, fruit and herb syrups, sweet and savoury jellies, vinegars and tempura). And you might even learn that some of those ornamental plants already taking up space in your garden are actually edible!

Top that off with beautiful photos, specific plant recommendations for the best choices for many fruits and world crops, and a supportive glossary on everything from anthers to watersprouts, and *Extraordinary Ornamental Edibles—100 Perennials, Trees, Shrubs and Vines for Canadian Gardens* is the ultimate guide to growing beautiful food

Darwin's barberry fruit.

plants that just keep on giving. With this stunning and delicious selection of perennials, Lascelle shows gardeners of all experience levels that growing your own food is rewarding and fun, and with this book in hand, it can be easy and beautiful too.

Carol Pope
Associate Editor

Introduction

HERBAL FOR THE 21ST CENTURY

I have an original hand-painted leaf from a 1565 Bock herbal that sits framed on my desk. It serves two purposes—firstly, as a reminder that my profession is an old and venerable one; secondly, to provide myself with encouragement when I write about gardening. My reasoning is that if humanity chose plants as the focus of the very first books of civilization, this topic must have relevance to our modern world too. No matter how sophisticated society becomes, the need for air, water and food remains the same—and all three of these fundamentals rely on plants.

I come by my love of edible plants honestly, as my grandmother had a small orchard at her Okanagan home where I spent all my summer vacations. The rest of the time, I lived on rather mundane army bases from British Columbia to Ontario, moving every three years. Boredom drove me out into adjacent parks, forests and empty city lots, where I found plenty of wild berries or abandoned fruit trees to snack on—and, somewhere along the line, the makings of a gardener were instilled in me.

During my 35 years in horticulture, I have been a garden designer, landscape foreman and estate gardener, but it is my present position as a nursery manager that most allows me a unique perspective on the ever-expanding edible trend. Not only do I work with new immigrants to Canada who are asking for plants they grew and ate back home, but also with young families being forced into increasingly smaller accommodations, who are looking for edibles that can thrive in tiny spaces or containers. They are making the need for edibles with ornamental attributes even more essential.

I purchase my plants from highly competent wholesale growers, most of whom welcome my opinion regarding potential crops and the overall value of the plant in the garden. When these new introductions

OPPOSITE, CLOCKWISE FROM TOP LEFT: A kiwi orchard; 'Bluecrop' blueberries; ladybugs on echeveria; bumblebee on butterfly weed; nodding onion.

Von der kreutter Underscheid/

der hat diß Zapffenkraut in gleicher meinung inn seinem kreutter gespräch angezeiget/ ist sonst von keinem nie angezeiget/wa diß kraut inn Diosco.wachse/ Gott wölle fleissige Männer schicken/ das hierinn der gemein nutz auch gefürdert werde/Amen. Diß Zapffenkraut bringen die Landfahrer auß Ungerland/ohn wurtzel/vnd sagen das es inn hohen Wälden wachse. Das kraut hat runde stengel/wie die Weißwurtz/spannen lang/ zů beiden seitten mit jhren dicken blettern bekleidet/ Schweitzer grün/die vergleichen sich beynahe den Lorbeer blettern/seind aber zarter/ ein jedes blatt hat auß jm selbs noch ein kleines bletlein wachsen/ anzůsehen wie ein Zünglein oder wie ein angehenncktes zäpfflein/daher es seinen Namen bey vns Teutschen vberkommen hat. Zwische den blettern vnd stengeln hab ich rohte körner gesehen als Erweissen/vmb S. Johanns tag zů Straßburg bey einem Zanbrecher/der hat es auß Ungerland also grün bracht/ettlichs mit frucht/das ander ohn frucht/doch waren sie einander vast gleich.

Von den Namen.

HJE haben wir das sighafftig kreutlein Alexandri/darmit er sich in seinem sieg hat lassen krönen/wie Marcellus Vergilius schreibet/daher disem Zapffenkraut (dz man auch Hockenblat nennet) sein nam Laurus Alexandrina ist worden/wiewol diser nam dem Chamädaphne auch zůgelegt würt in Diosco. Sonst heißt das Zapffenkraut auch Idea Laurus/vom Berg Ida/da dessen vil wächßt. Diosco.lib. iiij.cap.cxlij.nennets fürter Danaen/ Hippoglotton/Hippoglossion/ vmb des Zäpffleins willen/vnd Zaliam/ Stephanen/ Daphnon/ Samothracicen/ vnd Methrion/zů Latin Uuularia. Von Theophrasto würt es Epiphyllocarpon genennet/ vmb der körner willen so vnder den bletteren wachsen/lib.iij.cap.xvij. Die andern namen Apuleij stehn droben im Yngrün gezeichnet/vnder welchen auch Victoria der nam stehet des Sigs halben. Inn Serapione heissets Gar Alexandrie/cap.cccxxiiij.

Von der Krafft vnd Würckung.

LEFT: A hand-painted leaf from a 1565 herbal by German botanist Hieronymus Bock. RIGHT: Pineberry, a strawberry hybrid.

finally reach market, I have hundreds of customers whose feedback further tells me how these edibles are faring in the real world.

What's been lacking is a simple comprehensive guide to edible ornamentals—a 21st-century herbal for modern gardeners who want to know the full range of unique and exciting options available to them. With 100 in-depth sections on the most noteworthy edible ornamental plants, along with hundreds more presented in detail and ranging in hardiness from zones 2 to 8, *Extraordinary Ornamental Edibles* is *the* reference Canadians have been waiting for.

Meet the Plants

The 100 plant-selection chapters that follow have been designed for quick reference and easy efficiency. But before you plunge into the world of edible ornamentals, I would like to give you some quick notes on the standardized sections.

SPECIES:

This is the current botanical name of the plant in question and the one you should use for positive identification prior to eating it. Where relevant and still in common use, synonyms or former botanical classifications are also noted.

A.K.A.:

Non-scientific nicknames, or common names, have been included—but keep in mind that the same common name can apply to different species, some of which may not be edible, and that the botanical name should always be your first place of reference.

PLANT TYPE:

Understanding the plant type, or whether it is a tree, vine, shrub or perennial, will help you to integrate it properly into your edible landscape.

ORIGINS:

Knowing where a plant originates can help determine its cultural needs—such as Mediterranean species generally requiring sharp drainage.

HARDINESS:

I have adopted a simplified USDA zone rating system over our newly upgraded Canadian zones, because the latter has not been widely adopted and is, in my opinion, still a work in progress. You will find a basic numeric 1 to 8 plant zone–tolerance rating, with zone 1 the most tolerant of cold weather (averaging down to −50F or −45.6C) and zone 8 the least (10 to 20F or −12.2 to −6.7C). Plants chosen should be suited for the lowest temperatures of the area where they are to be planted. By way of example, the zone rating of a sampling of Canadian cities is Vancouver—zone 8, Calgary—zone 3, Winnipeg—zone 3, Toronto—zone 6, Montreal—zone 5, and Fredericton—zone 4. To find your zone rating, go to www.planthardiness.gc.ca, click "Plant Hardiness Zone by Municipality" and reference the 1961–1990 column. Hardiness zones are often further divided into

Oca (*Oxalis tuberosa*) tubers.

"a" and "b" ratings, with "a" zones being an average of 5F colder than "b" zones. By way of example, zone 5a has an average minimum temperature of −15 to −20F (−26 to −29C) while 5b is −10 to −15F (−23 to −26C). Where plants are annuals (which complete their life cycle within a year) or frost-tender, this is also noted.

SUN:
A basic classification of full sun, part sun, partial shade (more shade than sun) or shade is given to help you orient your plants properly—keep in mind that this refers to conditions in the growing season, not those dark winter months.

'Red Malabar' climbing spinach.

WATER:
Moisture and drainage needs for the specified plant are included.

ULTIMATE SIZE:
Average mature height and spread are provided (given in both imperial and metric measurements); keep in mind that this will vary with location, rootstock and soil fertility.

BLOOM:
The time of year or specific month(s) of bloom are noted to help with seasonal colour design or facilitate cross-pollination where necessary.

POLLINATION:
Plants are classified as self-fertile (one plant can produce fruit), dioecious (separate male and female plants required) or as requiring cross-pollination (from a compatible variety that blooms at the same time).

PRUNING:
Pruning is complicated, and this simplified overview is only meant to give you a casual glimpse into how much maintenance this plant requires.

WHAT'S EDIBLE:
All the parts of the plant that are edible, along with any cautions about eating it.

HARVEST TIME:
The average season or month of harvest can vary somewhat with weather and location; however, this will give you a pretty good idea.

TASTES LIKE:
My best description, based on my palate, of how these new and ancient foods taste.

Wherever possible, each plant selection includes visuals showing the ornamental aspect (flowering, fall colour), along with the ripened fruit or edible portion. All the plant photos have been taken in Canadian gardens.

Along with sharing my personal experiences with each plant, and describing its edible uses and ornamental value, I provide you with the names of the most popular cultivars. In some cases, similar species may also be given. In many of these listings, I've also noted small-space options for containers and patio spaces, along with specific cultivars for other growing challenges found in gardens across this great country.

Note: The names written in small capital letters refer to proprietary plant cultivars.

Akebia

I'll be the first to admit akebia fruit is a rarity in the home garden, but the taste and appearance of this crop is so unusual that it merits attention. When you consider that the minuscule purple flowers (reputed to smell like chocolate, although I sense more of a subtle sweet vanilla) can morph into huge lobed fruits measuring up to 8 inches (20 cm) across, it is truly a wonder of nature. Then there's the weird factor. When ripe, the often-clustered purple-skinned seed pods split open to reveal a gelatinous sack of black seeds against sky-blue flesh—looking like nothing you have ever seen before in your garden!

The edible portion is the pulp surrounding the black seeds, which like decaisnea fruit (to which it is related) is jelly-like in texture and tastes like lychee nut. The empty outer shell of the pod (which is bitter) is traditionally stuffed with ground meat and deep-fried in Japan, where akebia fruit is grown commercially.

Akebia is semi-evergreen in mild climates and quite vigorous in growth habit, quickly twining over arbours and trellises. While it does not get as woody as wisteria or trumpet vine, you will need a strong structure to support the weight of the palmate-shaped foliage. While akebia prefers full sun, it tolerates partial shade, and will even grow in deep shade although it rarely blooms there.

Two varieties of akebia are needed in your garden for cross-pollination and fruit set, and there are a number of good choices: 'Alba' (white flowers), 'Variegata' (splashed cream variegation), 'Shirobana' (white blooms), 'Rosea' (rose-pink flowers) and 'Silver Bells' (white to pale pink blooms).

WHAT'S EDIBLE:
Pulp or jelly surrounding seeds

TASTES LIKE:
Lychee nut

HARVEST TIME:
Early to mid-autumn

OPPOSITE: 'Rosea' Akebia in bloom.
ABOVE: Mature akebia fruit.

SPECIES:
Akebia quinata

A.K.A.:
Chocolate vine, fiveleaf akebia

PLANT TYPE:
Semi-evergreen woody vine

ORIGINS:
China, Japan, Korea

HARDINESS:
USDA zone 5

SUN:
Part to full sun

WATER:
Consistent soil moisture with good drainage

ULTIMATE SIZE:
23–33 feet (7–10 m) tall

BLOOM:
Early to mid-spring

POLLINATION:
Cross-pollination required

PRUNING:
Prune to form after flowering

Amaranth

ABOVE: Love-lies-bleeding flowers.
OPPOSITE: Joseph's coat foliage.

SPECIES:
Amaranthus caudatus; A. cruentus; A. tricolor

A.K.A.:
Love-lies-bleeding (*Amaranthus caudatus*); prince's feather, tassel flower (*A. cruentus*); Joseph's coat (*A. tricolor*)

PLANT TYPE:
Annual

ORIGINS:
Tropical regions of North and South America

HARDINESS:
Self-seeding annuals

SUN:
Part to full sun

WATER:
Consistent soil moisture with good drainage

ULTIMATE SIZE:
Up to 4 feet (120 cm) tall for *Amaranthus caudatus*; 6 feet (180 cm) tall for *A. cruentus*; 3 feet (90 cm) tall for *A. tricolor*

BLOOM:
Summer to frost

POLLINATION:
Self-fertile

PRUNING:
Young plants can be pinched to produce denser growth

WHAT'S EDIBLE:
Leaves and seeds

TASTES LIKE:
Young leaves are citrusy, seeds are nutty

HARVEST TIME:
Young leaves any time, seeds (eaten as grain) from late summer to early fall

While these beautiful summer flowers have long held a place in our gardens, in other parts of the world, such as India or South America, amaranth is grown for the edible leaves and seeds. The ornamental forms, such as love-lies-bleeding, produce spectacular displays of pendulous crimson-purple flowers (or green in such cultivars as 'Viridis'). Displayed in dreadlock-like clusters throughout the summer, blooms mature to seeds as tassels dry, and can be harvested or left for birds to enjoy.

Joseph's coat (*A. tricolor*) is the show-off of the family, with spectacular whorled foliage of red, green, yellow or purple (and there are several colour variations, with 'Splendens' being the best). It is primarily grown as a foliage plant, with the young leaves added to salads and older foliage cooked like spinach. The flowers of this species are insignificant and often obscured by the showy foliage, which is why it is not often grown for the seeds. On the other hand, prince's feather (*A. cruentus*) features striking upright terminal blooms of reddish purple or coppery brown ('Hot Biscuits'), which mature to abundant seed heads that are readily harvested. *A. hypochondriacus* is another species also known as prince's feather, used extensively for seed production.

Even if you aren't familiar with these showy annuals, chances are you still have them growing somewhere in your landscape in the form of pigweed (*Amaranthus retroflexus*), a noxious plant with edible foliage—so, yes, you can eat at least some of your weeds!

Apple

There are so many apples out there that it can be difficult to choose which ones to grow. The best principle to start with is "the right plant in the right place," meaning specific cultivars are better for wet coastal, colder prairie or drier interior climates—so you can be somewhat guided by where you live.

In coastal regions, west or east, diseases such as scab and canker are prevalent, so resistant varieties such as 'Liberty', 'Redfree' or 'Jonafree' are your best choice. For prairie settings, hardier cultivars have been bred to withstand cold winters, including 'September Ruby', 'Norland' and 'Haralson'.

Adequate pollination presents another common problem, as even partially self-fertile varieties, such as 'Gala', 'Cortland' and 'Golden Delicious', produce better with cross-pollination. Then there is the group known as triploids, which have three sets of chromosomes and are essentially pollen sterile. 'Belle de Boskoop', 'Gravenstein' and 'Bramley's Seedling' are notable examples and need a cross-pollination partner that is at least partially self-fertile.

People gardening on smaller landscapes or in containers should look to a pair of columnar apple cultivars developed in British Columbia and selected by Doug DeJong of Misty Meadow Nursery. I have both 'Scarlet Sentinel' and 'Golden Sentinel' growing in pots on my patio, the latter in its container (with one replanting) for eight years now, and both are producing just fine.

WHAT'S EDIBLE:
Fresh flowers and fruits (excluding seeds, which contain hydrogen cyanide and are toxic)

TASTES LIKE:
Tart or sweet, depending on cultivar

HARVEST TIME:
Late July to October, depending on location and cultivar

OPPOSITE: 'Golden Sentinel' apples.
ABOVE: 'Redfree' apples.

SPECIES:
Malus domestica (syn. *M. pumila*)

A.K.A.:
Apple

PLANT TYPE:
Deciduous tree

ORIGIN:
Central Asia

HARDINESS:
USDA zone 3 (depending on cultivar)

SUN:
Part to full sun (minimum 6 hours)

WATER:
Consistent soil moisture with good drainage

ULTIMATE SIZE:
Up to 25 feet (7.7 m) high and wide, depending on rootstock

BLOOM:
Early to late spring, depending on climate

POLLINATION:
Cross-pollination recommended

PRUNING:
Dormant structural pruning, head back new growth in summer

CLOCKWISE FROM TOP LEFT: 'Goodland' apples; 'Scarlet Sentinel' and 'Golden Sentinel' apple trees in bloom; 'Cox's Orange Pippin' apple; 'Elstar' apple.

Apple cultivars

You only have to attend a local apple festival, like the one held at the University of British Columbia Botanical Garden every year, to realize we have a long and complex relationship with apples. We have been storing, cooking, baking, drying, pressing and fermenting them since colonial times and, as a result, there are hundreds of varieties out there, some regional in availability and others being nearly obsolete. Given our special bond with apples, I am providing you with additional choices, including hardy selections, pie varieties (with firm flesh and tart flavour), dessert or superb fresh-eating choices, and cider apples, including one ('Empire') often used for hard cider.

The following list includes cultivar, harvest time and fruit description:

APPLES HARDY TO AT LEAST ZONE 3

'Goodland': Mid-September, light green with red blush

'Harcourt': Mid-September, bright red

'Honeycrisp': Late September, bright red over yellow

'Norkent': Late August to early September, green with red striping

'Parkland': Mid to late August, yellowish green with red blush

PIE APPLES

'Belle de Boskoop': Late September to early October, gold with red striping

'Bramley's Seedling': Early October, green with occasional red blush

'King of Tompkins County': Early to mid-October, yellow with red stripes

'Northern Spy': Late October, green with red flush

'Wealthy': Early September, pale yellow with red striping

DESSERT APPLES

'Ambrosia': Late September, cream with a bright pink overlay

'Cox's Orange Pippin': Late September, golden yellow with red stripes

'Elstar': Late September, yellow with red striping

'Mutsu' (syn. 'Crispin'): Mid-October, greenish yellow with a red blush

'Pink Lady': Late October, yellow with a bright pink blush

CIDER APPLES

'Cortland': Late September, yellow base with heavy red striping

'Empire': Mid-October, bright red

'Golden Russet': Late October, yellow with gold russeting

'Grimes Golden': Early October, yellow with copper russet dots

'Winesap': Late October, bright red over a yellow background

Apricot and Almond

ABOVE: 'Tilton' apricots.
OPPOSITE: Ripening 'Hall's Hardy' almonds.

Both apricot (*Prunus armeniaca*) and almond (*Prunus dulcis*) are spectacular in bloom, the only problem being that they flower so early they are often damaged by frosts in cooler areas.

While apricots are grown commercially in British Columbia's Okanagan Valley and parts of southern Ontario, those of us in the rest of Canada should be careful about cultivar selection. In coastal British Columbia, 'Puget Gold' apricot (self-fertile) does well. Most other varieties will have to be grown espalier-style under a west or south-facing eave, as they dislike wet weather. Prairie gardeners need hardier varieties, such as those derived from Siberian apricot (*Prunus sibirica*) or Manchurian apricot (*P. mandshurica*), with 'Scout', 'Westcot' and 'Prairie Gold' proving themselves over the years. Those living in geographical sweet spots can try commercial cultivars like 'Harglow', 'Goldbar', 'Rival' or good, old-fashioned, all-purpose 'Tilton'.

Almonds have always been an act of zone denial in Canada, with 'All-In-One' and 'Texas Mission' among our trials. Then along came 'Hall's Hardy', a peach-almond cross that blooms later and is self-fertile but has very thick shells. And there is a new find called 'Canadian Almond'—a peach-almond hybrid from Hungary—discovered on an old farm and offered by Green Barn Farm in Quebec. Seedlings from this tree are marketed as zone-5 hardy, self-fertile and very productive in the Canadian climate. Late-blooming Ukrainian cultivars NIKITA'S PRIDE, BOUNTY and ORACLE are also worth considering.

HARVEST TIME:
Midsummer for apricot; September to October for almond

WHAT'S EDIBLE:
Apricot fruits (but not its seeds, which are poisonous); almond seeds

TASTES LIKE:
Apricot fruits taste of musky peach and plum; almond seeds have a subtle sweet nutty flavour

SPECIES:
Prunus armeniaca; *P. dulcis*

A.K.A.:
Armenian plum (*Prunus armeniaca*); badam tree (*P. dulcis*)

PLANT TYPE:
Deciduous trees

ORIGINS:
Ancient garden origins, possibly Armenia (*Prunus armeniaca*); North Africa, Central and Southwest Asia (*P. dulcis*)

HARDINESS:
USDA zone 5 (*Prunus armeniaca*); zone 7 (*P. dulcis*)

SUN:
Full sun

WATER:
Consistent soil moisture with good drainage

ULTIMATE SIZE:
For apricot 15–30 feet (4.6–9 m) tall by 13–20 feet (4–6 m) wide (depending on rootstock); for almond 10–15 feet (3–4.6 m) high and wide

BLOOM:
Late winter to early spring

POLLINATION:
Apricot is usually self-fertile but yields increase with cross-pollination; both self-fertile almond trees and those requiring cross-pollination are available

PRUNING:
Best thinned in summer and pruned in late winter, preferably when not raining

Arbutus

ABOVE: Dwarf strawberry tree fruit cluster. INSET: Strawberry tree flowers.

WHAT'S EDIBLE:
Rounded red fruits

HARVEST TIME:
Autumn (approximately 1 year after flowering)

TASTES LIKE:
Mild apricot and guava

This is a lovely evergreen shrub I planted for decades as a landscaper before realizing the dangling red fruits are edible. The fruit itself has a reputation for being poisonous, but it is not. A complication is that under-ripe fruits induce nausea if ingested, while those left to over-ripen and ferment on the bush can cause mild intoxication—so pick fruits in peak form. The Portuguese highly prize this shrub for bee-keeping and the harvesting of "bitter honey," as well as to make a strong brandy called Medronho. Other treats from *Arbutus unedo* include strawberry tree jam and syrups. The long-suffering fruit takes about a year to ripen, changing from green to yellow to golden orange and finally red at just about the time it begins to flower again.

The ornamental aspects are many and include white to pale-pink urn-shaped blooms starting in October and often lasting until early December, when few flowers are in the garden. Then there are the glossy evergreen foliage and peeling cinnamon-brown bark, and the reputation for tolerating tough, drought-prone sites.

Dwarf cultivars grow well in large containers and provide important winter appeal on decks and patios. There are a number of available cultivars: 'Compacta', which at 6–10 feet (1.8–3 m) high and wide (even with pruning) is not that small a bush. 'Elfin King' (heavy fruit set) and 'Oktoberfest' (pink flowers) might be better choices for urban gardens, as both mature around 8 feet (2.5 m) tall. 'Elfin King', Oktoberfest' or 'Nana' all work in large pots. Last but not least, *Arbutus unedo f. rubra* reaches from 13–26 feet (4–8 m) and is a hard-to-find Royal Horticultural Society (RHS) Award of Garden Merit winner with rosy-pink flowers.

SPECIES:
Arbutus unedo

A.K.A.:
Strawberry tree

PLANT TYPE:
Broad-leaved evergreen shrub or tree

ORIGINS:
Southeast Europe, Ireland, Asia

HARDINESS:
USDA zone 7

SUN:
Part to full sun

WATER:
Drought tolerant once established

ULTIMATE SIZE:
8–15 feet (2.5–4.6 m) high and wide (larger in warmer climates)

BLOOM:
Late autumn

POLLINATION:
Self-fertile

PRUNING:
Light shaping in late winter

Aronia

SPECIES:
Aronia melanocarpa

A.K.A.:
Black chokeberry

PLANT TYPE:
Deciduous shrub

ORIGIN:
Eastern North America

HARDINESS:
USDA zone 3

SUN:
Part to full sun

WATER:
Consistent soil moisture with good drainage; tolerates slightly boggy sites

ULTIMATE SIZE:
4–6 feet (1.2–1.8 m) tall by 6–8 feet (1.8–2.5 m) wide (dwarf forms available)

BLOOM:
Late spring to early summer

POLLINATION:
Self-fertile

PRUNING:
Prune in late winter or after flowering

If you look closely at the ingredients list of your favourite blended juices, chances are you will find aronia. It is widely grown in Europe as an edible crop, with the berries often frozen for use in such smoothies as aronia-orange. They are also commonly dried as a currant replacement for tarts or muffins.

Aronia has the perfect balance of ornamental attributes and edible fruit production. These suckering deciduous shrubs are ideal for mass planting, where the white flower clusters contrast well against the glossy green leaves. The foliage shifts to brilliant autumn hues of scarlet, orange and yellow, and nicely highlights the dangling purplish-black berry clumps. It is also quite tolerant of a wide range of soil conditions, including slightly boggy sites or even those with drier soils, and the zone-3 hardiness means it can easily be grown throughout much of Canada.

This member of the rose family bears pea-sized berries that resemble blackcurrants. Although they appear to ripen (or darken) midsummer, wait until late August or early September to harvest when their sugar content rises, averaging 19 to 21 brix (Bx). The berries are notably high in antioxidants (more than blueberries) and taste quite tart when eaten fresh off the bush.

Proven Winners has introduced a pair of very useful cultivars: LOW SCAPE MOUND is a compact form (up to 24 inches/60 cm) useful for containers, while LOW SCAPE Hedger has a narrow columnar habit that makes it ideal for screening. A standard compact cultivar at 24–36 inches (60–90 cm) tall is IROQUOIS BEAUTY ('Morton'), while 'Autumn Magic' is well known for brilliant fall foliage. 'Viking' is a European variety primarily grown for berry production, with 'Nero' also cultivated commercially.

ABOVE: Compact 'Morton' aronia in bloom.
INSET: Aronia fall foliage and berries.

WHAT'S EDIBLE:
Berries

HARVEST TIME:
Late summer into autumn

TASTES LIKE:
Tart berry

Asian Pear

ABOVE: 'Chojuro' Asian pear fruits.
OPPOSITE: '20th Century' Asian pear flowers.

SPECIES:
Pyrus pyrifolia

A.K.A.:
Chinese pear, Korean pear, Japanese pear, Nashi pear, sand pear

PLANT TYPE:
Deciduous tree

ORIGIN:
East Asia

HARDINESS:
USDA zone 5

SUN:
Part to full sun

WATER:
Consistent soil moisture with good drainage

ULTIMATE SIZE:
20–26 feet (6–8 m) high by 16–20 feet (5–6 m) wide, depending on rootstock

BLOOM:
April

POLLINATION:
Most are partially self-fertile but crop better with cross-pollination

PRUNING:
Prune for form and to remove old wood in late winter

A

WHAT'S EDIBLE:
Fruits

HARVEST TIME:
Late summer

TASTES LIKE:
Mild pear

I used to think that Asian pears seemed juicy but a little bland, and then I tasted a perfectly ripened fruit and the delicate undertones (like a hint of apricot) became apparent—so it's best to allow them to mature on the tree. This is an immensely popular tree fruit in coastal British Columbia, borne out by the many cultivars available.

It's considered a traditional symbol of spring in its native Asia, and this tree's abundant April blooms of pure-white flowers contrasted by purple anthers are an impressive ornamental display. Most cultivars are at least partially self-fertile but best paired with another Asian pear that blooms at the same time, although even European species such as 'Bartlett' can be used as a pollinator. Another option is a multi-graft tree, which often has at least four cultivars that cross-pollinate each other, and is available in standard upright or espalier forms. Asian pears are very prolific trees, often bearing more fruit than the branches can hold, so some thinning is required and will allow for larger pears to form.

Most fruits are rounded in shape, rather than pyriform, with the exception being 'Ya Li' (*Pyrus* × *bretschneideri*), a hybrid. Some of the cultivars you are likely to find at your local garden centre include 'Chojuro' (sweet golden-brown fruits), 'Hosui' (sweet and tart flavour), 'Shinko' (russet golden brown), 'Shinseiki' or 'New Century' (yellow juicy white flesh), 'Kosui' (speckled golden-green skin), 'Seuri' (very cold hardy) and 'Nijisseiki' or '20th Century' (yellowish-green skin, sweet).

Bamboo

SPECIES:
Phyllostachys bambusoides; P. dulcis

A.K.A.:
Giant timber bamboo, madake (*Phyllostachys bambusoides*); sweetshoot bamboo (*P. dulcis*)

PLANT TYPE:
Evergreen perennial plant in the grass family

ORIGIN:
China

HARDINESS:
USDA zone 6 (*Phyllostachys bambusoides*); zone 7 (*P. dulcis*)

SUN:
Part to full sun

WATER:
Consistent soil moisture with good drainage

ULTIMATE SIZE:
Up to 40 feet (12 m) tall with indefinite spread (*Phyllostachys bambusoides*); 20–50 feet (6–15 m) tall with indefinite spread (*P. dulcis*)

BLOOM:
Bamboos have very long intervals between flowering cycles, with *P. bambusoides* averaging 120 years!

POLLINATION:
Not required for harvest

PRUNING:
Thin out old canes in late summer after new growth has matured

WHAT'S EDIBLE:
New shoots

HARVEST TIME:
Cut young shoots as they emerge from spring to early summer

TASTES LIKE:
Mild corn with asparagus, occasionally bitter

OPPOSITE: Emerging sweetshoot bamboo.
ABOVE: Japanese timber bamboo culms.

I had been eating bamboo shoots for most of my adult life, yet somehow never equated those pale slices from a can with the bamboo many of us have in our landscapes. Then I started a gardening position on an established estate (built in the 1930s), where the Japanese owner decided to plant a large field of edible bamboo shoots. The following spring, he or his wife would be out every morning harvesting young shoots, and I began to appreciate the importance of this plant as a food source.

Most bamboos are desirable ornamentals that can be quite expensive to purchase. But since many are running species (particularly *Phyllostachys*) that need control or thinning once mature, why not eat what you prune and get your money's worth? Many popular landscape specimens have delicious new shoots, including giant timber bamboo (*P. bambusoides*), *P. vivax* and the grey-stemmed black bamboo *P. nigra* 'Henon'. And moso bamboo (*P. edulis*) and sweetshoot bamboo (*P. dulcis*) are both considered delicacies as far as the young new shoots are concerned. Harvest from mature plants in spring when they are about 4 inches (10 cm) above ground, cutting 2 inches (5 cm) below soil level with a sharpened spade or pruning knife. The shoots contain natural cyanide and should be boiled until any bitter flavour has dissipated.

Banana

ABOVE: Mature hardy banana grove.
OPPOSITE: Hardy banana flower and ripening fruits.

Bananas are far from the ideal fruit-bearing plant for Canadian gardens, with the most obvious problem being that most are not hardy here except the Japanese fibre banana, and its tiny fruits are seedy and not very palatable. Then there's the often-overlooked obstacle that once a banana pseudostem has matured, flowered and produced fruit, it dies and is replaced by small offshoots or pups. I remember one red banana (*Ensete ventricosum* 'Maurelii') that we used in a tropical bedding scheme in a West Vancouver garden—every fall we dug it up and sent it to a greenhouse for overwintering. After four years of doing this, it finally flowered, fruited and died while still in greenhouse storage (this species produces no pups) and the owner was livid, assuming we did something to hasten its demise, but this is the norm with bananas.

Yet there are culinary reasons to have a banana plant in the garden. The leaves make a superb cooking wrap and infuse a subtle grassy flavour to fish (especially salmon), rice and tamales when steamed—and the fresh leaves are *so* much better than those commercially packaged ones. *Musa basjoo* foliage works well for this and you can even freeze your own for winter use. For those of you who insist upon growing your own banana for the fruit, try *M.* × *paradisiaca* 'Dwarf Cavendish', which reaches about 7 feet (2 m) in a pot, produces small but tasty bananas and can be grown as a houseplant year-round if you like.

WHAT'S EDIBLE:
Leaves are used to wrap foods for cooking or steaming

HARVEST TIME:
Harvest leaves for cooking in late spring to autumn

TASTES LIKE:
Imparts a subtle grassy flavour to foods

SPECIES:
Musa basjoo

A.K.A.:
Japanese fibre banana

PLANT TYPE:
Tender perennial

ORIGIN:
Japan

HARDINESS:
USDA zone 8 (6–7 with protection)

SUN:
Full sun

WATER:
Consistent soil moisture with good drainage

ULTIMATE SIZE:
16 feet (5 m) tall by 13 feet (4 m) wide (smaller if unprotected)

BLOOM:
Summer

POLLINATION:
Small fruits are not palatable, so pollination is not necessary for harvest; it is the leaves we want to harvest for eating

PRUNING:
In late autumn, prune off frost-damaged leaves and cut stem to the desired height for winter protection

Barberry

ABOVE: The hybrid golden barberry in bloom. OPPOSITE: Darwin's barberry ripening.

I became acquainted with *Berberis darwinii* on my first gardening job, working full-time on a 40-acre estate in the Fraser Valley of British Columbia. Mass planted by the driveway entrance, it was one of the few shrubs the resident deer left alone. In spring, the red-tinged buds opened to abundant apricot-orange flowers (with a light repeat bloom in autumn), in late summer the evergreen shrubs were covered in masses of dark bluish-black fruits, and in winter the glossy deep green foliage gleamed with frost in the morning sun. For these and many other reasons, this shrub is an RHS Award of Garden Merit recipient, and its namesake is none other than Charles Darwin, who discovered it in South America in 1835 while travelling on HMS *Beagle*. Although seedy, the fruits of *B. darwinii* have a pleasant flavour of fig and Oregon grape when perfectly ripened, and make a superb jelly.

Golden barberry (*B.* × *stenophylla*) is a hybrid of this species and of *B. empetrifolia*, with rich yellow flowers and a similar growth habit. The berries are also edible but not always as plentiful, unless there is a *B. darwinii* nearby for cross-pollination. There are several dwarf cultivars, including 'Compacta' (*B. darwinii*) and 'Corallina Compacta' (*B.* × *stenophylla*), which features coral-coloured flower buds opening to yellowish-orange blooms.

These are dense thorny shrubs often used around entrance gates or grown as hedging to form impenetrable barriers. They are quite drought tolerant once established and require little pruning except light shaping after flowering—just be sure to leave some of the developing berries.

WHAT'S EDIBLE:
Berries

HARVEST TIME:
Summer (*Berberis darwinii*); late summer to autumn (*B. × stenophylla*)

TASTES LIKE:
Acidic, fig and Oregon grape berries

SPECIES:
Berberis darwinii; B. × stenophylla

A.K.A.:
Darwin's barberry (*Berberis darwinii*); golden barberry (*B. × stenophylla*)

PLANT TYPE:
Evergreen shrub

ORIGINS:
Argentina, Chile (*Berberis darwinii*); garden origin (*B. × stenophylla*)

HARDINESS:
USDA zone 7 (*Berberis darwinii*); zone 6 (*B. × stenophylla*)

SUN:
Part to full sun

WATER:
Low to average, drought tolerant once established

ULTIMATE SIZE:
5–8 feet (1.5–2.5 m) high and wide for *Berberis darwinii*; 6–9 feet (1.8–2.7 m) high and wide for *B. × stenophylla*

BLOOM:
Mid to late spring

POLLINATION:
Self-fertile

PRUNING:
Lightly prune after flowering

Bay Laurel

In my opinion, there is no such thing as palatable beef stew without that subtle taste of bay laurel, even if we do discard the leaf after cooking. There are also those who wouldn't touch a bowl of soup or a Bloody Mary without that *je ne sais quoi* added by a little powdered bay. The ancient Greeks and Romans felt just as strongly about this broadleaf evergreen shrub; a crown of woven bay laurel leaves was awarded to victors and graduates, and is where the word "laureate" originated.

That's a lot of pressure on just one plant, and when you consider that it isn't the easiest to grow in Canada, you may want to ensure things are right from the get-go. The species is zone-8 hardy, meaning it isn't entirely hardy here, but bay laurel tolerates container culture rather well and can be grown as a houseplant to be brought outdoors from May to early October. It can also be trained into standard or pompom topiaries rather easily, making it a good choice for that pot by the front door.

In coastal British Columbia, some of us are growing it outdoors year-round and I have seen several substantial specimens (8 feet/2.5 m or more in height) thriving in-ground, in sunny sites with good drainage and protection from winter winds. I have a golden bay laurel (*L. nobilis 'Aurea'*) that stays out all winter, growing in a pot by my west-facing front door, and Proven Winners has introduced an improved gold-leaved form called SICILIAN SUNSHINE. There are even a few hardier cultivars rated for zone-7 climates, including 'Celtic Queen' and the thin-leaved *L. nobilis* f. *angustifolia*.

OPPOSITE: Gold-leaved bay laurel. ABOVE: 'Celtic Queen' bay laurel flowers.

WHAT'S EDIBLE:
Mature leaves as seasoning

HARVEST TIME:
2-year-old leaves in midsummer

TASTES LIKE:
Herbal essence of light oregano and thyme

SPECIES:
Laurus nobilis

A.K.A.:
Bay tree, sweet bay

PLANT TYPE:
Broadleaf evergreen shrub or tree

ORIGIN:
Mediterranean

HARDINESS:
USDA zone 8

SUN:
Part to full sun

WATER:
Consistent soil moisture with good drainage

ULTIMATE SIZE:
8–10 feet (2.5–3 m) tall by 5–7 feet (1.5–2 m) wide, larger in warmer regions

BLOOM:
March to May

POLLINATION:
Not required for harvest

PRUNING:
Prune anytime from late spring to midsummer

Bee Balm

SPECIES:
Monarda didyma; M. fistulosa (and hybrids)

A.K.A.:
Bergamot, Oswego tea (*Monarda didyma*); wild bee balm (*M. fistulosa*)

PLANT TYPE:
Hardy herbaceous perennial

ORIGIN:
Eastern North America

HARDINESS:
USDA zone 3

SUN:
Part to full sun

WATER:
Consistent soil moisture with good drainage

ULTIMATE SIZE:
3–4 feet (90–120 cm) tall by 2 feet (60 cm) wide or more for *Monarda didyma*; 4 feet (120 cm) tall by 18 inches (46 cm) wide or more for *M. fistulosa*

BLOOM:
Summer to early autumn

POLLINATION:
Not required for harvest

PRUNING:
Pinch in early spring for density, cut back when dormant

WHAT'S EDIBLE:
Flowers and foliage

HARVEST TIME:
Eat the flowers when in bloom and pick leaves for consumption in mid to late summer

TASTES LIKE:
Minty Earl Grey tea or bergamot

OPPOSITE: Wild bee balm in bloom.
ABOVE: 'Jacob Cline' bee balm, the hummingbird's favourite flower.

The common names of this hardy herbaceous perennial—bee balm, Oswego tea and bergamot—hint at the plant's uses and popularity with pollinators. Just plant a red-flowered bee balm, like 'Jacob Cline' or the compact 'Fireball' (18 inches/46 cm tall), in your garden and I guarantee hummingbirds will be fighting over it come summer.

Oswego tea references both *Monarda fistulosa* (lilac-purple blooms) and *M. didyma*, used by First Nations and early settlers as a refreshing brew with some medicinal (antiseptic) uses. The leaves of both species have a pleasant Earl Grey tea scent and can also be eaten fresh in salads (younger leaves) or used to season meats, with the blooms making spectacular garnishes for summer drinks. (Pregnant women should avoid eating *Monarda* or drinking its tea.)

Bee balm is normally easy to grow but is sometimes affected by powdery mildew where summer drought or poor air circulation is the case. If so, switch to mildew-resistant cultivars such as 'Marshall's Delight' or 'Raspberry Wine'. *M. fistulosa* is usually only available as the species, while *M. didyma* includes many worthy cultivars or hybrids, including 'Purple Rooster', 'Snow White', 'Blue Stocking' and 'Gardenview Scarlet'. Compact 'Fireball' or 'Petite Wonder' (a true pink) make great container specimens. Taller cultivars work well in a mixed border—just keep in mind these precocious perennials will often spread vigorously when conditions are ideal!

Black Locust

Black locust is a large deciduous tree with a long history in North America, being both a favoured ornamental and source of rot-resistant lumber going back to colonial times. Nowadays, it has gained notoriety for being susceptible to storm damage, and for bearing large thorns and being on the invasive plant list of many states and provinces, much in part due to its aggressive root suckers.

But every cloud has a silver lining—and in the case of *Robinia pseudoacacia*, this is the white pea-like flower clusters, which not only taste heavenly but are also an important nectar and pollen forage for wild and domestic bees. The crunchy, sweet-tasting flowers are reminiscent of young peas, and work well in soups, salads or spring rolls—though my preference is to eat them in fresh crêpes with a little blackcurrant syrup on top!

One of the better cultivars is 'Frisia', with both a growth rate more restrained than the species and brilliant chartreuse new-growth leaflets that shift to lime green by summer. For gardeners with smaller spaces, there are several contorted cultivars to choose from, including 'Tortuosa' and TWISTY BABY ('Lace Lady'), both of which mature slowly to about 15 feet (4.6 m) high and wide and are good candidates for large containers or raised beds. Their dormant silhouettes are truly spectacular, particularly after a light snowfall. The species or large cultivars need careful placement, as they are fast-growing and require room to grow; shelter from strong winds should also be considered. Expect some tip dieback on juvenile specimens; this can be pruned out when the tree is in leaf with dead portions readily visible.

SPECIES:
Robinia pseudoacacia

A.K.A.:
False acacia

PLANT TYPE:
Large deciduous tree

ORIGIN:
Eastern United States

HARDINESS:
USDA zone 4

SUN:
Full sun

WATER:
Consistent soil moisture with good drainage

ULTIMATE SIZE:
30–50 feet (9–15 m) tall by 20–36 feet (6–11 m) wide

BLOOM:
Late spring to early summer

POLLINATION:
Not required for harvest

PRUNING:
Prune out deadwood when in leaf

ABOVE: 'Frisia' black locust in flower.
INSET: Gold-leaved black locust tree.

WHAT'S EDIBLE:
Fresh flowers

HARVEST TIME:
May through June when in flower

TASTES LIKE:
Garden pea with honey

Blueberry

Blueberry Cultivars

'Blueray': Excellent flavour with high yields, mid-season

'Brigitta': Large and firm with good flavour, store well, late season

'Liberty': Produces just before 'Elliott' with better flavour, late season

'Patriot': Winter hardy with large firm fruits, mid-season

'Spartan': Large and firm with good flavour, early season

Picking blueberries in Canada can be a remarkably diverse experience, depending on where you live. My first venture was to Sandilands Provincial Forest (south of Winnipeg) where we picked lowbush blueberries (*Vaccinium angustifolium*). I remember incredibly delicious berries, a lot of bending over, and donating blood to ravenous mosquitos. Five years later, my family moved to Chilliwack, British Columbia, where the highbush blueberries (*V. corymbosum*) grew over my head and were loaded top to bottom with huge fruits—needless to say, the latter was a much more enjoyable experience.

The blueberries you pick will vary from region to region. Half-highs (a cross of low and highbush) such as 'Northsky', 'Chippewa' and 'Polaris' provide zone-3 hardiness for prairie gardeners, while those of us in milder climes can enjoy commercial highbush cultivars such as 'Bluecrop', 'Duke', 'Reka', 'Chandler' (huge berries) and the late-cropping 'Elliott', many of which have brilliant autumn foliage. There are even two pink-berried cultivars: 'Pink Lemonade' has bright citrus-flavoured berries that look great in fruit salads, while the newer PINK POPCORN has blush-pink berries and is zone-4 hardy. You should also keep an eye out for another new introduction, 'Razz', a powder-blue blueberry that has fruits that taste like raspberry.

For container gardeners, there are a lot of options available. Consider the half-highs, or the very compact 'Tophat' (2 feet/60 cm high and wide), also zone-3 hardy. And the Bushel and Berry series provides many cultivars specifically bred for growing in pots, including JELLY BEAN (sweet berries), PEACH SORBET (peachy-pink new growth) and BLUEBERRY GLAZE (wild blueberry flavour).

OPPOSITE: Lowbush blueberry fall colour and fruit. ABOVE: 'Pink Lemonade' blueberries.

WHAT'S EDIBLE:
Berries

HARVEST TIME:
Midsummer (*Vaccinium angustifolium*); midsummer to late summer (*V. corymbosum*)

TASTES LIKE:
Wild or musky (*Vaccinium angustifolium*); sweet yet tart (*V. corymbosum*)

SPECIES:
Vaccinium angustifolium; *V. corymbosum*

A.K.A.:
Lowbush blueberry (*Vaccinium angustifolium*); highbush blueberry (*V. corymbosum*)

PLANT TYPE:
Deciduous shrub

ORIGIN:
Eastern North America

HARDINESS:
USDA zone 2 (*Vaccinium angustifolium*); zone 4 (*V. corymbosum*)

SUN:
Part to full sun

WATER:
Consistent soil moisture with good drainage

ULTIMATE SIZE:
1–2 feet (30–60 cm) high and wide for *Vaccinium angustifolium*; 5–7 feet (1.5–2 m) tall by 5 feet (1.5 m) wide for *V. corymbosum*

BLOOM:
Late spring to early summer

POLLINATION:
Partially self-fertile, better crops with cross-pollination

PRUNING:
Requires regular rejuvenation pruning (*Vaccinium angustifolium*); remove old wood in late winter (*V. corymbosum*)

Cane Fruits

SPECIES:
Rubus × loganobaccus; R. fruticosus × idaeus

A.K.A.:
Loganberry (*Rubus × loganobaccus*); tayberry (*R. fruticosus × idaeus*)

PLANT TYPE:
Perennial

ORIGIN:
Garden origin

HARDINESS:
USDA zone 6

SUN:
Full sun

WATER:
Low to average soil moisture with good drainage

ULTIMATE SIZE:
7 feet (2 m) high

BLOOM:
Spring

POLLINATION:
Self-fertile

PRUNING:
Cut back canes that have fruited to the ground, and thin remaining new canes (for next year's berries) to a manageable grouping

While I'll agree that an unkempt cane fruit allowed to become a billowing tangled mess has no aesthetic qualities, when properly trained against a box lattice panel or tied to an ornamental obelisk, it can look good. Both the white spring blooms and maroon to bright red fruits show really well on an upright plane—so if things look messy you have no one to blame but yourself!

Aesthetics aside, both loganberry and tayberry offer delicious, abundant fruits that are easy to grow. They can be eaten fresh or processed into juices, wines and preserves, or just frozen for later use. And this is just the tip of the cane-fruit iceberg. There are numerous hybrids awaiting you at your local garden centre, including youngberry (blackberry × raspberry × dewberry), boysenberry (loganberry × raspberry × blackberry) and marionberry ('Chehalem' × 'Olallie' blackberries).

Blackberries present another front in British Columbia. The most common one in coastal regions is Himalayan (*Rubus armeniacus*), which has very tasty berries but is also highly invasive and choking out open forests and roadsides. As a home gardener, choose from some of the less precocious thornless varieties, including 'Black Satin' (slightly hardier), 'Loch Ness' (large fruits), 'Apache' (good flavour), 'Triple Crown' (sweet berries) and 'Navaho' (high yields)—all of which are hardy to zone 5, with some surviving in colder regions with protection.

Container culture is not generally practical with this group, although the new dwarf thornless blackberry, BABY CAKES from the Bushel and Berry series, is zone-4 hardy and only grows 3–4 feet (90–120 cm) tall, making it ideal for large pots.

ABOVE: Tayberry fruits.
INSET: Ripening loganberries.

WHAT'S EDIBLE:
Berries

HARVEST TIME:
Mid to late summer

TASTES LIKE:
Tart raspberry with hints of blackberry (*Rubus × loganobaccus*); raspberry-blackberry, sweeter than loganberry (*R. fruticosus × idaeus*)

Cardoon and Artichoke

WHAT'S EDIBLE:
Stems (*Cynara cardunculus*); young flower buds (*C. cardunculus* var. *scolymus*)

HARVEST TIME:
Late summer to fall

TASTES LIKE:
Slightly bitter artichoke (*Cynara cardunculus*); mild avocado and Brussels sprouts (*C. cardunculus* var. *scolymus*)

Cardoon (*Cynara cardunculus*) is a tall and showy plant with prominent silvery-grey foliage and an overall form reminiscent of giant thistle with its large purple blooms. It can be grown from seed by starting in late winter and setting plants out after danger of frost, although many gardeners just buy starter plants. Cardoon requires well-drained soil with plenty of compost, a full-sun exposure and shelter from prevailing winds; otherwise plants will be stunted. When it is at least 3 feet (90 cm) tall, you can blanch stems by pulling the leaves together and tying them in place with a piece of burlap, landscape fabric or newspaper over the top for three to six weeks, after which they are ready to harvest. They will need to be chopped into 1-inch (2.5-cm) segments and boiled in water with salt and lemon juice (to remove bitterness and retain colour), after which they can be added to soups or stews.

Artichoke (*C. cardunculus* var. *scolymus*) likes much the same growing conditions, with the flowers best harvested when terminal buds are still tight and firm and about 3 inches (7.5 cm) in diameter; secondary flowers can be harvested later. Artichokes usually grow vegetatively the first season and flower in their second; if overwintering is a problem in your zone, try 'Imperial Star', a short-season (85 to 90 days) thornless variety that blooms in its first year. Both cardoon and artichoke are tender perennials that can be overwintered by mulching the crown with straw or leaves, and removing mulch in April.

OPPOSITE: 'Purple Globe' artichoke.
LEFT: Cardoon in flower.

SPECIES:
Cynara cardunculus; *C. cardunculus* var. *scolymus*

A.K.A.:
Artichoke thistle (*Cynara cardunculus*); globe artichoke (*C. cardunculus* var. *scolymus*)

PLANT TYPE:
Perennial (*Cynara cardunculus*); short-lived perennial (*C. cardunculus* var. *scolymus*)

ORIGINS:
North Africa, Southwest Mediterranean (*Cynara cardunculus*); unknown (*C. cardunculus* var. *scolymus*)

HARDINESS:
USDA zone 7

SUN:
Full sun

WATER:
Consistent soil moisture with sharp drainage

ULTIMATE SIZE:
5–8 feet (150–250 cm) tall by 2–3 feet (60–90 cm) wide for *Cynara cardunculus;* 3–5 feet (90–150 cm) tall by 2–3 feet (60–90 cm) wide for *C. cardunculus* var. *scolymus* (smaller in cooler regions)

BLOOM:
Mid to late summer

POLLINATION:
Self-fertile

PRUNING:
Cut back to 8 inches (20 cm) when dormant, and mulch for winter

Chestnut

John Sousa, my Portuguese friend who lives across the street from the nursery where I work, is always walking me over to see his collection of old-world fruits, such as figs, grapes and plums, and his pride and joy—sweet chestnut (*Castanea sativa*), grown from seed and grafted. On cycling forays throughout my hometown, I often see an old chestnut tree thriving in an abandoned farm or overgrown country garden. In the here and now, though, they are just starting to gain traction as a popular edible ornamental.

The two most common nut-bearing species are sweet and Chinese chestnut (*C. mollissima*), both of which are handsome deciduous trees featuring arching branches and glossy deep green leaves with serrated edges that turn bronze or golden yellow in fall. I have seen solitary trees produce well but admit the individual nuts (often several per husk) are rather small, so you may have to rely on seedling stock for cross-pollination, as cultivars can be difficult to source—although any species of chestnut can pollinate the other, as long as the male and female flowers are in sync. There is also a *C. dentata* × *mollissima* hybrid called the Dunstan chestnut, bred to be resistant to the blight that nearly wiped out the American species. Other than that, look for *C. sativa* 'Marron de Lyon', a French cultivar with huge solitary nuts, or the beautifully variegated 'Albomarginata', an RHS Award of Garden Merit recipient.

OPPOSITE: Variegated sweet chestnut.
ABOVE: Ripening sweet chestnuts.

WHAT'S EDIBLE:
Nuts

HARVEST TIME:
Autumn, when they fall to the ground

TASTES LIKE:
Sweet potato and pecan

SPECIES:
Castanea sativa; *C. mollissima*

A.K.A.:
Spanish chestnut, sweet chestnut (*Castanea sativa*); Chinese chestnut (*C. mollissima*)

PLANT TYPE:
Deciduous tree

ORIGINS:
Southern Europe, North Africa (*Castanea sativa*); Southwest Asia, China (*C. mollissima*)

HARDINESS:
USDA zone 5 (*Castanea sativa*); zone 4 (*C. mollissima*)

SUN:
Part to full sun

WATER:
Consistent soil moisture with good drainage

ULTIMATE SIZE:
50–66 feet (15–20 m) high and wide (larger in warmer climates)

BLOOM:
June through July

POLLINATION:
Partially self-fertile, better crops with cross-pollination

PRUNING:
Light pruning and removal of deadwood in late winter

Chilean Guava

This exotic South American fruit is a relative newcomer to the local edible plant market and yet was introduced to England way back in 1844, becoming one of Queen Victoria's favourite snacks. It is also being grown commercially in both New Zealand and Australia, where it is marketed as Tazziberry. The plant itself is evergreen, with fine textured leaves similar to common myrtle (*Myrtus communis*) and easily trimmed to a tight form.

Since the attractive white to pink-tinged flowers are produced from young shoots, Chilean guava tends to bear its fruit conveniently on the contour of trimmed plants and even if it suffers a little winter damage, it still produces flowers later in spring. Which brings us to the only drawback, that being its zone-8 hardiness. However, these shrubs can be successfully overwintered in cool greenhouses and cold frames, which means they must be grown in containers in order to be moved inside and out. Your other options are to plant them in a very sheltered site (such as under a south- or west-facing eave) or offer protection over winter with a temporary frost blanket such as N-Sulate.

Is Chilean guava worth all this fuss? Queen Victoria would approve of my answer—a definitive yes! Not only do these shrubs come into bearing at a young age, they produce consistently large crops (up to 2.2 pounds/1 kilogram of fruit for a 3-year-old plant) with minimal care required. Then there's that incredible flavour, as these red berries of more than ⅗ inch (1.5 cm) across have a tang that combines strawberry and guava, a completely unique taste experience that everyone seems to enjoy. If any remain after all the fresh sampling, leftover berries can be made into flavourful jellies, used to top yogurt, or baked into homemade muffins.

SPECIES:
Ugni molinae (syn. *Myrtus ugni*)

A.K.A.:
Strawberry myrtle, Tazziberry

PLANT TYPE:
Evergreen shrub

ORIGINS:
Argentina, Chile

HARDINESS:
USDA zone 8

SUN:
Part to full sun

WATER:
Consistent soil moisture with good drainage

ULTIMATE SIZE:
5–6 feet (150–180 cm) tall by 3 feet (90 cm) wide

BLOOM:
Late spring

POLLINATION:
Self-fertile

PRUNING:
Prune to shape after fruiting

ABOVE: Chilean guava in flower.
INSET: Ripening Chilean guava berries.

WHAT'S EDIBLE:
Berries

HARVEST TIME:
Late August to October

TASTES LIKE:
Strawberry and guava

Chokecherry

ABOVE: Chokecherry in bloom.
OPPOSITE: Ripening chokecherry fruit.

SPECIES:
Prunus virginiana

A.K.A.:
Bitter-cherry, chokeberry

PLANT TYPE:
Large deciduous bush or small tree

ORIGIN:
North America

HARDINESS:
USDA zone 3

SUN:
Part to full sun

WATER:
Average moisture, drought tolerant once established

ULTIMATE SIZE:
20–30 feet (6–9 m) tall by 15–20 feet (4.6–6 m) wide

BLOOM:
Late spring

POLLINATION:
Self-fertile

PRUNING:
Thin in late winter

WHAT'S EDIBLE:
Red to purplish-black fruits (but toxic to horses and livestock)

HARVEST TIME:
Late summer

TASTES LIKE:
Intense sour cherry

Chokecherries are synonymous with the Prairies, and as a kid living in Saskatchewan and Manitoba I prided myself on my ability to eat straight off the tree—but I also learned why they are called chokecherries. Even when fully ripened, the tiny 0.04-inch (1-mm) burgundy-black fruits are highly astringent, so one too many usually meant a stomach ache. And be warned that this small deciduous tree or bush can be highly toxic to both horses and livestock when they browse the foliage or branches or bite down on the seeds, all of which contain some degree of cyanide—so keep pastures clear of this species.

That said, there are plenty of prairie farmers alive and kicking today who point to their prized chokecherry wine as one of the reasons for their good health and long lifespan, so who am I to argue with that? The point being that this fruit is best ingested by being cooked and processed (take care not to crush the seeds when separating them from the fruit) into delicious syrups, jellies and fruit leather. This was also an important food source for First Nations communities across the Prairies, who dried and ground the berries in order to add them to soups and to buffalo meat or other game as a key ingredient in pemmican.

Chokecherries can be found in many locales throughout Canada. In fact, I pass dozens of large bushes or small trees myself on the way to work each day, but only really notice them in late spring when they burst into flower, literally covering themselves in pendulous white racemes. For those of you who might like a more refined version of this species, there are several purple-leaved cultivars, including 'Midnight Schubert', which also has edible berries.

Citrus

ABOVE: 'Meyer' lemon espalier.
OPPOSITE: Ripening chinotto sour oranges.

If you've heard rumours about someone growing lemons outdoors in Canada, chances are they were referring to Bob Duncan and his Fruit Trees and More Nursery and Demonstration Orchard in North Saanich on Vancouver Island, British Columbia. Bob has been growing citrus for more than 20 years and has perfected systems of cultivating both acid (lemons, limes) and sweet citrus (navel orange, grapefruit), with the latter being grown in an unheated greenhouse. I saw a beautiful 'Meyer' lemon tree there, covered with large ripened fruits and espaliered under a glass overhang on the south side of his house. When the temperature drops in winter, Bob protects these trees with a string of old-fashioned Christmas lights (7-watt bulbs) and a curtain of Reemay cloth (pinned at the bottom) to insulate. He also uses Reemay from mid-March to April to trap heat and induce earlier flowering, and by using this system he is able to harvest lemons (which last on the bush for several months) year-round.

The rest of us not living in mild coastal regions will just have to grow our citrus in pots, bringing them out in spring (April or May) and putting them back inside a cool greenhouse or sunroom for winter from September to October. These trees need as much indoor sun as you can manage, and occasional repotting and root pruning, as well as a Miracid-type fertilizer. The selection is outstanding (which is why I have included a citrus addendum), with chinotto sour orange and 'Improved Meyer' lemon (virus free) being just a few.

WHAT'S EDIBLE:
Fruits including peel

HARVEST TIME:
Year-round for *Citrus × meyeri* (fruits last for several months on the bush); winter to spring for *C. aurantium* var. *myrtifolia*

TASTES LIKE:
Sweet lemon (*Citrus × meyeri*); sour orange, slightly bitter (*C. aurantium* var. *myrtifolia*)

SPECIES:
Citrus × meyeri (syn. *Citrus × limon* 'Meyer'); *C. aurantium* var. *myrtifolia* (syn. *C. myrtifolia*)

A.K.A.:
Meyer lemon (*Citrus × meyeri*); chinotto sour orange, myrtle-leaved orange (*C. aurantium* var. *myrtifolia*)

PLANT TYPE:
Semi-evergreen to evergreen shrub or tree

ORIGINS:
China (*Citrus × meyeri*); China, Myanmar (Burma) (*C. aurantium* var. *myrtifolia*)

HARDINESS:
USDA zone 9

SUN:
Part to full sun

WATER:
Consistent soil moisture with good drainage

ULTIMATE SIZE:
3–7½ feet (90–230 cm) tall by 2–5 feet (60–150 cm) wide (but larger in warmer climates and when protected)

BLOOM:
Late March to mid-October (*Citrus × meyeri*); mid to late spring, one year after pollination (*C. aurantium* var. *myrtifolia*)

POLLINATION:
Self-fertile

PRUNING:
Prune in late winter to thin out weak branches or deadwood and to improve light penetration

CLOCKWISE FROM LEFT: Variegated calamondin; 'Meyer' lemon; key lime.

Citrus cultivars

When one considers that the Orangerie in Versailles has been growing hundreds of citrus plants in large wooden containers that are brought inside from October to May every year, having a few potted kumquats or key limes in Canada shouldn't be too hard for us to handle. Home gardeners are just beginning to realize the amazing variety of citrus becoming available, and we can really thank the 'Meyer' lemon for starting this trend here. This hard-to-resist combination of delightfully perfumed flowers and delicious, sweet fruits that can be grown in most homes really caught our attention.

The following list includes common name, botanical name and description of fruit; * means appropriate for slightly smaller-sized container:

Bergamot Sour Orange: *Citrus bergamia,* peel used to flavour Earl Grey tea

Bouquet de Fleurs Sour Orange: *Citrus aurantium* 'Bouquet de Fleurs', sour orange cultivar used to flavour liqueurs and make marmalade

Buddha's Hand Citron: *Citrus medica* var. *sarcodactylis,* hand-shaped citron*

Calamondin: × *Citrofortunella mitis,* Mandarin orange × kumquat hybrid, fruit and edible peel used to flavour food and beverages*

Cocktail Grapefruit (syn. Mandelo): *Citrus × hybrida, Pummelo × Mandarin* cross, small grapefruit-sized citrus with sweet yellow flesh

Etrog Citron: *Citrus medica,* traditional citron used in Jewish rituals*

Kaffir Lime: *Citrus hystrix,* leaves and rind used in Thai cuisine*

Key Lime: *Citrus aurantifolia,* fruit used for pies and frozen desserts*

Limequat: *Citrus × floridana,* a key lime × kumquat cross, sliced and added to cocktails or used to flavour fish or chicken dishes

Lisbon Lemon: *Citrus limon* 'Lisbon', versatile commercial variety

Mexican Thornless Lime: *Citrus aurantifolia* 'Mexican Thornless', your typical bartender's lime for cocktails and drinks*

Nagami Kumquat: *Fortunella margarita* 'Nagami', small orange fruits

Oroblanco Grapefruit (syn. Sweetie): *Citrus × hybrida,* sweet seedless fruits*

Palestine Sweet Lime: *Citrus limettioides,* ripens to yellow, used to make beverages while peel used for seasoning

Persian Lime: *Citrus × latifolia,* a key lime × lemon hybrid used for making fresh drinks or to flavour frozen concentrates

Ponderosa Lemon: *Citrus limon × medica,* a bumpy lemon × citron hybrid with an unusual shape, a good lemon substitute

Rangpur: *Citrus × limonia,* a Mandarin orange × lemon cross, acid with orange peel and flesh, used for cooking*

Variegated Calamondin: × *Citrofortunella mitis* 'Variegata', resembles kumquat but with creamy-white edged leaves and striped juvenile fruit*

Variegated Kumquat: *Fortunella margarita* 'Centennial', sport of 'Nagami'

Variegated Pink Lemon: *Citrus limon* 'Eureka Variegated Pink', pink fleshed, makes a beautiful lemonade*

Clove Currant

I was introduced to clove currant by mistake: one year, I ordered *Ribes nigrum* (European blackcurrant) for my spring plant booking and received this shrub instead. All was fine until the flowers opened and in place of those inconspicuous racemes of yellowish-green to pale pink there were vibrant bright yellow tubular blooms with a spicy clove fragrance. While I found them delightful, my regular nursery customers were less impressed, as they wanted the traditional blackcurrant and had no idea what type of fruit this was. So, the plants hung around the nursery and by midsummer some good-sized shiny black berries started to take shape, with a fresh flavour that in my opinion exceeded *R. nigrum*, as they weren't as sharp tasting.

My stubborn customers still refused this self-redeeming fruit and by fall the bushes were ablaze with vibrant mahogany-red autumn foliage, at which time several regulars finally decided clove currant was worthy of a place in their gardens! So here we have a first-rate ornamental plant with good cold hardiness that also provides us with a tasty berry with a minimum of care—what more could one want from an edible ornamental?

Besides the species, the only cultivar you are likely to encounter is 'Crandall', a very old selection first discovered back in 1888; at 3–5 feet (90–150 cm) tall, it is reasonably compact and the berries are up to almost ¾ inch (2 cm) wide. The only downside to this species and all *Ribes* is that they are the alternate host to white pine blister rust, a fungus that requires two hosts to complete its life cycle and is responsible for destroying many five-needled pines—so plant with caution if this disease is present in your region.

WHAT'S EDIBLE:
Berries

HARVEST TIME:
Midsummer

TASTES LIKE:
Mild blackcurrant with spice

OPPOSITE: 'Crandall' clove currant berries.
ABOVE: Clove currant in flower.

SPECIES:
Ribes odoratum (syn. *R. aureum* var. *villosum*)

A.K.A.:
Buffalo currant

PLANT TYPE:
Deciduous shrub

ORIGIN:
Central United States

HARDINESS:
USDA zone 4

SUN:
Part to full sun

WATER:
Average moisture, drought tolerant once established

ULTIMATE SIZE:
6 feet (1.8 m) high and wide

BLOOM:
Early to mid-spring

POLLINATION:
Partially self-fertile, better crops with cross-pollination

PRUNING:
Prune out old wood in late winter

Cornelian Cherry

SPECIES:
Cornus mas

A.K.A.:
Cherry dogwood

PLANT TYPE:
Deciduous tree or large shrub

ORIGINS:
Europe, Western Asia

HARDINESS:
USDA zone 4

SUN:
Part to full sun

WATER:
Consistent soil moisture with good drainage

ULTIMATE SIZE:
15–23 feet (4.6–7 m) high and wide

BLOOM:
Late winter to early spring

POLLINATION:
Benefits from cross-pollination

PRUNING:
Structural pruning in winter

OPPOSITE, TOP: 'Golden Glory' Cornelian cherry in bloom.
INSET: Cornelian cherry drupes.

This tree rivals forsythia with its late-winter to early-spring display of bright yellow flowers borne abundantly on bare branches. And while we have been extolling Cornelian cherry's ornamental values for decades in North America, it is only recently with the arrival of many immigrants from Eastern Europe that we have become aware of its nutritious edible berries or drupes. These have been a food crop as far back as ancient Greece, with modern uses including jams, sauces and syrups, as well as homemade liqueurs that are often taken as a tonic due to their high vitamin-C content.

Some of the best cultivars come out of Ukraine, with most of these bearing an elongated pear-shaped fruit—these include ELEGANT (sweet, good for fresh eating), RED DAWN (sweet-tart flavour) and PIONEER (fruits up to 1½ inches/3.8 cm long, easier to process). SUNRISE is another large-berried cultivar that is equally good for fresh eating. Yellow fruits are also available either from the older cultivar 'Flava' or YELLOW, another Ukrainian introduction that is favoured for processing into juice or compote. Grafted trees begin bearing consistently after about three years and the species is long-lived, with many older specimens exceeding a century in age.

While partially self-fertile, Cornelian cherry crops much more consistently with cross-pollination. It is easily trained into standard or multi-stem bush form, with fruiting hedgerows also an option. Variegated and gold-leaved forms, such as 'Aureo-elegantissima', 'Variegata' and 'Aurea', are best placed out of locations with hot afternoon sun to avoid leaf scorch. While not sold as a fruiting cultivar, 'Golden Glory' is an RHS Award of Garden Merit winner, with abundant flowers, reddish-purple autumn foliage and pretty generous crops of rod-shaped berries.

WHAT'S EDIBLE:
Red or yellow drupes

HARVEST TIME:
Late August to early September

TASTES LIKE:
Cranberry and sour cherry

Crabapple

In the opinion of 12-year-old me, crabapples were the perfect fruit: portable (fitting nicely into any pocket size), a perfect thirst-quenching balance of sweet and sour, and—in a pinch—just right for self-defence without the associated guilt of throwing a rock. In fact, I might have taken this a little further by stating that crabapple should become our national tree instead of the sugar maple, because no matter where I lived in Ontario, Manitoba, Saskatchewan or British Columbia, I could always find one.

Adult Mike would concur with his juvenile self, simply because this is one of the easiest fruit trees to grow no matter where you live in this country, except the extreme north. Crabapples are self-fertile, have very attractive white to pink flowers and come into bearing at a young age. The only downside is that this old-fashioned fruit has fallen out of favour and can be a little hard to find at local garden centres.

Still, there are several good cultivars available, including 'Dolgo' with its fragrant white flowers and slightly rod-shaped 1½-inch (3.8-cm) fruits that make excellent jelly. A couple of other fairly common cultivars with larger round fruits are 'Chestnut' (2-inch / 5-cm nutty-flavoured fruits) and 'Whitney'. Also related is the apple-crab group, or hybrids between apples and crabapples, such as 'Kerr' ('Dolgo' × 'Haralson'), which are larger in size but require cross-pollination to produce a full crop. There are also modern ornamentals, such as the columnar EMERALD SPIRE or 'Jefgreen', that adapt well to growing in large containers and produce decent crops of 1¼-inch (3-cm) red fruits that taste good right off the tree.

WHAT'S EDIBLE:
Fruits (excluding seeds)

HARVEST TIME:
Late summer into autumn

TASTES LIKE:
Tart, acidic apple

OPPOSITE: EMERALD SPIRE crabapple in flower.
ABOVE: 'Dolgo' crabapples.

SPECIES:
Malus spp.

A.K.A.:
Wild apple

PLANT TYPE:
Deciduous tree

ORIGIN:
Bred domestically

HARDINESS:
USDA zone 3

SUN:
Full sun

WATER:
Consistent soil moisture with good drainage

ULTIMATE SIZE:
12–20 feet (3.7–6 m) high and wide, depending on rootstock

BLOOM:
Mid-spring

POLLINATION:
Self-fertile

PRUNING:
Prune in late winter for structure and suckers

Cranberry

SPECIES:
Vaccinium macrocarpon

A.K.A.:
American cranberry

PLANT TYPE:
Evergreen subshrub

ORIGIN:
Eastern North America

HARDINESS:
USDA zone 2

SUN:
Full sun

WATER:
Moist to wet soil

ULTIMATE SIZE:
6 inches (15 cm) tall by 3–4 feet (90–120 cm) wide

BLOOM:
Late spring into summer

POLLINATION:
Partially self-fertile, better crops with cross-pollination

PRUNING:
Lightly head back uprights and runners after harvest

Few of us think of cranberries in terms of the plant proper, as we usually only see them around Thanksgiving and Christmas as packaged berries. I am lucky enough to live in the Fraser Valley of British Columbia, one of the major cranberry-production areas in North America, and even pass a few fields on my daily commute. Few sights are as impressive as a "wet harvest" of cranberries, when the fields are temporarily flooded, with the surface of the water covered with bright red berries as far as the eye can see.

This evergreen subshrub is easily grown by homeowners in evenly moist soils and can even be trained into a reasonable ground cover with some light pruning. The white to pale pink flowers held on short stems have reflexed petals and begin showing in late spring. These are responsible for the common name, as early European settlers thought they resembled the neck of a crane and called the fruit "craneberry," eventually shortened to "cranberry."

Bumblebees are the primary wild pollinators, and fertilized flowers develop into large ¾-inch (2-cm) burgundy-red berries by late autumn. The green foliage also shifts to an attractive bronzy-purple in colder weather. This species is sometimes confused with wild cranberry or *Vaccinium oxycoccos*, a smaller-berried type that is found across the Northern Hemisphere and was harvested by First Nations communities who stored the fresh fruit in moss or dried it into cakes. A full-sun exposure is best, as cranberry tends to get thin and leggy with any shade. Different cultivars are not readily available to home gardeners, so you are likely to find only 'McFarlin' (an old variety from 1874) and 'Stevens', a 'McFarlin' hybrid with large deep red fruits.

OPPOSITE, TOP: 'Stevens' cranberries.
INSET: Recurved cranberry blooms.

WHAT'S EDIBLE:
Berries

HARVEST TIME:
Late autumn

TASTES LIKE:
Sharp, acidic flavour

Currant

ABOVE: 'Red Lake' currants.
OPPOSITE: 'Pink Champagne' currants.

Currants are the exception in edible ornamentals in that they are much more attractive when laden in fruit than when in full bloom. Nothing is quite as eye-catching as the translucent berries of red or pink currant glistening in the morning sun: so much so that it almost seems a shame to pick them, although the birds won't hesitate. Your standard fruit types include black (*Ribes nigrum*) and red (*R. rubrum*), as well as white and pink berries that are just sports of redcurrant.

They are usually self-fertile, but benefit from cross-pollination by producing larger fruits and heavier crops; they are pollinated by insects and, to a lesser degree, by wind. These deciduous shrubs are quite versatile and can be trained as informal fruiting hedges or small standard trees; they can even be espaliered flat against a wall or fence.

Currants are the alternate host to white pine blister rust, an introduced fungus that affects all five-needled pines and has nearly wiped out western white pine (*Pinus monticola*) in parts of British Columbia—so there may be planting restrictions in your area. Other than that, these productive berry bushes are hardy enough to be planted in most parts of Canada, with your standard blackcurrant cultivars being 'Consort' (rust resistant), 'Ben Sarek' (good flavour) and 'Coronet' (also rust resistant). For *R. rubrum*, choose 'Red Lake' (very productive), 'White Imperial' or 'Pink Champagne', with the latter two considered the best tasting of all currants by many fruit connoisseurs.

WHAT'S EDIBLE:
Berries

HARVEST TIME:
Mid to late summer

TASTES LIKE:
Sharp blackberry (*Ribes nigrum*); sweet berry with some tartness (*R. rubrum*)

SPECIES:
Ribes nigrum; *R. rubrum*

A.K.A.:
Blackcurrant (*Ribes nigrum*); pink currant, redcurrant, white currant (*R. rubrum*)

PLANT TYPE:
Deciduous shrub

ORIGINS:
Western Europe (*Ribes nigrum*); Europe and Northern Asia (*R. rubrum*)

HARDINESS:
USDA zone 3

SUN:
Part to full sun

WATER:
Consistent soil moisture with good drainage

ULTIMATE SIZE:
40–60 inches (1–1.5 m) tall by 40–50 inches (1–1.2 m) wide for *Ribes nigrum*; 50–60 inches (1.2–1.5 m) high and wide for *R. rubrum*

BLOOM:
April through May

POLLINATION:
Most *Ribes nigrum* are self-fertile; *R. rubrum* is self-fertile (cross-pollination increases yield)

PRUNING:
Remove weak shoots and head back long branches in late winter

Dead Man's Fingers

SPECIES:
Decaisnea fargesii

A.K.A.:
Blue bean tree

PLANT TYPE:
Deciduous tree

ORIGIN:
Western China

HARDINESS:
USDA zone 6

SUN:
Open shade to full sun

WATER:
Consistent soil moisture with good drainage

ULTIMATE SIZE:
16–20 feet (5–6 m) high and wide

BLOOM:
May through June

POLLINATION:
Self-fertile

PRUNING:
Requires little pruning beyond structural

When my youngest daughter, Madeleine, was about 10 years old, she was fascinated by the gruesome (think ghosts, monsters, vampires), quite typical for that age. So when she found out that a friend had given me several clusters of dead man's fingers at the nursery where I work, she begged me to bring them home. The 4–6-inch (10–15-cm) sausage-like fruits live up to their name by resembling a digit, and the indigo-blue skin colour certainly lends itself to stories of the undead.

The edible portion is the translucent pulp or jelly that surrounds the black seeds inside the pods; the only problem being that it is "snotty" in texture. Madeleine's older sisters wouldn't touch the fruits with a 10-foot pole, but she and I ate several pods' worth and were pleasantly surprised by the lychee-nut flavour. Of course, she had earned bragging rights and went to school the next day telling her friends that she had eaten dead man's fingers.

The other attributes of this large deciduous shrub are not nearly as macabre, as the elegant pinnate foliage and multi-stem habit give it the look of a sumac at a distance. The bell-shaped yellowish-green (with a tinge of blue) flowers are held in terminal racemes in late spring and the foliage turns a beautiful gold in the fall, which nicely contrasts the bright blue fruit. This relative of akebia is also a member of the Lardizabalaceae family, and seems to thrive in open shade but can be grown in full sun with even soil moisture and shelter from strong winds. For a truly stunning display, try pairing *Callicarpa* 'Profusion' with *Decaisnea fargesii*, as the unnatural contrast of purple berries and blue fruits is eye-catching, to say the least.

ABOVE: Dead man's fingers in bloom.
INSET: Dead man's fingers fruits and fall colours.

WHAT'S EDIBLE:
Jelly around seeds in the pod

HARVEST TIME:
Mid-autumn, around Halloween

TASTES LIKE:
Lychee nut

Dogwood

I like to think of the kousa dogwood as the fruit tree most of us don't realize we already have. This popular ornamental species has white to deep rose-pink flowers (or bracts) and is deciduous, with the foliage turning a brilliant reddish purple in the fall. The ascending branches and upright habit make it an ideal tree for the front yard and its resistance to anthracnose fungus is the reason it is often chosen over the susceptible eastern dogwood (*Cornus florida*).

Then there are the multitude of flowering and variegated cultivars available to us, with the most popular being 'Satomi', with its pink to rose-red bracts. Variegated forms include 'Summer Gold' (gold margins that flush pink in fall), SAMARITAN (thin white leaf margins), as well as 'Wolf Eyes' (creamy-white variegation with wavy leaf margins), which can be a little shy to bloom at times. For those impressive flower displays that literally cover the contour of the tree, consider *Cornus kousa* var. *chinensis* (large white bracts) or 'Milky Way' (heavy set of white flowers). With its abundant rose-pink bracts, HEART THROB is a good alternative to 'Satomi'.

All of these are worthy ornamentals for your garden, but the bonus becomes apparent in late summer when the fruit provides another display in itself. It is actually a dull red compound berry (about 1–1¼ inches/2.5–3 cm wide) that much resembles a warty cherry, dangling on 3-inch (7.5-cm) stems. When ripe, the fruit is slightly hard outside with a hint of peach scent, while the contents are soft and custard-like with a sweet mild mango taste. The processed fruits make a lot of puree (once run through a food processor) that can be baked into muffins, made into jam or added to a fresh smoothie.

WHAT'S EDIBLE:
Reddish-pink fruits

HARVEST TIME:
Late summer to early fall

TASTES LIKE:
Mild sweet mango

OPPOSITE: Chinese dogwood in bloom.
ABOVE: Dogwood fruit.

SPECIES:
Cornus kousa

A.K.A.:
Japanese dogwood, Korean dogwood, kousa dogwood

PLANT TYPE:
Deciduous tree

ORIGINS:
China, Korea, Japan

HARDINESS:
USDA zone 5

SUN:
Part to full sun

WATER:
Consistent soil moisture with good drainage

ULTIMATE SIZE:
23 feet (7 m) tall by 15–16 feet (4.6–5 m) wide

BLOOM:
Late spring

POLLINATION:
Self-fertile

PRUNING:
Prune for form after flowering

Elderberry

ABOVE: BLACK LACE elderberry in flower.
OPPOSITE: American elderberry fruits.

There are two preferred species of elderberries for fruit production, black elder (*Sambucus nigra*) and American (*S. canadensis*), although the latter is now considered a variety of the European native and can be found as *S. nigra* var. *canadensis*—but we will keep these separate, as that is how they are currently marketed. Both are large deciduous shrubs that have edible flowers and berries, with the European species producing many highly prized ornamental forms, such as BLACK LACE or 'Eva' (pink flowers, jet-black cutleaf foliage), 'Pulverulenta' (mottled green and white foliage, but light on berries) and *S. nigra* f. *laciniata*, which much resembles a green cutleaf Japanese maple. American elderberries require cross-pollination, so 'Nova' and 'York' are your best bets, while 'Korsor' is a popular Danish cultivar of *S. nigra* grown for its large fruit clusters.

The flowers from both *S. canadensis* and *nigra* make a unique cordial, which when combined with sparkling water or even champagne can only be described as "spring in a glass." This can be made by boiling 6 cups (1.4 L) water with 5 cups (1.2 L) sugar to make a syrup, letting it cool before pouring into large mason jars. Divide between the jars the zest of 4 medium-sized lemons, slicing the remaining fruits and adding them too. Lastly, mix in 15 large elderberry flower heads (lightly shaken, not washed) with stems removed. Cover and store in the refrigerator for 2 days, then strain through cheesecloth, and you have your elderflower cordial base. The berries make delicious juices, wines and preserves, and are high in antioxidants and vitamin C.

WHAT'S EDIBLE:
Flowers and berries

HARVEST TIME:
Late summer

TASTES LIKE:
Flowers are sweetly herbal, berries when processed taste like wild grape with blackberry

SPECIES:
Sambucus nigra; *S. canadensis*

A.K.A.:
European elderberry, black elder (*Sambucus nigra*); American elderberry (*S. canadensis*)

PLANT TYPE:
Deciduous shrub

ORIGINS:
Europe, North Africa, Southwest Asia (*Sambucus nigra*); North America (*S. canadensis*)

HARDINESS:
USDA zone 4 (*S. nigra*); zone 3 (*S. canadensis*)

SUN:
Part to full sun

WATER:
Consistent soil moisture

ULTIMATE SIZE:
7½–15 feet (2.3–4.6 m) high and wide for *Sambucus nigra*; 6–12 feet (1.8–3.7 m) high and wide for *S. canadensis*

BLOOM:
May through June (*Sambucus nigra*); June through July (*S. canadensis*)

POLLINATION:
Sambucus nigra is partially self-fertile, cross-pollination increases yield; cross-pollination required for *S. canadensis*

PRUNING:
Prune in late winter to thin out weak branches or deadwood

Fig

My introduction to figs was a bush my grandmother kept in an old Chinese egg crock at her Okanagan home, one that thrived in the summer heat but needed to be brought into her covered porch to survive the cold winters. I also have a 'Petite Negra' growing in a pot on my back porch and as I was enjoying the sweet, strawberry-coloured flesh of my first fruit from it, my Gran came to mind and that fig instantly tasted twice as good.

We grow the plants we love and if sales are any indication, we love our figs, as I am currently selling more each season. We don't have the long Mediterranean summers required to ripen the second or main crop, so in Canada we have to be content with those that produce a heavy first or "breba" crop on one-year wood. Standard varieties over the years have included 'Italian Honey', 'Brown Turkey' and 'Desert King', with the latter being the most prolific for coastal gardens. 'Ronde de Bordeaux' is another good choice, as it is highly productive and has absolutely delicious figs with violet-black skin, while 'Little Ruby' and 'Negronne' (a.k.a. 'Violette de Bordeaux') are both compact and work well in containers. 'Peter's Honey' is considered one of the best for fresh eating, while 'Chicago Hardy' (zone 5) is a good choice for those climate-zone deniers.

WHAT'S EDIBLE:
Entire fruit is edible, but most people just eat the pulp inside as some are allergic to the skin

HARVEST TIME:
Late July to August for "breba" or first crop; the second or main crop will probably not ripen in our shorter Canadian summers

TASTES LIKE:
Fresh figs taste like sweet honey with hints of fruit jams (varies with cultivar)

OPPOSITE: 'Ronde de Bordeaux' figs.
ABOVE: Ripening 'Brown Turkey' figs.

SPECIES:
Ficus carica

A.K.A.:
Common fig

PLANT TYPE:
Deciduous tree or shrub (evergreen in warmer climates)

ORIGINS:
Middle East, Western Asia

HARDINESS:
USDA zone 6 (with some cultivars being more tender)

SUN:
Full sun

WATER:
Consistent soil moisture with good drainage

ULTIMATE SIZE:
10–13 feet (3–4 m) high and wide (larger in warmer regions)

BLOOM:
Flowers are unseen inside the fruit, so no bloom period *per se*

POLLINATION:
Does not require pollination for the fruit to develop

PRUNING:
Train to standard or bush form in the first few years, and remove weak or old wood in late winter to allow for more productive growth

Filbert

ABOVE: Contorted red hazelnut.
OPPOSITE: Recently harvested 'Barcelona' hazelnuts.

SPECIES:
Corylus avellana

A.K.A.:
Cobnut, common hazel, hazelnut

PLANT TYPE:
Deciduous tree or shrub

ORIGINS:
Europe, Turkey

HARDINESS:
USDA zone 3

SUN:
Part to full sun

WATER:
Consistent soil moisture with good drainage

ULTIMATE SIZE:
15 feet (4.6 m) tall by 12–15 feet (3.7–4.6 m) wide

BLOOM:
Late winter to early spring

POLLINATION:
Cross-pollination is required, wind pollinated

PRUNING:
Remove old wood on mature trees in late winter

WHAT'S EDIBLE:
Nuts

HARVEST TIME:
Mid to late autumn

TASTES LIKE:
Buttery sweet nut flavour when fully ripened

Filberts used to be the "go-to" nut tree—the easiest to grow and fit into average urban gardens. There were even ornamental forms, such as the fantastically twisted Harry Lauder's walking stick (*Corylus avellana* 'Contorta') and a purple-leaved version called 'Red Majestic'. In British Columbia, all this garden bliss came to a screeching halt with the arrival of eastern filbert blight to the Fraser Valley around 2000. Over the course of 10 years, this fungus (which also affects Eastern Canada) wiped out entire orchards and even decimated our contorted filberts (the newer 'Red Dragon' is resistant). Rigorous pruning and sprays to suppress this disease failed to hold it back and all the local commercial cultivars, such as 'Ennis', 'Barcelona' and 'Butler', were highly susceptible.

There is, however, a way forward and it involves forgetting the past and turning to new resistant filbert cultivars coming out of Oregon State University. Of the varieties that have been introduced here, both 'Sacajawea' and 'Lewis' are partially resistant, 'Jefferson' (large nuts like 'Barcelona') is highly resistant and 'Yamhill' (compact growth habit) appears impervious.

As with traditional cultivars, these new varieties will need to be paired with a partner in order to cross-pollinate and bear nuts, such as 'Sacajawea' with 'Yamhill'. They will also need to be in close proximity, as filberts are wind pollinated, with the maximum spacing between trees being 15–20 feet (4.6–6 m) apart. I am still waiting for 'Red Dragon' to become more widely available, as contorted hazelnuts are no longer available from local wholesale nurseries due to high infection rates—but like any other obstacle in gardening, we almost always find a way around it.

Fish Mint

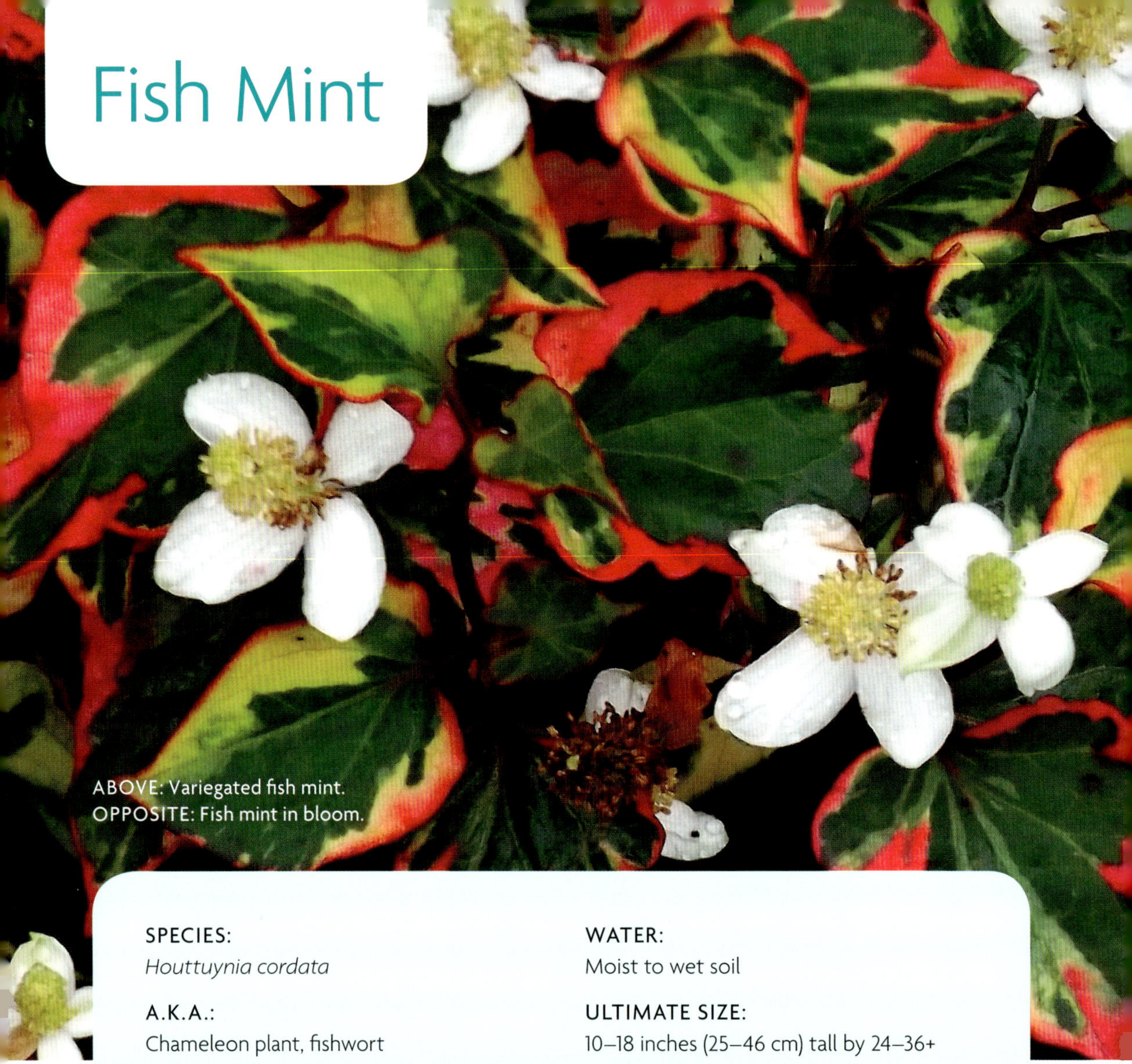

ABOVE: Variegated fish mint.
OPPOSITE: Fish mint in bloom.

SPECIES:
Houttuynia cordata

A.K.A.:
Chameleon plant, fishwort

PLANT TYPE:
Herbaceous perennial

ORIGIN:
Eastern Asia

HARDINESS:
USDA zone 5

SUN:
Part to full sun

WATER:
Moist to wet soil

ULTIMATE SIZE:
10–18 inches (25–46 cm) tall by 24–36+ inches (60–90+ cm) wide

BLOOM:
Early summer

POLLINATION:
Self-fertile

PRUNING:
Cut back after dormancy

I had been planting the variegated form (*Houttuynia cordata* 'Chameleon') of fish mint as a landscaper for decades before realizing it was an edible plant. What I learned in those interim years is that this aggressive species (it is considered an invasive plant in many countries) is best grown in containers or used as a potted shallow marginal in a pond or water feature, as once rooted in ground it spreads rapidly and can be difficult to control. When fish mint is grown as a marginal plant in a pond, its crown can be maintained anywhere between 1–2 inches (2.5–5 cm) below the surface of the water.

The green-leaved species is rarely seen (except as reversions), although why one would plant this in preference to the beautifully variegated rose-red, green and yellow foliage of 'Chameleon' would be a mystery to me—just keep in mind that a full-sun exposure is required to bring out the best leaf colouration. Small white four-petaled flowers begin appearing in late spring but are in full force in early summer, when they sit just above the foliage.

Fish mint is quite unique in scent and flavour, both of which remind me of orange and cilantro. Others detect a fishy-mint taste (hence the common name) and, whatever the case, you either love it or hate it—there doesn't seem to be any culinary middle ground. Regardless, it should be used very sparingly, with fresh leaves treated as an eye-catching garnish or finely chopped and added to fruit salads for a little zest. Fish mint is cooked as a pot herb in Vietnam and is a key ingredient in many Thai dishes. It is also used extensively in Indian cuisine, where it is cooked with vegetables or made into chili dishes and chutneys.

WHAT'S EDIBLE:
Young shoots and leaves

HARVEST TIME:
Anytime when in leaf

TASTES LIKE:
Orange and cilantro

Flowering Quince

ABOVE: 'Simonii' quince fruits. INSET: 'Pink Lady' quince flowers.

WHAT'S EDIBLE:
Irregular fruits

HARVEST TIME:
Late autumn

TASTES LIKE:
Tart true quince with cooking

SPECIES:
Chaenomeles speciosa; *C. japonica*

A.K.A.:
Flowering quince (*Chaenomeles speciosa*); japonica (*C. japonica*)

PLANT TYPE:
Deciduous shrub

ORIGINS:
China (*Chaenomeles speciosa*); Japan (*C. japonica*)

HARDINESS:
USDA zone 5

SUN:
Part to full sun

WATER:
Average moisture, drought tolerant once established

ULTIMATE SIZE:
40–120 inches (1–3 m) high and wide

BLOOM:
Early spring, as leaves emerge

POLLINATION:
Self-fertile

PRUNING:
Thin or shape after flowering

Flowering quince is an unruly old-fashioned deciduous shrub—usually found in older neighbourhoods or abandoned farms—that has not really found a place in the modern garden. One thing that can be said for those often long-abandoned shrubs is that they seem to take care of themselves, readily blooming despite an obvious lack of attention. It is these neglected thickets that effortlessly produce the irregular bright yellow fruits (often with a red blush) that persist into winter and are quite visible after leaf drop. While they are hard as a rock and too acidic to be eaten in a raw state, if you can collect enough of them, they make an absolutely delicious jelly that is a lovely rose-pink in colour.

Most of what we see in older gardens or available at our local garden centres are from one of three species or hybrids, including *Chaenomeles speciosa*, *C. japonica* and *C.* × *superba* (a cross of *speciosa* and *japonica*). These provide a vast array of flower colours, including reddish orange ('Orange Delight'), pure white ('Jet Trail'), pale pink ('Apple Blossom'), scarlet ('Rowallane'), coral pink ('Pink Lady') and blood red ('Simonii'), with both double and single blooms.

Compact varieties are available, but even the larger cultivars can be trained flat against a wall or fence line as informal espaliers, where the flowers are produced on the contour and fruit is much easier to pick (many flowering quince are thorny). They also make excellent, impenetrable hedges, tolerating shearing and becoming quite dense over time. While I'll admit that few gardeners are likely to plant *Chaenomeles* for fruit production, if you already have it in your garden, you might as well enjoy both the blooms (which make good cut flowers) and the incidental edible pomes.

Fuchsia

All fuchsia flowers and berries are edible, but I chose these two because *Fuchsia magellanica* is one of the hardiest and the Bolivian fuchsia has the best-tasting berries, in my opinion. One of my favourite garden memories is of a bank of hardy fuchsia that covered a sheltered south-facing slope on one of the estates I used to work on. Once the fuchsia was in bloom, there was no getting near it, as the rather territorial hummingbirds would dive-bomb us (you could feel them brushing your hair) any time we approached.

F. magellanica is a deciduous subshrub here in Canada, dying back in the cold but recovering from its base in spring. Some zone-5 gardeners have had some success with it by heavily mulching the base. There are many cultivars available, including 'Aurea' (gold foliage), 'Alba' (pale pink blooms) and 'Versicolor' (grey-green, cream and pink foliage).

The flowers are slightly bitter but make a beautiful garnish, while the berries need to be picked at peak ripeness for best flavour. *F. boliviana* is a bit of a rarity but well worth looking for, as the purple rod-shaped berries are juicy, much resembling and tasting like a red grape. There is also a new hybrid coming out of Thompson & Morgan in England—bred just for delicious fruit, it is called FUCHSIABERRY and I am hoping to see it in Canada soon.

OPPOSITE, TOP: 'Riccartonii' hardy fuchsia. INSET: Bolivian fuchsia berries and blooms.

SPECIES:
Fuchsia magellanica; *F. boliviana*

A.K.A.:
Hardy fuchsia (*Fuchsia magellanica*); Bolivian fuchsia (*F. boliviana*)

PLANT TYPE:
Deciduous subshrub (evergreen in warmer climates)

ORIGINS:
Argentina, Chile (*Fuchsia magellanica*); Argentina, Bolivia, Peru (*F. boliviana*)

HARDINESS:
USDA zone 6 (*Fuchsia magellanica*); zone 9 (*F. boliviana*)

SUN:
Part to full sun (*Fuchsia magellanica*); shade to partial shade (*F. boliviana*)

WATER:
Even soil moisture with good drainage

ULTIMATE SIZE:
2–4 feet (60–120 cm) tall by 3 feet (90 cm) wide (larger in warmer climates) for *Fuchsia magellanica*; 7–13 feet (2–4 m) tall by 3 feet (90 cm) wide where native (much smaller when grown in containers) for *F. boliviana*

BLOOM:
Summer to fall

POLLINATION:
Self-fertile

PRUNING: Hard prune in early spring when new growth begins to emerge, pinch afterwards to increase density

WHAT'S EDIBLE:
Flowers and berries

HARVEST TIME:
Flowers in bloom (usually retained for berry production), berries midsummer to fall

TASTES LIKE:
Flowers can be slightly bitter, and berries have a sweet yet subtle red-grape flavour when fully ripe, while others provide a peppery citrus taste, so expect some variation

Gaultheria

I had no idea salal berries were edible until my grandmother told me about how she used to hike British Columbia's North Shore mountains with her dad in the 1930s; this was before the Lions Gate Bridge was built, when there was little up there but forest trails and shingle mills. She recalled that their favourite on-the-fly snack was salal berries, which when eaten at peak ripeness tasted better than blueberries. She was right—those ripe dark bluish-purple berries have a wild flavour reminiscent of blueberry and an undertone that some describe as the tang of a concord grape, but pick them a little late and they are bland and mealy.

The plant itself is a useful evergreen subshrub with glossy deep green leaves and attractive white bell-shaped flowers. It forms a highly variable ground cover that I have seen grow 8 feet (2.5 m) tall in moist shade and a mere foot (30 cm) in full-sun exposures with limited moisture.

Prickly heath is a related evergreen shrub that used to be called *Pernettya*, and has separate male and female plants. The females produce attractive edible berries in white, pale pink and deep rose, which often cover the contour of the plant in early fall. The slightly prickly foliage makes both males and females a good barrier shrub. 'Bell's Seedling', PINK SNOWDROP and WHITE SNOWDROP are self-fertile, but most of the older female cultivars require a nearby male for pollination and berries. *Gaultheria × wisleyensis* 'Wisley Pearl' is a self-fertile *G. shallon* × *G. mucronata* hybrid that also produces tasty purplish-pink fruits.

WHAT'S EDIBLE:
Berries

HARVEST TIME:
Late summer to early fall

TASTES LIKE:
Mild blueberry (*Gaultheria shallon*); mild wintergreen (*G. mucronata*)

OPPOSITE: Salal berries.
ABOVE: *Gaultheria* × *wisleyensis* 'Wisley Pearl' fruits.

SPECIES:
Gaultheria shallon; *G. mucronata* (syn. *Pernettya mucronata*)

A.K.A.:
Salal (*Gaultheria shallon*); prickly heath (*G. mucronata*)

PLANT TYPE:
Evergreen shrub

ORIGINS:
Western North America (*Gaultheria shallon*); Argentina, Chile (*G. mucronata*)

HARDINESS:
USDA zone 6 (*Gaultheria shallon*); zone 7 (*G. mucronata*)

SUN:
Shade to full sun (*Gaultheria shallon*); part to full sun (*G. mucronata*)

WATER:
Evenly moist to dry (*Gaultheria shallon*); even moisture with drainage (*G. mucronata*)

ULTIMATE SIZE:
1–6 feet (30–180 cm) tall by 1½–4 feet (46–120 cm) wide for *Gaultheria shallon*; 4 feet (120 cm) tall and wide for *G. mucronata*

BLOOM:
May to June

POLLINATION:
Gaultheria shallon is self-fertile; some cultivars of *G. mucronata* require cross-pollination

PRUNING: Remove deadwood and shape in spring (*Gaultheria shallon*); light pruning in early spring (*G. mucronata*)

Goji Berry

While there is no denying the taste of fresh goji berries is a love or hate proposition (much in part due to its strange blend of tomato and other fruit flavours), the health benefits cannot be ignored. These raisin-sized red berries are an ancient Chinese herbal medicine packed with antioxidants proven to reduce joint inflammation and boost immunity. The only problem being that most of the goji berry crop is grown in China, where pesticide regulations are inconsistent at best. This has resulted in shipments (even those labelled "organic") being denied access to outside markets due to chemical residues—so maybe it's time to grow your own.

Thankfully, these deciduous shrubs are not difficult to handle and some colder-weather zone-3 gardeners are having great success, so the potential for production across Canada is pretty good. The essentials of cultivation include well-drained soil (they languish or die in wet conditions) and a full-sun exposure if you want good fruit production. Aesthetically, the bush itself is not particularly beautiful, but when the arching branches are full of violet flowers and orange to red berries it really redeems itself.

For those of you with limited garden space, goji berries adapt well to growing in containers and can even be trained to a weeping standard form. The closely related *Lycium chinense* is reported to have sweeter berries, although both species are often marketed as the same fruit. *L. barbarum* is readily available at most garden centres, with CRIMSON STAR (large red fruits), SWEET LIFEBERRY (exceptionally sweet berries) and BIG LIFEBERRY (extra-large fruit) being the most common cultivars.

SPECIES:
Lycium barbarum

A.K.A.:
Chinese box thorn, Chinese wolfberry

PLANT TYPE:
Deciduous shrub

ORIGIN:
China

HARDINESS:
USDA zone 5 (but grown in colder zones)

SUN:
Full sun

WATER:
Even soil moisture with good drainage, tolerates drought but fruit quality may suffer

ULTIMATE SIZE:
7½–10 feet (2.3–3 m) tall by 5–7 feet (1.5–2 m) wide, smaller when pruned

BLOOM:
June through August

POLLINATION:
Self-fertile

PRUNING:
Head back main branches in late winter to encourage new wood, increasing flowers and fruit

OPPOSITE, TOP: Ripe goji berries.
INSET: Goji berry flowers and fruit.

WHAT'S EDIBLE:
Red berries

HARVEST TIME:
Midsummer to late fall, before first frost

TASTES LIKE:
Fresh berries taste of cranberry, tomato and sour cherry

Gooseberry and Jostaberry

ABOVE: 'Hinnonmaki Red' gooseberry.
OPPOSITE: Ripe jostaberry fruits.

While gooseberries are not as popular as they have been in the past, they were essentials on my wife's grandparents' farm in Ste. Anne, just south of Winnipeg. *Groseille* (as they are known to French Canadians) tolerated the brutally cold winters and blistering summers, all the while producing a heavy crop of tart red berries that were the key ingredient in the family's quintessential jam. Most gooseberries are derived from either European (*Ribes uva-crispa*) or American species (*Ribes hirtellum*), with fruits varying in size from ½–1 inch (1.25–2.5 cm) and berry colours ranging from green, red, yellow and reddish purple.

Most of these deciduous bushes are quite thorny, which can make harvesting a challenge, but if properly pruned to allow essential light penetration the picking is much easier. Cultivars that thrive in Canada include the Finnish varieties 'Hinnonmaki Red' and 'Hinnonmaki Yellow', along with 'Captivator' (almost spineless, good flavour), 'Invicta' (very productive) and 'Pixwell' (disease resistant).

Jostaberry (*R.* × *nidigrolaria*) is a blackcurrant-gooseberry hybrid that is thornless and produces black fruit that doesn't taste quite as sharp as fresh blackcurrant. While there are several cultivars available (such as 'Jostina'), you are only likely to find a generic jostaberry at your local garden centre. These deciduous shrubs are usually quite erect, with a strong upright branching habit; however if left unpruned they bear heavily but with smaller, poorer-quality fruits. One advantage of this hybrid is that it is resistant to white pine blister rust.

WHAT'S EDIBLE:
Berries

HARVEST TIME:
Midsummer

TASTES LIKE:
Sour grape to floral, with a hint of strawberry (*Ribes uva-crispa*); blackcurrant and gooseberry, with subtle blueberry (*R. × nidigrolaria*)

SPECIES:
Ribes uva-crispa; *R. × nidigrolaria*

A.K.A.:
European gooseberry (*Ribes uva-crispa*); josta (*R. × nidigrolaria*)

PLANT TYPE:
Deciduous shrub

ORIGINS:
Europe, North Africa, Asia (*Ribes uva-crispa*); garden origin (*R. × nidigrolaria*)

HARDINESS:
USDA zone 3–4, depending on cultivar (*Ribes uva-crispa*); zone 4 (*R. × nidigrolaria*)

SUN:
Part to full sun

WATER:
Average soil moisture with good drainage

ULTIMATE SIZE:
3–6 feet (90–180 cm) high and wide for *Ribes uva-crispa*; 4–6 feet (120–180 cm) high by 4 feet (120 cm) wide for *R. × nidigrolaria*

BLOOM:
Early to mid-spring (*Ribes uva-crispa*); mid-spring (*R. × nidigrolaria*)

POLLINATION:
Ribes uva-crispa is self-fertile, often wind pollinated; *R. × nidigrolaria* is self-fertile with exceptions

PRUNING:
Prune out weak branches or deadwood in late winter, shorten new growth in summer

Goumi Berry

Goumi berry is a fruiting shrub I rarely encounter except on older properties where edible plants were obviously the priority, but I am hoping that more gardeners familiarize themselves with this useful species. Growing them has environmental benefits—the fragrant pale yellow flowers (scented like lilac) support native pollinators such as mason bees, and this plant is capable of fixing its own nitrogen with symbiotic soil bacteria.

The species usually forms a large multi-stemmed shrub that is deciduous here in Canada, with tapered foliage that is deep green on top with an attractive silvery reverse. While there are a few thorns, these are not hard to see and work around. It is a disease-resistant species with few problems other than mouse and rabbit bark girdling, which is easily remedied with a hardware cloth barrier.

Although it is said to be only partially self-fertile, the few established shrubs I know of locally seem to produce just fine without a cross-pollinator. The translucent rod-shaped fruits turn red when ripe and have subtle silver speckles on the skin. It is important to harvest only when it is fully ripened for the best sweetness and taste—a tangy cross of rhubarb and redcurrant. The berries process well into fruit leather, preserves such as jam, and even wine. The nuts are also edible and occasionally eaten with the berries, but some find the seed coat rather stringy. There are not many cultivars available, as most specialty nurseries offer seedling stock. RED GEM (very productive) and SWEET SCARLET (large sweet berries) are both from Ukraine and can be used to cross-pollinate each other, while the rare 'Monez' has very large fruits.

WHAT'S EDIBLE:
Fruits and seeds

HARVEST TIME:
Midsummer

TASTES LIKE:
Sweet to tart rhubarb and redcurrant

OPPOSITE: Ripening goumi berries.
ABOVE: Goumi berry shrub in flower.

SPECIES:
Elaeagnus multiflora

A.K.A.:
Cherry silverberry, gumi

PLANT TYPE:
Deciduous shrub

ORIGINS:
China, Korea, Japan

HARDINESS:
USDA zone 5

SUN:
Part to full sun

WATER:
Moderate with good drainage

ULTIMATE SIZE:
6–10 feet (1.8–3 m) high and wide

BLOOM:
Spring

POLLINATION:
Partially self-fertile, better crops with cross-pollination

PRUNING:
Remove old wood in late winter and lightly shape after harvest

Grape

ABOVE: Purpleleaf grape's autumn tones.
OPPOSITE: PIXIE 'Pinot Meunier' grape cluster.

SPECIES:
Vitis vinifera

A.K.A.:
Common grape, European wine grape

PLANT TYPE:
Deciduous vine

ORIGINS:
Europe, Southwestern Asia, Morocco

HARDINESS:
USDA zone 6 (hardier cultivars exist)

SUN:
Full sun

WATER:
Consistent soil moisture with good drainage

ULTIMATE SIZE:
10–20+ feet (3–6+ m) tall, depending on pruning

BLOOM:
May to early July

POLLINATION:
Self-fertile

PRUNING:
In late winter, prune mature vines by removing old wood and cutting back 1-year wood (pencil thickness) to 2 to 4 buds, in summer prune for light penetration by heading back excessive new growth

While my grandmother's garden was her space, anything that pertained to wine-making was my grandfather's domain. He was a no-nonsense Austrian and often greeted his grandchildren by opening the refrigerator to show us multiple crispers filled with leftover wine grapes and warning us that we should not let these go to waste—so I come by my grape palate honestly.

Choosing the right grape varieties is important and largely based on where you live. Prairie gardeners are limited to table grapes such as 'Beta' and 'Valiant', which are hybrids of FOX (*Vitis labrusca*) and RIVERBANK GRAPE (*V. riparia*)—although new cold-hardy wine grapes such as 'Marquette' (red), 'Frontenac Gris' (amber juice) and 'La Crescent' (white) are now available. In coastal regions with cooler summers, 'Himrod' (green seedless), 'Vanessa' and 'Canadice' (both red seedless) are good eating choices, while local vintners have been having some success with 'Marechal Foch' (red wine) and 'Siegerrebe' (white wine).

Those in Canada's wine regions, such as British Columbia's Okanagan Valley, Ontario's southern Niagara and Nova Scotia's Annapolis Valley, can all grow the classic 'Chardonnay', 'Riesling' and 'Pinot Noir'—although each region definitely has its own microclimate. There is even a nice ornamental purpleleaf grape (*V. vinifera* 'Purpurea'), with burgundy new growth and tart dark blue grapes that can make a good jelly. For those of you looking for the ideal container specimen, try one of the PIXIE series, which maxes out at 2 feet (60 cm) tall and produces miniature bunches of green or blue grapes.

WHAT'S EDIBLE:
Leaves and fruits

HARVEST TIME:
Late summer to early fall

TASTES LIKE:
Leaves are slightly herbal, usually taking on the flavour of the foods they're cooked with, and fruits are sweet or tart, with fruit, spice or musky flavours depending on growing conditions and cultivar

LEFT: 'Sovereign Coronation' grapes. RIGHT: 'Niagara' grapes.

Grape cultivars

Grapes can become collector items for vintners looking for that subtle hint of fruit or spice that will distinguish their blends from the rest of the crowd, which is why I have included more cultivars here that can be grown in wine regions across Canada. That same search for perfection also applies to table or eating grapes—while those subtle hints of musk or strawberry may be lost in a blended wine, they are certainly present when the fruit is eaten fresh.

The following list includes cultivar name and description of fruit:

TABLE GRAPES

'Bath': Blue seeded with mild 'Concord' flavour for fresh eating and jellies

'Einset': Pink seedless with a subtle strawberry flavour

'Niagara': Seedless green grape good for juicing, fresh eating or wine-making

'Sovereign Coronation': Blue seedless with a slightly musky flavour

'Suffolk Red': Red seedless with a subtle spicy-sweet aftertaste

WINE GRAPES

'Baco Noir': Hybrid red with berry and spice flavours

'Cabernet Franc': Black grape used for blending or ice wine production

'Gewürztraminer': Pink to red-skinned white wine grape for cooler climates

'Kerner': Aromatic white wine grape with citrus and peach flavours

'Seyval Blanc': Hardy white wine grape with pear and citrus overtones

A grapevine can be an elegant addition to the garden. *Photo © Pix / Adobe Stock*

Green Tea

When you consider that most of the commercial tea grown is from China and India, it hardly seems possible that a Canadian crop would be feasible—and yet the Westholme Tea Farm located in Vancouver Island's Cowichan Valley is already harvesting a pure locally grown leaf called Tree Frog Green. Tea is brewed from the leaves of *Camellia sinensis*, which has both large-leaf (var. *assamica*) and small-leaf (var. *sinensis*) forms. At zone 7, it is not hardy everywhere in Canada, but can be grown as a houseplant if you like.

The new flush (the top two leaves and bud) is traditionally harvested in spring, early summer and fall. Green tea is usually just steamed and dried, while black tea is crushed and fermented, with the former method being the most common means of processing utilized by home gardeners (see my step-by-step green tea instructions on pages 257–58).

I am familiar with four cultivars, including 'Korean Tea Seedling' (from Boseong, South Korea) and 'Sochi Tea Seedling', an extremely hardy cultivar from the most northern tea plantation in Russia. Two older introductions, 'Teabreeze' (1989) and *Camellia sinensis* var. *rubra* 'Blushing Maiden' (1992, pink flowers) are Canadian introductions from Piroche Plants in Pitt Meadows, British Columbia. I have a nursery client who grows all four cultivars in his Fraser Valley garden and he rates 'Blushing Maiden' as a producer of the tastiest local green tea.

As far as aesthetics are concerned, these broadleaf shrubs have glossy green foliage that can be trimmed quite tightly, while the white to pink flowers (1–1½ inches/2.5–3.8 cm in diameter) are borne in autumn and often hidden in the foliage. The shrubs can be grown in containers in milder regions, but will need shelter from strong winter winds and should be brought in as a houseplant when it becomes colder.

SPECIES:
Camellia sinensis

A.K.A.:
Tea camellia

PLANT TYPE:
Evergreen shrub

ORIGINS:
Southeast Asia, China

HARDINESS:
USDA zone 7

SUN:
Part to full sun

WATER:
Consistent soil moisture with good drainage

ULTIMATE SIZE:
6–10 feet (1.8–3 m) high and wide (depending on pruning)

BLOOM:
September to November

POLLINATION:
Not required for harvest

PRUNING:
Prune or shape bushes when harvesting

ABOVE: 'Blushing Maiden' green tea flowers.
INSET: Hardy 'Sochi Tea Seedling' camellia in bloom.

WHAT'S EDIBLE:

Leaves

HARVEST TIME:

Spring flush, as well as new growth in early summer and fall

TASTES LIKE:

Slightly bitter and mildly nutty tea, depending on brewing

Hardy Orange

ABOVE: Fall colours of contorted hardy orange.
INSET: Hardy orange fruits.

WHAT'S EDIBLE:
Small fruits

HARVEST TIME:
Late fall to early winter

TASTES LIKE:
Sour tangerine

At USDA zone 5, this is the hardiest of the *Citrus*, but the reason you may not be familiar with this species is that it fruits sparingly in our climate, and the thorns make barberry look positively wimpy. These prominent barbs, at 1¼–2 inches (3–5 cm) long, blend in well with the bright green new wood, which is why the species is often fashioned into impenetrable hedges that are favoured by nesting birds. The small trifoliate leaves almost appear as an afterthought, although many people find the open, wiry aesthetic of this large shrub quite pleasing.

There is another compact contorted form known as *Poncirus trifoliata* var. *monstrosa* or 'Flying Dragon', depending on the supplier (although these are identical in nature). Both the species and contorted form are used extensively as root understock for other citrus plants, where they improve hardiness and dwarf the topgraft, respectively. 'Flying Dragon' makes a superb container specimen with its fantastically twisted form and curved thorns that resemble huge fish hooks, although you do have to be careful with its placement so that passers-by don't get snagged.

The lightly fragrant white blooms are borne from late spring to early summer, and followed by golf ball–sized orange fruits that ripen in late fall through to early winter. These are quite seedy and not particularly good fresh eating, but when stored for several weeks can be juiced or made into a zesty marmalade. Small slices are also said to be good company for gin and tonic. *P. trifoliata* prefers a sheltered, sunny site away from cold winter winds, with sharp soil drainage, as wet soils are likely to result in plant mortality. Expect stunning autumn foliage of peachy-orange and bare bright green stems all winter.

SPECIES:
Poncirus trifoliata (syn. *Citrus trifoliata*)

A.K.A.:
Japanese bitter orange

PLANT TYPE:
Deciduous shrub

ORIGINS:
China, Korea

HARDINESS:
USDA zone 5

SUN:
Full sun

WATER:
Average moisture, drought tolerant once established

ULTIMATE SIZE:
8–12 feet (2.5–3.7 m) high by 6–10 feet (1.8–3 m) wide

BLOOM:
Late spring to early summer

POLLINATION:
Self-fertile

PRUNING:
Lightly shape after flowering

Haskap

SPECIES:
Lonicera caerulea

A.K.A.:
Blue honeysuckle, honeyberry

PLANT TYPE:
Deciduous shrub

ORIGIN:
Northern Hemisphere

HARDINESS:
USDA zone 2

SUN:
Part to full sun

WATER:
Consistent soil moisture with good drainage

ULTIMATE SIZE:
3–5 feet (90–150 cm) tall by 3–4 feet (90–120 cm) wide

BLOOM:
March to early May, depending on variety and location

POLLINATION:
Requires cross-pollination from a different cultivar that blooms at the same time

PRUNING:
Thin out and remove old wood on mature plants in late winter

While I still believe this fairly recent introduction is an important edible crop, there are several problems that have hindered it from becoming more widely accepted. The first was the unrealistic descriptions of the berry's flavour, touted as a cross between blueberry and raspberry. Home consumers expecting a highly palatable fresh-eating fruit were sorely disappointed with their first harvest, as most berries have a sharp blackcurrant aftertaste that lends itself to smoothies or fruit leather. The other problem was that the Russian-Canadian varieties of honeyberries (*Lonicera caerulea* var. *edulis* and *kamtschatica*) fared very poorly in coastal gardens, with foliar problems or issues with early blooming and an accompanying lack of pollinators.

Thankfully, the Japanese haskaps (*Lonicera caerulea* var. *emphyllocalyx*) grow much better in coastal regions and flower three to four weeks later. The standard honeyberry cultivars are great for interior or prairie gardens and include 'Tundra' (good flavour, firm fruit), 'Borealis' (best flavour, softer berries) and 'Honey Bee' (tart, excellent pollinator).

The University of Saskatchewan's newer introductions, 'Boreal Blizzard' (huge flavourful berries) and 'Boreal Beauty' (late cropping), are crosses of Russian and Japanese varieties. BLUE VELVET (compact spreading form), BLUE MOON (large flavourful fruit) and BLUE HOKKAIDO (popular with commercial growers) are Japanese varieties that fare well in coastal climates, as do the newer YEZBERRY SOLO (self-fertile) and SUGAR PIE (very compact) from Proven Winners. The terminology for this species is often convoluted, with old names such as *Lonicera villosa* and *edulis* turning up, as well as cultivars being classified as different varieties in various catalogues . . . so consider it a work in progress.

ABOVE: Ripening haskap berries.
INSET: 'Tundra' haskap in bloom.

WHAT'S EDIBLE:
Dark blue berries

TASTES LIKE:
Blueberry, raspberry and blackcurrant, often with a sharp aftertaste

HARVEST TIME:
June to mid-July, depending on variety and location

Highbush Cranberry

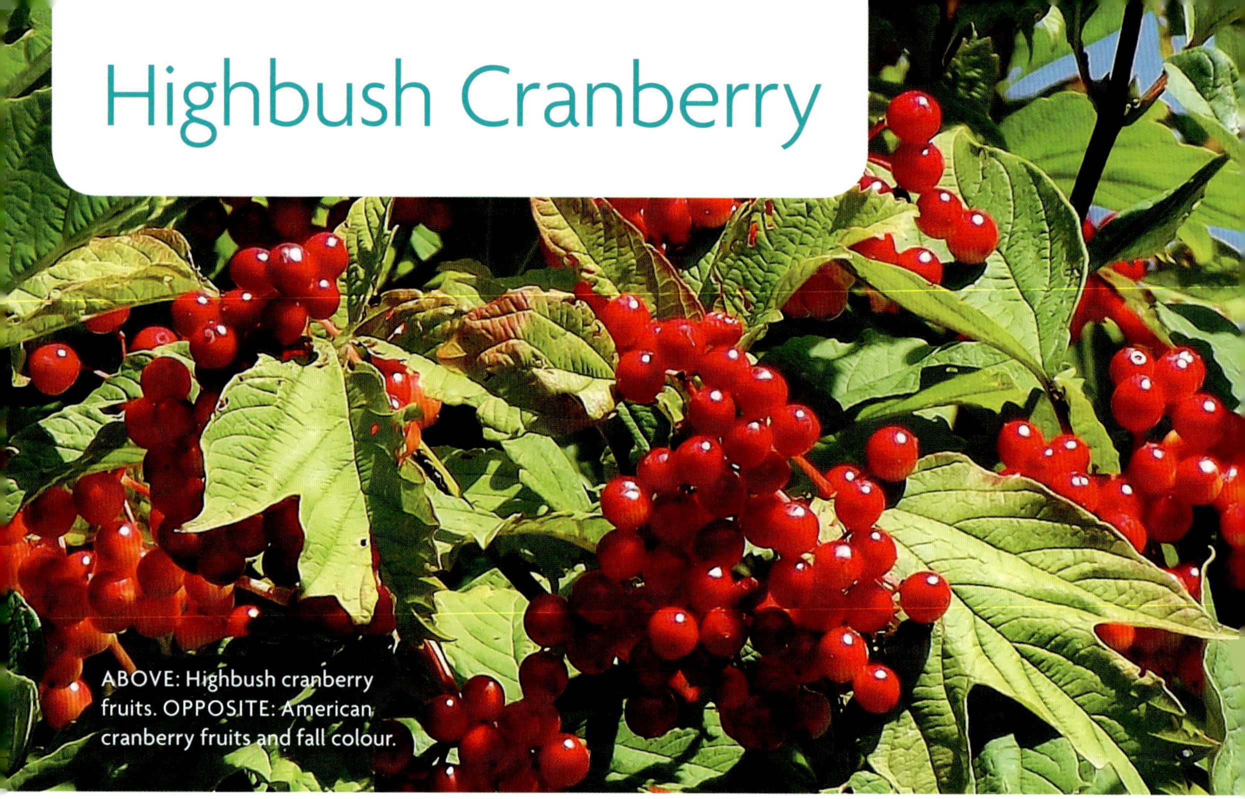

ABOVE: Highbush cranberry fruits. OPPOSITE: American cranberry fruits and fall colour.

This is the fruit of an older generation that once harvested highbush cranberry to make delicious jellies and wines—to the French Canadians it was known as *pembina* and to early Ukrainian immigrants *kalyna*. Both species are closely related and some just consider them the North American and European versions, although many regard the berries of *Viburnum trilobum* to be superior in flavour.

These are large deciduous shrubs that lend themselves to ornamental landscaping, with white lacecap blooms in spring, brilliant scarlet to burgundy autumn tones and drooping clusters of red translucent berries. They can be planted in the back of a mixed border or at the corner of a fence line, and dwarf cultivars such as 'Compactum' (5 feet/1.5 m high and wide) are available in both species. There is also a new *V. opulus* variety from Ukraine called KALINKA, which is self-fertile and features large tasty berries.

You should be looking out for one pest in particular, viburnum leaf beetle (*Pyrrhalta viburni*)—this European native first arrived in Canada back in 1947 and is now entrenched in Ontario, the Maritimes and coastal British Columbia. It is very difficult to control and its larvae can quickly make Swiss cheese of the foliage. The only low-impact control is to prune the overwintering eggs off the branches and destroy them, which effectively removes the flowering wood. So my advice is to check with your local garden centre or look around your neighbourhood for symptoms of this pest before you decide to plant.

SPECIES:
Viburnum opulus; *V. trilobum* (syn. *V. opulus* var. *americanum*)

A.K.A.:
European cranberry bush, guelder rose (*Viburnum opulus*); American cranberry bush (*V. trilobum*)

PLANT TYPE:
Deciduous shrub

WHAT'S EDIBLE:
Berries when processed (remove seeds before cooking to prevent bitterness)

HARVEST TIME:
After a light frost

TASTES LIKE:
Cranberry with black cherry

ORIGINS:
Europe, North Africa, Central Asia (*Viburnum opulus*); North America (*V. trilobum*)

HARDINESS:
USDA zone 3 (*Viburnum opulus*); zone 2 (*V. trilobum*)

SUN:
Part to full sun

WATER:
Consistent soil moisture, tolerates wet soils

ULTIMATE SIZE:
12–16 feet (3.7–5 m) tall by 10–13 feet (3–4 m) wide

BLOOM:
Late spring

POLLINATION:
Partially self-fertile, better crops with cross-pollination

PRUNING:
Rejuvenate mature plants after flowering by hard pruning 20 percent of the main branches annually

Hops

WHAT'S EDIBLE:
Female cones (used to flavour beer and make tea), leaves and roots

HARVEST TIME:
Late August to September, depending on variety and location

TASTES LIKE:
Bitter herbal, citrus, resinous pine or floral

When I was growing up, pretty much every clothesline pole in the neighbourhood was adorned with a hops vine, so when we moved to Chilliwack in British Columbia's Fraser Valley in the mid-1970s, I was impressed to see vast acres of hops strewn on huge support systems. That local industry has since all but disappeared, with production moving down to Washington and Oregon, but the renaissance of craft- and home-beer brewers has certainly revived interest in growing hops.

This perennial herbaceous vine is an extremely fast grower and has a reputation for rampant spreading unless you lift and split the rhizome every few years. It is technically a bine (clinging with prickly hairs) that twines for support, so simple growing systems can be created on the west or south side of any two-storey home with temporary stringers anchored on the ground near the hop's crown, slightly angled away from the building and secured just below the roofline; these stringers can be cut at harvest time. Hop cones are ready when they feel dry and papery to the touch, with the dust-like yellow lupulin showing.

Finding specific varieties can be difficult, as most garden centres only carry standard cultivars such as 'Cascade', 'Centennial' (strong citrus aroma), 'Nugget' (floral resinous flavour) and the primarily ornamental 'Aureus' (which also produces cones) with its brilliant chartreuse foliage. Specialty hop cultivars to consider include 'Fuggle' (English-style beers and stouts), CITRA (citrus and fruit flavour), 'Northern Brewer' and 'Willamette', with the latter two being used for ales and lagers.

OPPOSITE: Golden hops growing on an arbour.
ABOVE: Ripening hop cones.

SPECIES:
Humulus lupulus

A.K.A.:
Common hop

PLANT TYPE:
Herbaceous vine

ORIGINS:
North America, Europe, West Asia

HARDINESS:
USDA zone 4

SUN:
Part to full sun

WATER:
Consistent soil moisture with good drainage

ULTIMATE SIZE:
15–20 feet (4.6–6 m) tall

BLOOM:
Mid to late summer

POLLINATION:
Not required, as cones develop on female plants without pollination

PRUNING:
Thin excess shoots in spring, head back to accommodate harvest, cut back dead top growth after a hard frost

Hosta

Hosta has been eaten for centuries in Japan, where it was grown on the edges of the rice fields and known as *urui*. Both the young shoots and flowers are edible, with *Hosta sieboldii* and *H. montana* being preferred for their shoots—these are harvested in early spring before they unfurl (older leaves are bitter) by snapping or cutting them off at the base, working from the outer edge of the crown. Smaller shoots can be lightly stir-fried and served over rice with soy sauce, while larger ones should be boiled for a few minutes and used a vegetable. The mild flavours of asparagus and green bean should come as no surprise, as hosta is a member of the Asparagaceae family.

The buds and flowers are another taste treat, with *H. plantaginea* being the traditional choice, but I have found that many modern cultivars such as 'Rainforest Sunrise', 'First Frost' and 'Royal Standard' all have delicious blooms, reminiscent of honeysuckle and young pea in flavour. In fact, one taste takes me back to elementary school in Winnipeg, where I would diligently suck the delicious nectar out of the tiny yellow flowers of the bush honeysuckle (*Diervilla lonicera*).

Of course, shade gardeners will welcome an additional edible crop and those restricted to container culture will appreciate hosta's winter hardiness and tolerance of being root bound. The only downside is that dog and cat owners should note this plant can be toxic to pets (including horses), due to its saponin content, so foraging animals should be kept at bay.

WHAT'S EDIBLE:
Flowers and young shoots (but toxic to pets and horses, due to saponin content)

HARVEST TIME:
Midsummer for flowers, harvest new shoots in spring before they unfurl

TASTES LIKE:
Flowers taste of honeysuckle and young pea, shoots have flavours of mild asparagus and green bean

OPPOSITE: 'Rainforest Sunrise' hosta flowers and foliage.
ABOVE: 'Royal Standard' hosta in bloom.

SPECIES:
Hosta montana; *H. plantaginea*; *H. sieboldii*

A.K.A.:
Plantain lily, funkia

ORIGINS:
Eastern Asia and Japan

HARDINESS:
USDA zone 3

SUN:
Part to full shade

WATER:
Consistent soil moisture

ULTIMATE SIZE:
28 inches (71 cm) tall by 48 inches (120 cm) wide; 20–24 inches (50–60 cm) tall by 36–48 inches (90–120 cm) wide; 12–18 inches (30–46 cm) tall by 24 inches (60 cm) wide

BLOOM:
Midsummer

POLLINATION:
Not required

PRUNING:
Remove spent flower stalks, cut back dead foliage after fall dormancy

Huckleberry

ABOVE: New flush on evergreen huckleberry.
OPPOSITE: Ripe red huckleberry fruits.

Huckleberry is the common name for two of my favourite local berries, *Vaccinium ovatum* (evergreen huckleberry) and *V. parvifolium* (red huckleberry). In many ways, they are worlds apart, with one being evergreen with bluish-black berries and the other deciduous with translucent red fruit.

Evergreen huckleberry is a very useful ornamental shrub, bearing attractive pink bell-shaped flowers as new growth emerges a coppery red. It tolerates heavy pruning and can be grown anywhere from deep shade to full sun. While it will fruit sporadically in the shade, the plant form will be tall and leggy; those in full sun have vibrant new growth and are naturally compact. The tasty berries have a musky blueberry flavour and do sweeten a little after a light frost if they can still be found on the bush. Two cultivars are available, including 'Thunderbird', a clonal selection from the University of British Columbia, and SCARLET OVATION ('Vacsid1'), a compact cultivar (3 feet/90 cm high and wide) with brighter new growth.

Red huckleberries are often found in open shade, growing out of old rotting stumps. These have a wispy tiered growth habit and new bright green stems with small rounded leaves that drop in autumn. The flowers are not as showy, being a pale pink to yellowish-green, and are often hidden on the underside of the branches. That said, it is an elegant-looking shrub regardless of season.

Both species provide berries for a wide range of wildlife and serve as a nectar source for hummingbirds and wild bees. Last but not least on their list of attributes to emphasize is shade tolerance, which can be a difficult obstacle to overcome when it comes to fruit production.

WHAT'S EDIBLE:
Berries

HARVEST TIME:
Late summer to fall (*Vaccinium ovatum*); midsummer (*V. parvifolium*)

TASTES LIKE:
Intense blueberry (*Vaccinium ovatum*); tangy-tart berry (*V. parvifolium*)

SPECIES:
Vaccinium ovatum; *V. parvifolium*

A.K.A.:
Evergreen huckleberry (*Vaccinium ovatum*); red huckleberry (*V. parvifolium*)

PLANT TYPE:
Evergreen shrub (*Vaccinium ovatum*); deciduous shrub (*V. parvifolium*)

ORIGIN:
West Coast of North America

HARDINESS:
USDA zone 7 (*Vaccinium ovatum*); zone 6 (*V. parvifolium*)

SUN:
Open shade to full sun

WATER:
Consistent soil moisture with good drainage

ULTIMATE SIZE:
Averages 4–6 feet (1.2–1.8 m) high and wide depending on exposure

BLOOM:
Spring

POLLINATION:
Self-fertile

PRUNING:
Lightly prune in late winter

Japanese Silverberry

This close relative of goumi berry (*Elaeagnus multiflora*) and Russian olive (*Elaeagnus angustifolia*) was first introduced to the United States in 1830 and eventually utilized extensively for roadside erosion control. It quickly escaped into the wild and is now considered an invasive plant in many states, as well as Alberta—so do your research before you plant.

In coastal British Columbia, this has not been a problem and the species has been adopted by many in permaculture circles as an ideal berry bush that even thrives on lean mineral soils because it fixes its own nitrogen. It can also be found as naturalized plants in Ontario, Quebec, New Brunswick, Nova Scotia and Newfoundland. These fast-growing deciduous bushes come into bearing in their second year, with mature crops of the smaller red berries (speckled with silvery dots) often enveloping the branches and causing them to bend under the weight of the fruit. They have a pleasant tart flavour when eaten fresh (the seeds are also chewable) and are often processed into wine and preserves—with the berries being very high in lycopene, about 15 to 18 times more than the average tomato. If fostering wildlife is important to you, then it is worth considering that the fragrant pale yellow blooms are a favourite of bees and that the fruit will need to be picked promptly or you can consider it a bird feast.

Practical landscape uses include training autumn olive as a berry hedge or even growing it in containers on rooftop gardens, where cold hardiness comes into play. While RUBY (heavy crops of large red berries), AMBER (pale yellow fruit), 'Cardinal' (an older variety), Portuguese 'Super Hero' (good fruit quality) and TITAN (dense growth habit) are the most common cultivars available, selection varies with region.

SPECIES:
Elaeagnus umbellata

A.K.A.:
Autumn olive

PLANT TYPE:
Deciduous shrub

ORIGINS:
China, Himalayas, Japan

HARDINESS:
USDA zone 3

SUN:
Part to full sun

WATER:
Average moisture, drought tolerant once established

ULTIMATE SIZE:
10–16 feet (3–5 m) high and wide

BLOOM:
Late spring to early summer

POLLINATION:
Self-fertile

PRUNING:
Shape, thin or remove deadwood in late winter

ABOVE: Japanese silverberry fruit.
INSET: Japanese silverberry in bloom.

WHAT'S EDIBLE:

Berries and seeds

HARVEST TIME:

Late summer into fall

TASTES LIKE:

Tart rhubarb and redcurrant, much sweeter when fully ripened

Jasmine

ABOVE: Gold-leaved common jasmine in bloom.
INSET: Green tea with jasmine flowers.

WHAT'S EDIBLE:
Flowers

HARVEST TIME:
When in flower

TASTES LIKE:
Sweet and floral

It is hard to find a more universally loved flower than the common jasmine, and a lot of this admiration is to do with its being naturalized through much of the world, including southern Europe, the West Indies, China and Central America. The pure, sweet scent of this semi-evergreen vine in full bloom brings many of us back to our childhoods, which is why this plant is highly sought after, despite being a little tender in Canada. Getting it to thrive here means finding a sunny, sheltered site against a south- or west-facing wall, with fertile well-drained soil. Any exposure to cold winter winds will only kill it outright or beat it back to the ground, where it will have to regrow entirely.

There are several forms or cultivars to choose from besides the fragrant white-flowering species, with one of my favourites being 'Fiona Sunrise', a gold-leaved variety that really stands out in the garden. 'Argenteovariegatum' (syn. 'Variegatum') is an RHS Award of Garden Merit winner, with grey-green foliage generously edged in creamy-white, while the form *Jasminum officinale* f. *affine* (also known as *grandiflorum*) bears larger white flowers that emerge from pale pink buds. Common jasmine is frequently grown as a houseplant and I have seen many beautiful hanging baskets in full bloom.

Traditional culinary uses for jasmine flowers include flavouring maraschino cherries and creating a specialty tea. Jasmine tea is made by blending or layering either green or black tea with fresh jasmine flowers. *J. officinale* is used, along with *J. sambac* (Arabian jasmine), which in Canada can only be grown as a houseplant, as it is zone-9 hardy. I like to make a little green tea and add a few fresh jasmine flowers to make my own version of this traditional beverage.

SPECIES:
Jasminum officinale

A.K.A.:
Common jasmine, white jasmine

PLANT TYPE:
Semi-evergreen vine

ORIGINS:
Asia, Middle East

HARDINESS:
USDA zone 7

SUN:
Part to full sun

WATER:
Consistent soil moisture with good drainage

ULTIMATE SIZE:
10–13 feet (3–4 m) tall by 4 feet (1.2 m) wide

BLOOM:
Early summer into fall

POLLINATION:
Not required for harvest

PRUNING:
Prune to shape after flowering, remove damaged wood in spring

Jerusalem Artichoke

This relative of the sunflower has a nice balance of beauty and sustenance, as it is quite productive, easy to grow and bears attractive terminal clusters of bright yellow daisies (2–4 inches/5–10 cm across) in late summer. The edible portions are the underground tubers that look like ginger root but taste like artichoke and water chestnut, and come in a variety of colours, including white, purple, tan and red. They can be eaten raw when thinly sliced and added to salads, used as a vegetable in a stir-fry or cooked much the same way you would a potato.

You can blame Italians and Samuel de Champlain for the confusing common name, as de Champlain discovered First Nations communities eating these tubers in 1605 and had some sent back to Europe with the comment that they had a flavour reminiscent of artichoke. Once they received it, the Italians named this new vegetable "sunflower artichoke" or *girasole articiocco*, which eventually morphed into "Jerusalem artichoke." The one problem people encounter with this species is its invasive nature, as it can be difficult to eradicate once left to its own devices. You may think yourself an expert in finding wayward tubers but—trust me—when it comes to this species, we are all rank amateurs. Give them their own space (or better yet a very large container) and harvest with care.

General growing instructions include springtime planting of the tubers 4–6 inches (10–15 cm) deep and 16 inches (40 cm) apart in enriched soil, mounding the base of the stems with 6 inches (15 cm) of earth when they are 3–4 feet (90–120 cm) tall. Cutting the flowers off will divert energy to the tubers, which are often harvested after a frost (making them sweeter), with those left in-ground re-growing the following year.

SPECIES:
Helianthus tuberosus

A.K.A.:
Earth apple, sunchoke

PLANT TYPE:
Herbaceous perennial

ORIGIN:
Eastern North America

HARDINESS:
USDA zone 3

SUN:
Part to full sun

WATER:
Consistent soil moisture with good drainage

ULTIMATE SIZE:
10 feet (3 m) tall by 3 feet (90 cm) wide

BLOOM:
August to September

POLLINATION:
Not required for harvest

PRUNING:
Cut back the dead stalks of overwintering plants

OPPOSITE, TOP: Jerusalem artichoke in flower.
INSET: Jerusalem artichoke tubers.

WHAT'S EDIBLE:
Underground tubers

HARVEST TIME:
120–150 days after planting, or late fall to early winter

TASTES LIKE:
Artichoke and water chestnut

Juglans and Carya

ABOVE: Ripening butternut cluster.
OPPOSITE: Ripening shagbark hickory nuts.

I wanted to include at least two representatives of these important nut species in this book, even though their large ultimate size may preclude them from use in urban gardens where space is limited. *Juglans cinerea* is the most cold resistant of the walnuts, making it useful for prairie gardeners. It is fast growing but often short-lived (averaging 75 years) and can be difficult to transplant, as it has a deep taproot. Like other members of its family, such as black walnut (*Juglans nigra*), it is allelopathic, meaning it releases a chemical called "juglone" from its roots and decomposing foliage to stop the growth of competing plants, so keep these leaves out of the compost. That said, the nuts are superior to walnut in flavour, and the large compound leaves and elegant arching branches give it an exotic appeal.

Carya ovata, or shagbark hickory, is related to pecan (*C. illinoinensis*) and is a native of Ontario and Quebec. Deep taproots make it difficult to transplant in a nursery scenario, so these plants are often grafted or seed grown, although with the latter method it can take up to 10 years to mature and bear nuts. 'Wilcox' and 'Yoder No 1' (which may be a hybrid) are good cultivars for Eastern Canada.

WHAT'S EDIBLE:
Nut kernels

HARVEST TIME:
Harvest the nuts of Juglans after a hard frost; harvest Carya as soon as nuts drop

TASTES LIKE:
Sweet buttery walnut (*Juglans cinerea*); mix of sweet pecan and walnut (*Carya ovata*)

SPECIES:
Juglans cinerea; *Carya ovata*

A.K.A.:
Butternut, white walnut (*Juglans cinerea*); shagbark hickory (*Carya ovata*)

PLANT TYPE:
Deciduous tree

ORIGIN:
Eastern United States

HARDINESS:
USDA zone 3 (*Juglans cinerea*); zone 4 (*Carya ovata*)

SUN:
Full sun (*Juglans cinerea*); part to full sun (*Carya ovata*)

WATER:
Consistent soil moisture with good drainage (*Juglans cinerea*); consistent moisture with good drainage, tolerates seasonal drought (*Carya ovata*)

ULTIMATE SIZE:
40–60 feet (12–18 m) tall by 40 feet (12 m) wide for *Juglans cinerea*; 82 feet (25 m) tall by 50 feet (15 m) wide for *Carya ovata* (both grow larger in the wild)

BLOOM:
Mid to late spring

POLLINATION:
Juglans cinerea is self-fertile, but male catkins often mature before female flowers on the same tree, making cross-pollination necessary, wind pollinated; *Carya ovata* is also self-fertile but cross-pollination increases yield, wind pollinated

PRUNING:
Prune after leafing out to prevent excessive bleeding (*Juglans cinerea*); requires only minor structural pruning in late winter (*Carya ovata*)

Jujube

Jujube is a relative newcomer to Canadian gardens, but one need only shop a few minutes in Vancouver's Chinatown to discover that the dried fruits are immensely popular. They have a pleasant date-apple flavour and come in a range of sizes (averaging 1–2 inches/2.5–5 cm long). Just be sure not to eat the large pit. The ones to avoid are the smoked jujubes (a delicacy in Vietnam), which are the second-worst thing I have ever put in my mouth, right behind sea cucumber.

Jujube trees and shrubs have only been available in the Fraser Valley for the past few years, so the long-term potential is yet to be determined. Zone-6 hardy, they have been producing fruit in coastal British Columbia, although not fully ripening until very late in the season, usually October. So I don't think Canada has the potential for the fruits to dry on the tree as they do in China and Asia. But while jujube fruits don't ripen once picked and prefer hot summers, the fresh undried fruits have a nice green-apple flavour and are a worthwhile crop. The roundish to rod-shaped fruits ripen from green to pale yellowish-green with mahogany spotting, and are mature when they are a solid reddish-brown colour—but these never finish all at once.

The tree itself is attractive enough, with glossy deep green foliage that turns yellow in fall, tiny white to yellowish-green flowers and a few spines (especially on root suckers) to deal with. The most common cultivars are 'Li' (large rounded fruits) and 'Lang' (large pear-shaped fruits), both originally brought back by the famous plant collector Frank Meyer. While these are reported to be self-fertile, they can be used to pollinate each other too. An early-ripening cultivar from Ukraine, MASSANDRA, also seems to be doing well in British Columbia.

SPECIES:
Ziziphus jujuba

A.K.A.:
Chinese date, red date

PLANT TYPE:
Deciduous shrub or small tree

ORIGIN:
Southern Asia

HARDINESS:
USDA zone 6

SUN:
Full sun

WATER:
Average moisture with sharp drainage

ULTIMATE SIZE:
8–12 feet (2.5–3.7 m) tall by 6–8 feet (1.8–2.5 m) wide, larger in warmer climates

BLOOM:
Midsummer

POLLINATION:
Partially self-fertile, better crops with cross-pollination

PRUNING:
Prune for shape and size in late winter

ABOVE: 'Lang' jujube flowers and green fruit.
INSET: Ripening MASSANDRA jujube fruit.

WHAT'S EDIBLE:
Fresh or dried fruits

HARVEST TIME:
October

TASTES LIKE:
Fresh jujube is green apple, dried jujube is apple and date

Kiwi

ABOVE: Fuzzy kiwi fruits. OPPOSITE: 'Ananasnaya' hardy kiwi fruits. *Photo courtesy Tree Eater Nursery*

These vigorous deciduous vines are dioecious in nature, which means you will need both sexes for cross-pollination and for viable fruits on the females. A few exceptions are *Actinidia arguta* 'Issai' and *A. deliciosa* 'Jenny', both self-fertile females that can produce without a male, with fruits being larger when cross-pollinated.

For successful growth, kiwis need to be carefully sited in fertile well-drained soil with a full-sun exposure and some protection from cold or strong prevailing winds. They also need very sturdy support, such as an arbour or pergola, as they are extremely vigorous in their growth habit.

Hardiness varies widely, with *A. arguta* and *A. kolomikta* thriving in colder climates while the larger-fruited fuzzy kiwi (*A. deliciosa*) is only zone-7 hardy. The variegated kiwi vine is shade tolerant and has attractive white, pink and green foliage (more so on the males), and the cultivar 'Arctic Beauty' is hardier at zone 3. *A. arguta* cultivars to look for include 'Ananasnaya' or 'Anna' (red-skinned, intense flavour) or the hybrid 'Ken's Red' (*arguta* × *melanandra*). Better *A. deliciosa* varieties include 'Hayward' (female), 'Saanichton 12' (large fruit), 'Tomuri' (male) and the self-fertile 'Blake'. Two quirks I would like to leave you with include the close-range "skunky" smell of *A. deliciosa* at times (plant away from the patio) and the fact that cats love *A. kolomikta* and will often tear up the foliage.

WHAT'S EDIBLE:
Fruits

HARVEST TIME:
Late fall (*Actinidia deliciosa*); late summer to fall (*A. arguta*); late summer (*A. kolomikta*)

TASTES LIKE:
Tart to sweet kiwi with hints of melon, banana and pineapple

SPECIES:
Actinidia deliciosa (syn. *A. chinensis*); *A. arguta*; *A. kolomikta*

A.K.A.:
Fuzzy kiwi (*Actinidia deliciosa*); hardy kiwi (*A. arguta*); variegated kiwi vine (*A. kolomikta*)

PLANT TYPE:
Deciduous vine

ORIGINS:
China, East Asia

HARDINESS:
USDA zone 7 (*Actinidia deliciosa*); zone 3 (*A. arguta*); zone 4 (*A. kolomikta*)

SUN:
Part to full sun

WATER:
Consistent soil moisture (particularly when fruit is forming) with good drainage

ULTIMATE SIZE:
16–26 feet (5–8 m) tall for *Actinidia deliciosa*; 20–30 feet (6–9 m) tall for *A. arguta*; 13–23 feet (4–7 m) tall for *A. kolomikta*

BLOOM:
Late spring to early summer

POLLINATION:
Male and female plants required, with some self-fertile cultivars available

PRUNING:
Male = head back after flowering. Female = dormant prune old wood, leaving 1-year-old canes that are headed back, lightly summer prune excessive growth

Lavender

SPECIES:
Lavandula angustifolia; *L.* × *intermedia*

A.K.A.:
English lavender (*Lavandula angustifolia*); lavandin (*L.* × *intermedia*)

PLANT TYPE:
Evergreen subshrub

ORIGINS:
Western Mediterranean (*Lavandula angustifolia*); garden origin (*L.* × *intermedia*)

HARDINESS:
USDA zone 5

SUN:
Full sun

WATER:
Low moisture with sharp drainage

ULTIMATE SIZE:
18 inches (46 cm) tall by 24 inches (60 cm) wide for *Lavandula angustifolia*; 24–36 inches (60–90 cm) tall by 30–36 inches (76–90 cm) wide for *L.* × *intermedia*

BLOOM:
Midsummer

POLLINATION:
Not required

PRUNING:
After flowering but never into old wood

WHAT'S EDIBLE:
Fresh flowers and dried buds

HARVEST TIME:
Just as the flowers open

TASTES LIKE:
Much like the flower fragrance

OPPOSITE: 'Loddon Blue' English lavender. ABOVE: 'Hidcote Pink' English lavender.

I love lavender when it is added as a culinary spice, but I'll be the first to admit it needs to be used sparingly, as it is quite a strongly flavoured herb. All three of my daughters cook with it and as a result I am the beneficiary of such culinary delights as Earl Grey tea and lavender cookies, lavender aioli and lavender-vanilla ice cream—the potential for this underused herb is yet to be exploited, in my opinion.

So let's start with the appropriate culinary species, which are English lavender (*Lavandula angustifolia*) and lavandin (*L.* × *intermedia*), with the latter being a *L. angustifolia* × *L. latifolia* cross. Of these, some of the edible preferences are for 'Munstead' and 'Hidcote' in the English lavenders and 'Provence' and 'Grosso' for the lavandins—thankfully all are easy-to-obtain cultivars. What should be avoided are the species with high camphor content, including French (*L. dentata*) and Spanish (*L. stoechas*) lavenders, both of which are too strongly flavoured to be used in the kitchen.

Lavender the ornamental plant is an evergreen subshrub that works well in foreground mass plantings (English) as part of a mixed border or even as an informal flowering hedge (lavandin) along a property line. It is extremely drought tolerant once established and requires sharp drainage to overwinter well. Numerous colour variations are available, including pink ('Rosea', 'Hidcote Pink', 'Jean Davis') and white ('Ellagance Snow', 'Nana Alba'), as well as compact English lavenders such as BLUE CUSHION. The intoxicating fragrance also brings in beneficial pollinators, such as bumblebees, butterflies and honeybees—which will move on to pollinate other edible plants in your garden.

Lesser Celandine

There are two things you need to know about lesser celandine before you grow it. First, it is a member of the Ranunculus family, known for its toxicity to horses and livestock; second, it is often quite invasive in nature. Those points made, it is a beautiful ornamental perennial, yet another edible option for the shade garden, and harvesting some of it to eat can be a part of its control program. This herbaceous plant spreads by bulbils and often forms low carpets of glossy deep green heart-shaped leaves (frequently with bronze or silver highlights) and yellow to orange buttercup flowers borne in early spring. As its profile is usually low, it blends well with taller woodlanders, and it also goes summer dormant.

The only edible portions I recommend are the delicious young leaves (picked before flowering)—older leaves can be toxic to humans—which can be eaten raw or boiled like spinach. The other taste treat is the multi-branched bulbils found underground at the base of the stem. They can be harvested after summer dormancy and carefully washed, after which they must be cooked either by boiling for two minutes, then changing the water and repeating, or by coating them in tempura batter and frying—you can expect a pleasant carrot-parsnip flavour, although some just taste like young potato.

While this is a choice plant for foraging chefs, mature clumps should not be left where horses and livestock graze, as this runs the risk of poisoning them. A few varieties I have sold over the years include 'Primrose' (pale yellow blooms), 'Flore Pleno' (double yellow flowers), 'Coppernob' (orange blooms, bronze foliage), 'Collarette' (anemone-form flowers, mottled foliage) and 'Brazen Hussy' (purplish-black foliage).

SPECIES:
Ficaria verna (syn. *Ranunculus ficaria*)

A.K.A.:
Fig buttercup

PLANT TYPE:
Herbaceous perennial

ORIGINS:
Europe, North Africa, Southwest Asia

HARDINESS:
USDA zone 4

SUN:
Shade to part shade

WATER:
Consistent soil moisture with good drainage

ULTIMATE SIZE:
2 inches (5 cm) tall by 12+ inches (30+ cm) wide

BLOOM:
Early spring

POLLINATION:
Not required

PRUNING:
None required

ABOVE: 'Collarette' lesser celandine in bloom.
INSET: Harvested lesser celandine bulbils.

WHAT'S EDIBLE:

Young leaves, bulbils (but toxic to horses and livestock)

HARVEST TIME:

Very young leaves in early spring before flowering, harvest bulbils after plant goes summer dormant

TASTES LIKE:

Young leaves have a nutty flavour, bulbils taste like mild carrot and parsnip

Lilac

ABOVE: 'Sensation' French lilac.
OPPOSITE: 'Primrose' French lilac.

SPECIES:
Syringa vulgaris

A.K.A.:
Common lilac, French lilac

PLANT TYPE:
Deciduous shrub

ORIGIN:
Eastern Europe

HARDINESS:
USDA zone 3

SUN:
Full sun

WATER:
Consistent soil moisture with good drainage

ULTIMATE SIZE:
7½–15 feet (2.3–4.6 m) tall by 6–12 feet (1.8–3.7 m) wide

BLOOM:
April to May

POLLINATION:
Not required

PRUNING:
Prune after flowering and remove root suckers

WHAT'S EDIBLE:
Flowers

HARVEST TIME:
April to May

TASTES LIKE:
Floral with a hint of citrus and violet

In all my years of living on army bases across Canada, the only time we actually had a plant in the yard was in Winnipeg, when we had a lilac hedge between us and the neighbour. I distinctly remember two things about that lilac, the first being the heady fragrance of those deep purple flowers and the second that it was often covered top to bottom with gorgeous monarch butterflies in the summer. Most of us are familiar with this old-fashioned favourite, and for those of you who came from colder climates and remember them doing better there, you are right. These large deciduous shrubs need room to grow and a neutral to slightly alkaline pH, so forget peat moss as a soil amender and be sure to add lime from time to time.

That heady fragrance that I mentioned earlier made my mouth water and if I had known lilacs were edible back then, I certainly would have tried them. They can be used to make jelly, infuse honey or flavour ice cream, and when my wife and oldest daughters came back from a trip to France, candied lilacs made the flight back with them. One of my favourite uses is lilac syrup, which can be added to tea or cold summer drinks. Making it is easy: just dissolve 1 cup (250 mL) sugar in the same amount of water and bring to a boil, add 1 cup (250 mL) lilac flowers (removed from stems) and a few blueberries or blackberries for colour. Cook over a low heat for 10 to 15 minutes, strain through cheesecloth and pour into a sterile jar—it will keep for 2 weeks in the refrigerator.

For those of you looking for some choice French lilac cultivars, consider 'Sensation' (variegated flowers), 'Congo' (dark purple), 'Krasavitsa Moskvy' (double white with pink buds), 'Primrose' (pale yellow) and 'Prairie Petite' (a lavender-pink dwarf form).

Linden

You have an elderly German gardener to thank for this chapter, because when I asked my friend Wolfgang if he had ever tasted elderflower cordial he said, "Of course, but linden is better." So I looked into it, and the linden was a revered tree in ancient Germanic times and served as the place for the community to meet under to make important decisions or celebrate and dance.

Both the young leaves and flowers (which are often made into tea or cordial) are edible, with the latter remaining a popular drink to this day. Linden flowers can be dried and made into a calming tea (1–2 teaspoons/ 5–10 mL per cup of hot water) or a cordial (often made with limes instead of the lemons used for the elderflower cordial) that can be frozen into ice cubes and added to carbonated water or your favourite summer beverage. The young leaves make a delicious addition to any salad and have a lettuce-like sort of crunch, although you may want to chop them up.

Lindens are relatively common street trees in urban areas, so even if you don't have room for another tree in your garden there is the possibility of local foraging. While the littleleaf linden (*Tilia cordata*) is considered the best tasting of the family, there are other species with the same edible young leaves and flowers, including large-leaved lime (*T. platyphyllos*), the hybrid *T.* × *europaea* (*cordata* × *platyphyllos* cross) and American basswood (*T. americana*).

SPECIES:
Tilia cordata

A.K.A.:
Littleleaf linden, small-leaved lime

PLANT TYPE:
Deciduous tree

ORIGINS:
Europe, Southwestern Asia

HARDINESS:
USDA zone 3

SUN:
Part to full sun

WATER:
Consistent soil moisture with good drainage

ULTIMATE SIZE:
50–70 feet (15–21 m) tall by 30–50 feet (9–15 m) wide, depending on cultivar

BLOOM:
Early summer

POLLINATION:
Self-fertile, but not required for flower harvest

PRUNING:
While tolerant of heavy pruning, this species keeps its form with minimal late-winter trimming

ABOVE: Linden flowers.
INSET: Linden blossom cordial.

WHAT'S EDIBLE:
Flowers, young leaves

HARVEST TIME:
Early summer for flowers, young foliage at any time

TASTES LIKE:
Flowers taste sweetly herbal, similar to elderflower, and young leaves are tender and slightly sweet

Lingonberry

ABOVE: Lingonberry in flower.
INSET: 'Koralle' lingonberry.

WHAT'S EDIBLE:
Red berries

HARVEST TIME:
After a hard frost

TASTES LIKE:
Cranberry

Most people have only heard of lingonberry as being a specialty jam that can be bought at IKEA. As a nursery manager, I sell many of these plants from late fall to Christmas, when they are in high demand for their display of dangling red berry clusters that are ideal for seasonal planters. Few consider it an edible plant, which is a shame because it is an undemanding species that requires little pruning and, once established, produces consistent crops of tasty ¼-inch (6-mm) berries that taste like cranberry and get sweeter with exposure to a few frosts.

This evergreen subshrub is very attractive with its glossy green foliage and the white to pale pink heather bells are a welcome addition to any landscape. It makes a reliable small-scale ground cover and is extremely hardy, although it does require snow cover in cold regions to prevent wind burn. Lingonberry prefers acidic organic soils that are evenly moist but well drained and, if berry production is the priority, a full-sun exposure would be best.

I have encountered several cultivars over the years, including 'Koralle' (also known as the Koralle Group), an older variety and RHS Award of Garden Merit winner that is slow to establish but makes up for this with flavourful berries that are slightly larger than the species. The other is a subspecies called *Vaccinium vitis-idaea* subsp. *minus* that is often sought out as a native plant, rather than a true ornamental. That said, it often has deep pink flowers that sharply contrast with the compact green foliage that only grows ¾–4¾ inches (2–12 cm) tall. Lingonberries flower twice a year, but heavy fruit set usually occurs with the second bloom, with cross-pollination increasing yields and berry size.

SPECIES:
Vaccinium vitis-idaea

A.K.A.:
Cowberry, partridgeberry

PLANT TYPE:
Evergreen subshrub

ORIGINS:
Northern Hemisphere, Japan

HARDINESS:
USDA zone 2

SUN:
Part to full sun

WATER:
Consistent soil moisture with good drainage

ULTIMATE SIZE:
10–16 inches (25–40 cm) tall by 18+ inches (46+ cm) wide

BLOOM:
Spring and midsummer

POLLINATION:
Self-fertile

PRUNING:
Light pruning on mature plants

Loquat

I can remember seeing young loquat bushes showing up in Vancouver gardens back in the 1990s, when the tropical landscape trend was peaking. They were almost always accompanied by palms, bananas and timber bamboo, but what really made them stand out were the massive deep green leaves (often reaching 12 inches/30 cm long). This broadleaf evergreen wasn't being planted for its good looks but its fruiting potential, which I had always believed to be just wishful thinking.

At least that was until I toured Fruit Trees and More on southern Vancouver Island. There, in a sheltered southern exposure, were several loquats in a row, each bearing perfectly ripened yellow pear-shaped fruits (about 1¼–2 inches/3–5 cm long). The owner, Bob Duncan, was kind enough to let me sample, and it instantly became my favourite fruit thanks to its juicy texture and exotic peach-mango flavour. This experience convinced me that given enough time to figure out the best cultivars and localized growing conditions, we can grow loquats in Canada.

Its zone-8 hardiness will probably limit mass production to British Columbia's Fraser Valley and southern Vancouver Island, but loquats adapt quite well to growing in large containers, so gardeners elsewhere can enjoy them too. In colder climates, loquats need to be overwintered indoors and hand-pollination would be necessary. For outdoor plants, the fall-to-winter flowering may also call for hand-pollination if insect pollinators are lacking, and the fruits need protection from frost as they ripen over winter, so choose an in-ground site carefully. The white fragrant flowers emerge from woolly brown buds, with seedy fruits ripening in late spring—these are amazing for fresh eating or can be used for jellies, jams or baking. 'Tanaka' and 'Gold Nugget' are reliably self-fertile cultivars, with grafted loquats taking two to three years and seedlings five to eight years to bear fruit.

SPECIES:
Eriobotrya japonica

A.K.A.:
Biwa, Chinese plum, Japanese medlar, pipa

PLANT TYPE:
Evergreen tree or shrub

ORIGINS:
China, Japan

HARDINESS:
USDA zone 8

SUN:
Full sun

WATER:
Consistent soil moisture with good drainage, drought tolerant once established

ULTIMATE SIZE:
Averages 10–13 feet (3–4 m) high and wide here, larger in warmer climates

BLOOM:
Late fall to early winter

POLLINATION:
Best production with cross-pollination but self-fertile cultivars exist

PRUNING:
Lightly prune for form after harvest

ABOVE: Ripe loquat fruits.
INSET: Loquat in bloom.

WHAT'S EDIBLE:
Yellowish-orange fruits, excluding seeds

HARVEST TIME:
Late spring

TASTES LIKE:
Peach and mango, with citrus

Mayapple

Have shaded forest floor, will travel. That's the motto of the spreading herbaceous perennial commonly known as mayapple. This rhizomatous species readily spreads to form a dense carpet of glossy deep green palmate leaves, usually just two large ones per stem. Those with a single leaf do not produce the fragrant white flowers, which emerge from the axis between the two leaves and are often hidden by the foliage. Mayapple pollination is not well understood but suffice to say its fruit set can be low in the wild, so growing this species is more about being able to harvest edibles in the shade than it is about actual production.

That said, the ripe mayapple fruit (which is yellow) has a tasty pulp with a flavour reminiscent of apple, melon and tropical fruit—and is often used to make jelly and a traditional punch. The common name refers to the blooming time, usually May, with the apple being the fruit that develops sometime in midsummer, and picking time being when it turns from green to yellow.

So why haven't you heard about using mayapple for eating? Because, besides the ripe fruit pulp, the rest of the plant is poisonous (including the unripe fruit), hence the other common name, American mandrake. But I would like to make the argument that there are many common edibles with toxic parts, including rhubarb (leaves can cause kidney failure), apricot (pits contain high amounts of cyanide) and kidney beans (highly toxic if ingested raw). We simply need to exercise caution with regard to how we eat edible plants with poisonous properties.

SPECIES:
Podophyllum peltatum

A.K.A.:
American mandrake, ground lemon

PLANT TYPE:
Herbaceous perennial

ORIGIN:
Eastern North America down to Texas

HARDINESS:
USDA zone 3

SUN:
Part to full shade

WATER:
Consistent soil moisture with good drainage

ULTIMATE SIZE:
18 inches (46 cm) tall by 4 feet (120 cm) wide

BLOOM:
Spring

POLLINATION:
Limited pollination by bumblebees

PRUNING:
None required

ABOVE: Mayapple flower.
BELOW: Mayapple fruit.

WHAT'S EDIBLE:

Ripe fruit pulp (but not unripe fruits, toxic skin, seeds or plant)

HARVEST TIME:

Midsummer, when fruit colour is yellow

TASTES LIKE:

Melon and green apple, with a hint of tropical fruit

Maypop

ABOVE: Maypop bloom.
INSET: Maypop fruit.

WHAT'S EDIBLE:
Pulp that surrounds the fruit seeds

HARVEST TIME:
Late autumn

TASTES LIKE:
Mild lemon apricot

The maypop is the hardiest of the passionflowers and generally acts as an herbaceous perennial vine here in Canada, dying back to the ground with the heavy frosts, and sprouting again when the soil warms the following spring—which is why careful siting is important with this species. First, you require a sharply drained spot to overwinter maypop, as it tends to rot wherever soils remain overly wet during winter. And you will need a site where the spring sun can warm the soil early to break dormancy, so a sheltered south or west exposure would be ideal. If neither of these work for you, then consider growing maypop in a large pot with a trellis support and overwintering it in a cool greenhouse or shed, moving it out to a sunny site in spring.

While the growing conditions may seem a little demanding, you will be rewarded with fragrant purplish-pink flowers all summer, followed by goose egg–sized green fruits with a delicious edible pulp that can be used for jellies and juices.

There is some debate as to whether this species is self-fertile, which I think may vary with the clone. My local supplier only grows one variety of maypop (with no other *Passiflora* species on site) and they seem to bear fruit just fine. That said, cross-pollination will definitely increase fruit set and size, but our only option in Canada is the blue crown passionflower (*Passiflora caerulea*), which is not as hardy (zone 7), or a containerized tropical species overwintered in a heated greenhouse. *P. caerulea* occasionally produces egg-shaped orange fruits here, but the edible rind is bland (even when cooked) and pulp content usually minimal.

SPECIES:
Passiflora incarnata

A.K.A.:
Wild apricot

PLANT TYPE:
Herbaceous vine

ORIGIN:
Southeast United States

HARDINESS:
USDA zone 6

SUN:
Part to full sun

WATER:
Consistent soil moisture with sharp drainage

ULTIMATE SIZE:
6–10 feet (1.8–3 m) high and wide

BLOOM:
July to September

POLLINATION:
Partially self-fertile

PRUNING:
Cut back dead growth in early spring

Medlar

SPECIES:
Mespilus germanica

A.K.A.:
Common medlar

PLANT TYPE:
Deciduous tree

ORIGINS:
Southeast Europe to Southwest Asia

HARDINESS:
USDA zone 6

SUN:
Part to full sun

WATER:
Consistent soil moisture with good drainage

ULTIMATE SIZE:
15–20 feet (4.6–6 m) high and wide

BLOOM:
Late spring to early summer

POLLINATION:
Self-fertile

PRUNING:
Lightly prune mature trees for form in late winter

OPPOSITE: Medlar fruit.
ABOVE: Medlar in bloom.

WHAT'S EDIBLE:
Bletted fruits

HARVEST TIME:
Late autumn

TASTES LIKE:
Spiced apple butter

If you could take a time machine back to a European orchard in the Middle Ages, chances are you wouldn't be looking at apples or pears. Instead, you would be staring at the very unfamiliar medlar. What is a medlar, you ask? It is a mid-sized deciduous tree with very attractive five-petalled white flowers and a fruit that is the polar opposite—brown and really ugly. The French used to call it cul-de-chien, or "dog-butt" when loosely translated, and I have to say that is an apt description of the fruit form.

But wait, it actually gets worse . . . medlar fruit is not ready for consumption until it almost rots on the tree, a process known as bletting. Now I know that most of you are waiting for the inevitable upside (otherwise you would have no possible reason to grow this fruit) and here it is. The soft brown insides of a medlar fruit taste just like spiced apple butter and make what many consider to be a gourmet jelly.

When it comes to the ripening or bletting process, I should give you fair warning that my attempt at fruit ripening one year was foiled by marauder grey squirrels or raccoons that stripped the tree bare before the medlars were ready. So afterwards I kept a close eye on the crop and picked it when it was still firm, letting the fruit ripen in my garage, which took about two weeks. Once the fruit was soft to the touch with the skin slightly puckered, I cut it open to find ripened brown flesh that could be scooped out from around the large seed in the centre to be eaten fresh. So not only do you get a history lesson with every medlar tree, it is self-fertile, hardy and disease resistant—essential attributes for any edible plant worth having in our gardens.

Mulberry

Mulberries have been around for a long time and yet have never really caught on as a desirable fruit tree for the home garden. The first problem is messiness, particularly with black mulberry, as the ripened dark fruits readily drop (usually assisted by birds), often staining driveways and sidewalks—so plant them elsewhere. The second problem is availability; even as a nursery manager, I find it difficult to stock enough fruiting mulberries to meet my limited customer demand.

What is available are the weeping *Morus alba* 'Chaparral' (a non-fruiting male clone) and 'Unryu' (a contorted form with very few berries)—both great ornamentals but neither produce a crop to speak of. There have been a few new introductions of late, including M. × 'Illinois Everbearing', an *alba* × *rubra* hybrid that is self-fertile and produces 1½-inch (3.8-cm) black fruits when fully ripened. One cultivar that works particularly well in large containers or smaller urban gardens is M. *alba* 'Pendula', also known as 'Teas Weeping'. This graceful pendulous form is the female version of 'Chaparral' and features glossy simple to lobed leaves and red to black fruits, maxing out at 6–10 feet (1.8–3 m) tall, depending upon the height of the graft.

As far as flavour is concerned, I find black mulberry the tastiest, with 'Black Beauty' being the most common cultivar. While our native red mulberry is usually only available as the species, the berries have a good flavour and are often used for making wine. One newer cultivar of M. *alba* to look out for is 'Pakistan', which is from that country but features zone-6 hardiness and berries that average 3 inches (7.5 cm) long!

WHAT'S EDIBLE:

Berries

HARVEST TIME:

Mid to late summer

TASTES LIKE:

Sweet and tart mild blackberry and currant

OPPOSITE: Hybrid 'Illinois Everbearing' mulberry fruit.
ABOVE: Ripening black mulberries.

SPECIES:
Morus alba; *M. nigra*; *M. rubra*

A.K.A.:
White mulberry (*Morus alba*); black mulberry (*M. nigra*); red mulberry (*M. rubra*)

PLANT TYPE:
Deciduous tree

ORIGINS:
China (*Morus alba*); Southwest Asia (*M. nigra*); Canada and Eastern US (*M. rubra*)

HARDINESS:
USDA zone 4 (*Morus alba*); zone 5 (*M. nigra*); zone 5 (*M. rubra*)

SUN:
Part to full sun

WATER:
Consistent soil moisture with good drainage

ULTIMATE SIZE:
16–40 feet (5–12 m) tall by 16–50 feet (5–15 m) wide, weeping forms smaller

BLOOM:
Mid-spring

POLLINATION:
Generally self-fertile

PRUNING:
Prune for form when dormant

Nanking Cherry

I was a cold-weather gardener for a brief period during the early 1980s in Winnipeg, and one of the landscapes I maintained included a beautiful church entrance courtyard. Two-storey brick walls surrounded this garden and these were covered in Virginia creeper (*Parthenocissus quinquefolia*), but the real highlight of this space was a pair of Nanking cherries, both when they were in flower and berry. These bush cherry plants from China literally smother themselves in fragrant white flowers emerging from pink buds in early spring, followed in midsummer by an abundance of translucent scarlet berries that look just like maraschino cherries.

The flavour is certainly there but they are definitely less sweet than traditional *Prunus avium*, and you are going to have to pick pretty fast to be ahead of the birds. While the delicate fruits don't keep well (which is why you don't see them at the supermarket), they make delicious jams and jellies, as well as wines, if you can procure enough berries. Self-pollination is generally very poor, as solitary plants or even nursery blocks of the same clone produce sparsely. The difficulty here is that while there have been many cultivars in the past, these are few and far between now, with the only named one I've come across being 'Leucocarpa', a white-berried variety. One solution here might be to search out seedling stock for cross-pollination purposes.

That aside, this deciduous shrub is extremely cold hardy and actually does better in interior climates than on the "wet" coast of British Columbia. As previously mentioned, the flower display is quite impressive (so much so that it is considered a choice bonsai specimen), and mature specimens exhibit attractive reddish-brown exfoliating bark.

SPECIES:
Prunus tomentosa

A.K.A.:
Chinese bush cherry, Manchu cherry

PLANT TYPE:
Deciduous shrub

ORIGINS:
China, Japan

HARDINESS:
USDA zone 2

SUN:
Part to full sun

WATER:
Average moisture, drought tolerant once established

ULTIMATE SIZE:
6–8 feet (1.8–2.5 m) high and wide

BLOOM:
Early spring

POLLINATION:
Cross-pollination recommended

PRUNING:
Thin in late winter

OPPOSITE, TOP: Nanking cherry in flower.
INSET: Nanking cherry fruit.

WHAT'S EDIBLE:
Translucent red berries

HARVEST TIME:
Midsummer

TASTES LIKE:
Sour cherry with improved sweetness

Olive

ABOVE: European olive in flower.
INSET: 'Eddy's Winter Wonder' olive.

WHAT'S EDIBLE:
Small green to dark purple fruits

HARVEST TIME:
October to December

TASTES LIKE:
Salty, as raw olives need to be brine-cured

Growing olives in Canada is what most people used to consider a pipe dream of a few stubborn Italians, Greeks, Portuguese and Spaniards—and yet it appears that this persistence has finally paid off in coastal British Columbia. One need only take a drive through east Vancouver to see numerous well-established olive trees thriving alongside figs and grapevines. Then there's Waterlea Farm on Pender Island where owner Andrew Butt has an established olive grove from which he is already harvesting and curing, with the ultimate goal of producing Canada's first vintage of extra virgin olive oil once higher production is achieved. The Saturna Olive Consortium (established in 2009) has also been busy promoting the planting of olives and was created to select, grow and distribute cold-hardy varieties in coastal British Columbia.

To be successful, you need a perfect location that involves full sun, well-drained soil, reasonable air drainage and shelter from heavy winds (particularly winter). Protection from deer is also recommended. While olives are drought tolerant once established, juveniles require even moisture as do mature plants while the fruit is developing on the tree.

Many olive cultivars are self-fertile but benefit from cross-pollination, so trees should be planted about 16 feet (5 m) apart, as they are wind pollinated (although I saw many tiny pollinators about when my nursery trees were in bloom). 'Leccino' (cold-hardy) and 'Frantoio' (self-fertile) are considered a perfect pairing, while 'Taggiasca' (self-fertile), 'Pendolino' (universal pollinator) and 'Maurino' (tolerates cool summers) also work well. 'Arbequina' (self-fertile) is the most common olive found at garden centres, while a Swiss cultivar 'Eddy's Winter Wonder' (self-fertile) is reputed to be the hardiest. When it comes to green versus black olives, green olives have been picked before ripening while black olives have been allowed to mature.

SPECIES:
Olea europaea

A.K.A.:
European olive

PLANT TYPE:
Evergreen tree

ORIGIN:
Mediterranean

HARDINESS:
USDA zone 8

SUN:
Full sun

WATER:
Average moisture with sharp drainage

ULTIMATE SIZE:
7½–12 feet (2.3–3.7 m) high and wide, larger in warmer regions

BLOOM:
Late spring (often delayed in coastal British Columbia)

POLLINATION:
Some are self-fertile, the rest require cross-pollination

PRUNING:
Remove deadwood and lightly thin in late spring

Oregon Grape

Oregon grape is a versatile broadleaf evergreen shrub that can be grown as an understory plant, an informal hedge or even an ornamental specimen. I have seen them thrive in a wide range of exposures from deep shade to full sun, although in the latter you will need even soil moisture and shelter from winds to prevent foliage burn. The holly-like deep green foliage is nowhere near as prickly as holly (*Ilex aquifolium*) and usually turns an attractive bronze-purple in the colder weather. The bright yellow flower clusters in early spring are an important pollen and nectar source for bumblebees and hummingbirds, and followed by generous terminal clusters of very tart deep blue berries that begin ripening midsummer. It should be noted that berry production is much better on plants grown in part- to full-sun exposures.

Harvested by First Nations communities in the past, the berries can be made into a very tasty jelly with a few additional ingredients. Start with 6 cups (1.4 L) rinsed fresh berries that have been brought to a boil in 2 cups (475 mL) water and allowed to simmer on low heat for 15 minutes. After you've separated the pulp, this should yield about 3 cups (710 mL) jelly base, which you bring to a full boil for 1 minute with the juice of half a lemon, 3 cups (710 mL) sugar and 1 oz (30 mL) pectin, and then place in sterile jelly jars for preserving.

There are several other species of lower-growing Oregon grape that also have edible berries, including *Mahonia nervosa* (longleaf Oregon grape) or *M. repens* (creeping Oregon grape), and if height is an issue, there is a dwarf form of *M. aquifolium* called 'Compactum' that only grows 2–3 feet (60–90 cm) tall. Given its status as a Canadian native plant, four-season ornamental and source of edible berries, Oregon grape deserves a more prominent place in our gardens.

SPECIES:
Mahonia aquifolium

A.K.A.:
Oregon grape holly

PLANT TYPE:
Evergreen shrub

ORIGIN:
Western North America

HARDINESS:
USDA zone 5

SUN:
Shade to full sun

WATER:
Consistent soil moisture with good drainage

ULTIMATE SIZE:
4–8 feet (120–250 cm) tall by 3–5 feet (90–150 cm) wide

BLOOM:
Early to mid-spring

POLLINATION:
Self-fertile

PRUNING:
Prune for form after flowering

ABOVE: Oregon grape in bloom.
INSET: Ripe Oregon grape berries.

WHAT'S EDIBLE:
Brilliant blue berries

HARVEST TIME:
Midsummer to early fall

TASTES LIKE:
Tart blackcurrant, blueberry, and Oregon grape

Oso Berry

ABOVE: Ripening oso berry fruits.
INSET: Early blooming oso berry.

WHAT'S EDIBLE:
Ripened plum-like fruits (in small quantities)

HARVEST TIME:
Early summer

TASTES LIKE:
Black cherry, plum and melon

Almost every day, I cycle through a forest path near my home—it often accommodates bears and the natural foods they tend to seek, including salmonberry, wild hazelnuts, blackberries and oso berry. The latter is the first of these to come into flower, with its multitude of late-winter greenish-white bells that are a critical nectar source for Anna's hummingbird and other early native pollinators.

The flowers are found on separate male and female plants, although these are rarely sexed at garden centres, so it can be difficult to know what you are purchasing unless it is in bloom. The male flowers are reputed to have an offensive cat-urine fragrance at close range (I've never personally smelled it), so you may want to plant these a few feet away from the front door. Another bit of scent trivia is that the leaves have a distinct cucumber smell when bruised.

In any case, oso berries are one of the first forest fruits to ripen and they are quite beautiful, like tiny clusters of plums that shift from salmon orange to a deep purplish-black in early summer. They were eaten fresh, cooked and preserved by local First Nations communities. Even when the fruit has turned purplish-black, it may still be a bit unripe, as indicated by a bitter almond flavour. When oso berries are given a little time to soften and ripen on the bush though, sweetness emerges, with complex flavours of black cherry, melon and plum. Because of that strong flavour (and natural toxins that should be ingested only in small quantities), these berries are best made into syrup and added sparingly to salad dressings, preserves or even cocktails—and are quite possibly that distinctive new taste you have been looking for.

SPECIES:
Oemleria cerasiformis (syn. *Osmaronia cerasiformis*)

A.K.A.:
Indian plum, Oregon plum

PLANT TYPE:
Deciduous shrub

ORIGIN:
British Columbia to California

HARDINESS:
USDA zone 6

SUN:
Open shade to full sun

WATER:
Consistent soil moisture with good drainage

ULTIMATE SIZE:
10–15 feet (3–4.6 m) tall by 8–12 feet (2.5–3.7 m) wide

BLOOM:
Late winter to early spring

POLLINATION:
Dioecious, pollen from male plants required

PRUNING:
Prune in spring after flowering

Ostrich Fern

You won't get a more delicious tasting and versatile ornamental plant than ostrich fern. Despite its "shady" reputation, I can remember seeing huge blocks of this species growing at one of my suppliers (Van Vloten Nurseries Ltd.) and thriving in full sun with no foliage scorch to be seen, due much in part to consistent watering. Bare-root ostrich fern crowns had been brought in from up north, shipped in moist burlap sacks; they were potted up and away they grew.

The fern itself is herbaceous but extremely cold hardy, so most of us in Canada can enjoy it. It has an elegant funnel-shaped form and combines well in the background with mass plantings of larger woodland perennials, such as hosta, bleeding heart and *Brunnera macrophylla*. You can also use it in bogs or as a pond-side planting, as it tolerates saturated soils rather well. Separate fertile fronds emerge midsummer and eventually mature to a more rigid brown stalk. 'The King' and 'Jumbo' are two larger cultivars that can both potentially reach heights of 6 feet (1.8 m).

The edible portions of this plant are the newly emerging sterile or foliage fronds, which are picked from early to mid-spring (depending on location) by being snapped off by hand when they are still tightly curled and less than 4 inches (10 cm) in height. For fresh eating, these fronds are rinsed and boiled (for 15 minutes) or steamed (for 10–12 minutes) to remove the natural toxins—they are not edible in their raw state. For future use, they can be blanched for 2 minutes, rinsed in cool water, dried, packaged and frozen, where they will keep for up to a year until you are ready to cook them. Fiddleheads go really well with fresh linguini and a little lemon, or as the vegetable in cream-based soups.

OPPOSITE, TOP: Fully emerged ostrich ferns.
INSET: Unfurling ostrich fern crozier.

SPECIES:
Matteuccia struthiopteris

A.K.A.:
Fiddlehead fern, shuttlecock fern

PLANT TYPE:
Herbaceous perennial

ORIGIN:
Indigenous across the Northern Hemisphere

HARDINESS:
USDA zone 3

SUN:
Part to full shade

WATER:
Moist to wet soil

ULTIMATE SIZE:
Averages 4 feet (120 cm) tall by 3 feet (90 cm) wide (rhizome spread)

BLOOM:
Fertile fronds in mid-summer

POLLINATION:
Not required

PRUNING:
Cut back dead fronds in late winter

WHAT'S EDIBLE:

Emerging sterile fronds before they uncurl (must be cooked to remove toxins)

HARVEST TIME:

Early spring as fronds emerge

TASTES LIKE:

Mild asparagus and artichoke

Pawpaw

ABOVE: Pawpaw flower.
INSET: .'Sunflower' pawpaw fruit cluster.

WHAT'S EDIBLE:
Fruits (excluding seeds)

HARVEST TIME:
September to October

TASTES LIKE:
Sweet banana mango

The first time I heard about *Asimina triloba* was about 20 years ago, when one of my local nursery suppliers mentioned he had some Michigan mangoes for sale. The common name is a suitable one, as this species is a member of the custard apple family (*Annonaceae*), which branches out to numerous tropical fruits, many of which feature flavours of pineapple, banana and mango. In the wild, it ranges from southern Ontario all the way down to Texas and is commonly found as an understory tree, meaning it tolerates partial shade rather well. The dark purple flowers open just as the leaves emerge, face downwards and have a fetid scent—so flies and beetles are the main pollinators.

The problem with the Michigan mango is that most cultivars are self-sterile and as the perfect pawpaw flowers mature, the female portion is ready first and not always able to receive the male pollen, which ripens later. Hand-pollination (with a camel-hair brush) is highly recommended if you want a decent fruit set—use an older flower with ripe pollen from one cultivar on a different tree with younger flowers still bearing a receptive stigma. The fruits, often multi-lobed, will develop soon after and be ready for harvest in fall, at which time you can simply cut them in half and use a spoon to scoop out the delicious tropical-flavoured pulp (discarding the seeds).

This small deciduous tree is quite attractive, usually taking on a pyramidal form with long pendulous green leaves that shift to golden yellow in fall. Some of the recommended cultivars include 'Shenandoah' (large fruits), 'Sunflower' (one of the few self-fertile varieties), 'Pennsylvania Golden' (early ripening, good for cooler regions), SUSQUEHANNA (few seeds) and 'Prolific', which comes into bearing early.

SPECIES:
Asimina triloba

A.K.A.:
Michigan mango

PLANT TYPE:
Deciduous tree

ORIGIN:
Eastern North America

HARDINESS:
USDA zone 5

SUN:
Part to full sun

WATER:
Consistent soil moisture with good drainage

ULTIMATE SIZE:
15–20 feet (4.6–6 m) high and wide

BLOOM:
April to May

POLLINATION:
Cross-pollination required

PRUNING:
Structural pruning from late winter to early spring

Peach and Nectarine

SPECIES:
Prunus persica; *P. persica* var. *nucipersica*

A.K.A.:
Peche; nectarine

PLANT TYPE:
Deciduous tree

ORIGIN:
China (*Prunus persica*); garden origin (*P. persica* var. *nucipersica*)

HARDINESS:
USDA zone 5

SUN:
Full sun

WATER:
Consistent soil moisture with good drainage

ULTIMATE SIZE:
13–25 feet (4–7.7 m) tall by 13–20 feet (4–6 m) wide, depending on rootstock, smaller genetic dwarfs also available

BLOOM:
Early spring

POLLINATION:
Most peaches and nectarines are self-fertile

PRUNING:
Prune to an open vase form in late winter when cold weather has passed

WHAT'S EDIBLE:
Fruits (excluding pits)

HARVEST TIME:
Mid to late summer

TASTES LIKE:
Both have a true peach flavour

OPPOSITE: Dwarf 'Golden Prolific' nectarine in flower. LEFT: Dwarf 'Empress' peach fruit.

Depending on where you live, peaches (*Prunus persica*) and nectarines (*Prunus persica* var. *nusipersica*) can be a bit of a challenge to grow, as they are quite susceptible to peach leaf curl, particularly in wet coastal climates. Your options here are to keep them out of the rain by training them into a fan espalier form under a south- or west-facing eave (if foliage is kept dry, this fungus is not an issue) or grow FROST, a resistant cultivar that some consider to be less flavourful than older varieties such as 'Red Haven'.

Another good option is genetic dwarfs, such as 'Empress' peach and 'Golden Prolific' nectarine, both of which grow well in containers and reach a maximum height of about 5 feet (1.5 m). These can be kept under cover during the rainy spring weather and brought into the sun when the wet subsides, or you can simply temporarily protect them with a large beach umbrella. I have had a containerized 'Golden Prolific' for several years now and get juicy little nectarines if raccoons don't raid my tiny 30-inch (76-cm) tree.

To be honest, I would keep a peach or nectarine tree in my garden just as an ornamental, as the early-spring display of bright magenta-pink flowers is quite impressive. Nectarines are simply a smooth-skinned mutation of peaches and while some consider them more flavourful, the truth is that the taste has more to do with ripeness, weather and the cultivar grown. Your best flavour choice for nectarine is 'Red Gold' (yellow-fleshed freestone), while 'Glohaven' (freestone), 'Harken' (yellow-fleshed) and 'Cresthaven' (nearly fuzzless) are all lovely peach cultivars to consider.

Pear

ABOVE: Ripening 'Bosc' pears.
INSET: 'Red Bartlett' pears.

WHAT'S EDIBLE:
Fruits (excluding seeds)

HARVEST TIME:
Midsummer to late autumn

TASTES LIKE:
Generally sweet with light citrus

When I was a young boy living in southern Ontario, we had a grumpy old neighbour who had a pear tree in his front yard. While he never harvested those juicy golden fruits, he also tolerated no other pickers and was constantly spying out his window when his pears ripened. One day, I just climbed the tree and started filling my coat pockets, hoping to make a quick getaway. He was waiting for me (with willow switch in hand) at the bottom of the tree, demanding I get down, but when I realized I was going to be punished either way, I decided to stay perched and eat my fill—thus earning my punishment and beginning a life-long love affair with pears.

Fresh pears are still one of my favourite fruits (along with loquats), but these seem to have fallen out of favour with home gardeners of late. Much of this has to do with disease issues that can be addressed with proper maintenance (pruning and dormant sprays), but another common problem is poor quality caused by people picking the fruit too late, as pears ripen better in storage at room temperature.

For prairie gardeners, there are zone 3–hardy pears bred from *Pyrus ussuriensis*, such as EARLY GOLD ('Jefgold'), 'Golden Spice' and 'Ure'. The rest of us in warmer climes have myriad choices, including the scarlet 'Red Bartlett', the rough-skinned long-necked 'Bosc' (which is very productive) or the fat and juicy 'Comice', with more selections listed on the following page. Aesthetically, the abundant white blossoms of pears rival those of a flowering cherry and these trees really do deserve a more prominent place in our gardens.

SPECIES:
Pyrus communis

A.K.A.:
Common pear, European pear

PLANT TYPE:
Deciduous tree

ORIGIN:
Southern Europe to Southwest Asia

HARDINESS:
USDA zone 4

SUN:
Part to full sun (at least 6 hours of sun)

WATER:
Consistent soil moisture with good drainage

ULTIMATE SIZE:
Up to 25–30 feet (7.7–9 m) tall by 15–20 feet (4.6–6 m) wide, depending on rootstock

BLOOM:
March to April

POLLINATION:
Cross-pollination is recommended

PRUNING:
Structural winter pruning, light thinning in summer

LEFT: Bartlett pear. CENTRE: 'Clapp's Favorite' pear in flower. RIGHT: 'Clapp's Favorite' pear.

Pear cultivars

Although European pears are not as popular as they once were as a backyard fruit tree, a visit to Annie's Orchard in Aldergrove, British Columbia, and a good talk with owner Jim Rahe reminded me that this fruit is still immensely popular for fresh eating. Yes, we have had our problems with scab, fire blight and pear trellis rust—but when we look at the sheer production one can get out of a single pear tree, and its longevity of 50 years or more, it is still a very frugal investment.

The following list includes cultivar name, description of fruit and uses:

'Anjou': Light green skin, good for fresh eating, long storage life

'Bartlett': Smooth yellow skin with juicy flesh, fresh eating and canning

'Beurré Hardy': Traditional French pear with a delicious fresh flavour

'Clapp's Favorite': Large yellow fruits with slight red blush, cold hardy

'Conference': Elongated yellowish-green fruits with brown russeting

'Flemish Beauty': Large yellowish-green fruits with a red cheek

'French Bartlett' (syn. 'Doctor Jules Guyot'): Rough-skinned yellow pear

'Harrow Delight': Greenish-yellow fruits with a red blush, easy to grow

HARROW SWEET: Similar to 'Bartlett' but with a red blush, juicy flesh

'Seckel': Small yellowish-brown fruits with a red blush, often used for pickling

CLOCKWISE FROM TOP: 'Highland' espalier pear formerly growing in UBC Botanical Garden. 'Conference' pear. 'Comice' pear.

Persimmon

While global warming is a concern for all of us, the change in weather is having some positive effects with regard to bigger harvests where I live now in coastal British Columbia. The summer of 2015 in particular saw persimmons leap from a fringe fruit into the mainstream when people with trees started reaping record-breaking bumper crops—and with that came a huge resurgence in public interest. Unfortunately, demand quickly outstripped supply and we are still dealing with a persimmon-tree shortage.

Japanese persimmon is the most common, and almost all available cultivars are self-fertile, including 'Fuyu' (your typical supermarket variety), 'Early Jiro', 'Izu' (early ripening) and FIRE CRYSTAL (compact growth habit). The *Diospyros virginiana* × *kaki* hybrid known as NIKITA'S GIFT is another excellent choice, as it is also self-fertile, produces tasty red fruits and at zone 5 is quite cold hardy. The flowers are tiny on Japanese persimmons and don't really show well, but the new growth is an attractive yellowish-green and this often shifts to gold or a brassy red in autumn. Fruit can be harvested in fall when fully coloured and, because it is often raided by squirrels or birds if left on trees, can be matured indoors by storing with other ripening fruits in a cool room.

Another species option includes the American persimmon (*D. virginiana*), with smaller fruit and increased hardiness (zone 4), although except for self-fertile 'Meader' you will need both male and female cultivars. Two new hardy self-fertile American persimmons, PRAIRIE SUN and PRAIRIE STAR, should be more widely available in the near future. Beyond that, we are left with the date-plum (*D. lotus*), a tiny-fruited zone 6–hardy species often used as rootstock.

SPECIES:
Diospyros kaki

A.K.A.:
Japanese persimmon

PLANT TYPE:
Deciduous tree

ORIGINS:
China, Korea

HARDINESS:
USDA zone 7

SUN:
Part to full sun

WATER:
Consistent soil moisture with good drainage

ULTIMATE SIZE:
15–21 feet (4.6–6.5 m) high and wide

BLOOM:
Summer

POLLINATION:
Some cultivars are self-fertile

PRUNING:
Light structural pruning in late winter

ABOVE: New growth of 'Fuyu' Japanese persimmons. INSET: 'Meader' American persimmon fruit.

WHAT'S EDIBLE:
Yellow to reddish-orange fruits

HARVEST TIME:
Late autumn

TASTES LIKE:
Plum and sweet potato, varies with variety

Pheasant Berry

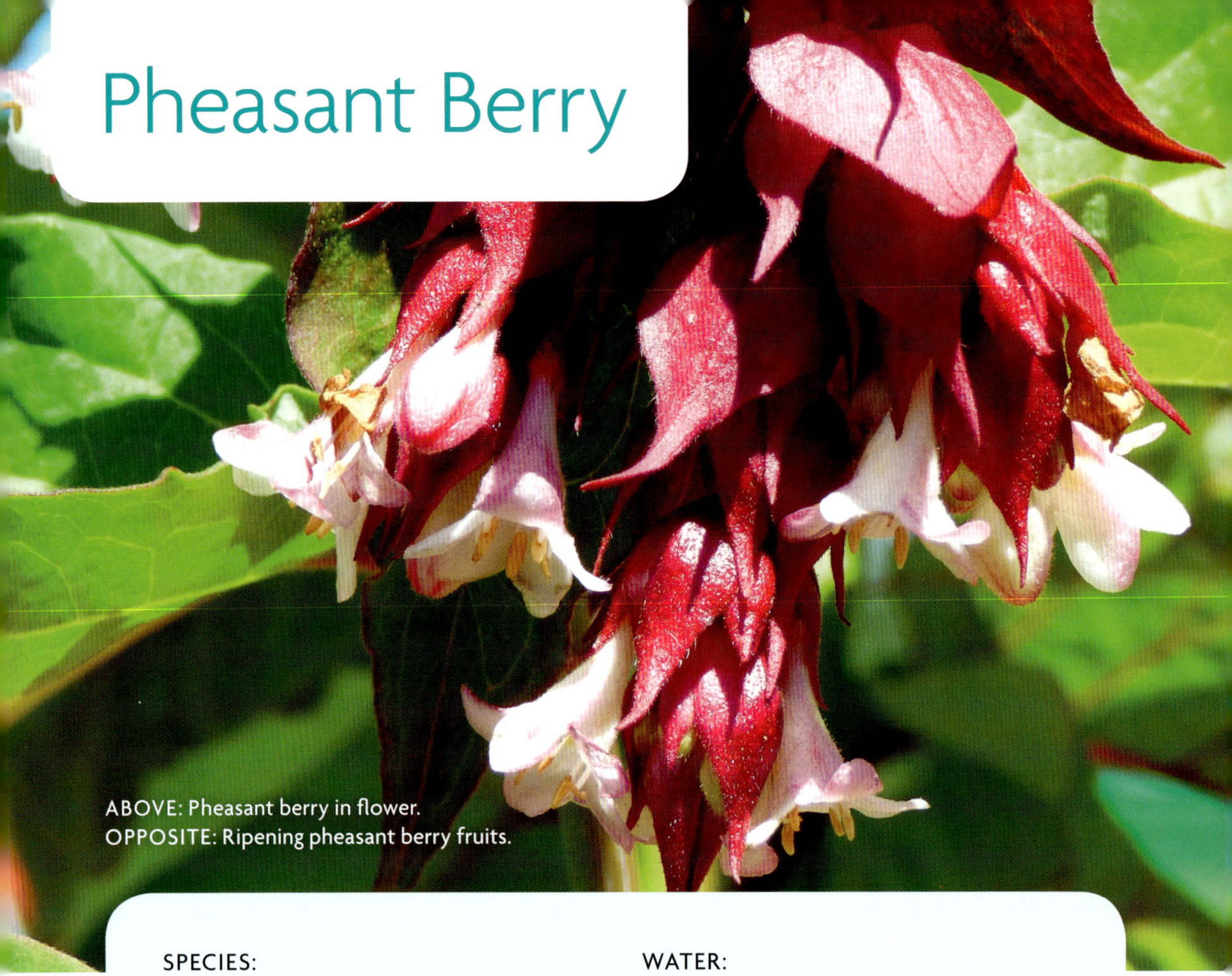

ABOVE: Pheasant berry in flower.
OPPOSITE: Ripening pheasant berry fruits.

SPECIES:
Leycesteria formosa

A.K.A.:
Flowering nutmeg, Himalayan honeysuckle

PLANT TYPE:
Deciduous shrub

ORIGINS:
Western China, Himalayas

HARDINESS:
USDA zone 7

SUN:
Prefers partial shade, tolerates sheltered sun

WATER:
Consistent soil moisture with good drainage

ULTIMATE SIZE:
7 feet (2 m) tall by 5–7 feet (1.5–2 m) wide

BLOOM:
Summer to early autumn

POLLINATION:
Self-fertile

PRUNING:
Cut back damaged or older stems in early spring, after the danger of heavy frost has passed

WHAT'S EDIBLE:
Dark reddish-purple berries

HARVEST TIME:
Autumn

TASTES LIKE:
Fig, bitter chocolate and burnt caramel

Pheasant berry is relatively unknown both for its aesthetic qualities and the fact that the berries can be eaten, even though it was a highly popular shrub during the Victorian era. It is a member of the honeysuckle family and much resembles bamboo with hollow segmented stems and thinly tapered simple leaves. Due to its suckering nature, it has become an invasive species in warmer countries, such as New Zealand, but that is not an issue here in Canada.

The clusters of white flowers surrounded by sharply contrasting deep purple bracts appear throughout the summer. These are followed by glossy reddish-purple berries, often being borne at the same time as the blooms later in the season. As the common name implies, the berries are highly sought after by birds, so much so that this species is often planted as cover for game birds in England. Some gardeners cut this deciduous shrub back entirely (to 6 inches/15 cm) in late spring to allow it to rejuvenate each year, as the stems are rather short-lived, only lasting a few years before they die back entirely. A more compact gold-leaved form called GOLDEN LANTERNS is also available.

The reasons you have likely not heard of this species as an edible are twofold. First, its berries are difficult to pick at peak ripeness; they often do not hold form and tend to bleed everywhere. Second, the flavour is quite variable (and this may have something to do with our individual palates), being superb at peak form—described as bitter chocolate with burnt caramel—but tasting awful at other times. In any case, it is strong (I taste smoked toffee) and probably lends itself to occasional fresh eating or blending with other fruits in baking and preserves.

Physalis

ABOVE: Peruvian groundcherry fruit.
OPPOSITE: 'Purple de Milpa' tomatillo flowers and fruit pods.

WHAT'S EDIBLE:
Ripe yellow to golden fruits (*Physalis peruviana*); green, yellow or purple fruits (unripe fruits are toxic) (*P. ixocarpa*)

HARVEST TIME:
Late summer to fall (*Physalis peruviana*); late summer to frost (*P. ixocarpa*)

TASTES LIKE:
Sweet and tart with citrus overtones (*Physalis peruviana*); tangy-tart with herbal and fruit flavours (*P. ixocarpa*)

SPECIES:
Physalis peruviana; *P. ixocarpa*

A.K.A.:
Peruvian groundcherry, cape gooseberry, Inca berry (*Physalis peruviana*); tomatillo, Mexican husk tomato (*P. ixocarpa*)

PLANT TYPE:
Tender perennial

ORIGINS:
Colombia, Ecuador, Peru (*Physalis peruviana*); Southern United States, Mexico (*P. ixocarpa*)

HARDINESS:
USDA zone 8, frost tender annual (often self-seeding)

SUN:
Part to full sun (*Physalis peruviana*); full sun (*P. ixocarpa*)

WATER:
Consistent soil moisture with good drainage

ULTIMATE SIZE:
24–48 inches (60–120 cm) high by 24–40 inches (60–100 cm) wide for *Physalis peruviana*; 36–48 inches (90–120 cm) high and wide for *P. ixocarpa*

BLOOM:
Late spring to midsummer (*Physalis peruviana*); midsummer to frost (*P. ixocarpa*)

POLLINATION:
Physalis peruviana is self-fertile; *P. ixocarpa* requires cross-pollination

PRUNING:
Pinch to produce more compact plants, remove suckers to increase light penetration

Both these plants are members of the nightshade family and, despite being closely related to tomatoes and eggplants, are not too common in Canadian gardens. Peruvian groundcherry is grown as an annual here, with young plants (either started from seed or purchased from a nursery) set out after danger of frost has passed. The delicious fruits begin to ripen in late summer but one must wait until they drop or shift to a bright gold and the husk turns brown, as the unripe berries are toxic. They are great for fresh eating or adding to fruit salads, or for dipping in chocolate, using the husk as a handle. A similar dwarf species, *Physalis pruinosa*, is also available.

Tomatillos are becoming more popular, but one has to remember to plant at least two varieties for cross-pollination or there will be no fruit. These are large sprawling plants, so some sort of support system or tomato cage is appropriate. *P. ixocarpa* is indeterminate, meaning that it flowers and produces until frost—with the blooms being a lovely pale yellow dotted with purple markings. Harvest begins in late summer and these are often picked green (for salsa verde) when the fruit fills out the husk and flavour is optimal. 'Purple de Milpa' (superb flavour), 'Toma Verde' (large fruits), 'Pineapple' (yellow fruits, pineapple flavour) and wild tomatillo (*P. philadelphica*) are also worth looking for.

Pine

ABOVE: Japanese white pine.
OPPOSITE: Bristlecone pine.

We don't often think of conifers as being a potential food source, and yet First Nations communities across Canada consumed pine and taught these traditional uses to early settlers. One good example is white pine tea, made from the steeped needles of *Pinus strobus*—it is high in vitamins A and C, making a natural tonic for the common cold (except for pregnant women, who should avoid it).

Pine nuts are another edible that might already be growing in your garden, as many ornamental species have small yet tasty seeds. The most common of these is the Japanese white pine (*P. parviflora*), a popular Asian species that comes in many interesting cultivars, such as 'Bergman' (slow growing with twisted blue needles), 'Ogon-janome' (gold-banded needles) and 'Glauca Nana' (dwarf with blue needles). While the pine nuts of this species are rather small once hulled, they are every bit as delicious as the store-bought variety but should be refrigerated to keep them from going rancid.

Two other fairly common landscape specimens are *P. cembra* (Swiss stone pine, zone 3) and *P. aristata* (bristlecone pine, zone 4), both of which have edible seeds. There is, however, one species of pine whose nuts (which are also sold in stores) you might want to avoid, as they can cause a taste disturbance, that being *P. armandii* or Chinese white pine—symptoms include an unpleasant metallic taste lasting anywhere from a few days to several weeks and which eventually resolves itself without treatment.

WHAT'S EDIBLE:
Seeds (*Pinus parviflora*); needles (for tea), seeds (*P. strobus*)

HARVEST TIME:
Cones ripen in October of the following year

TASTES LIKE:
Seeds have a buttery nut flavour, tea has a sweet pine flavour

SPECIES:
Pinus parviflora; *P. strobus*

A.K.A.:
Japanese white pine (*Pinus parviflora*); eastern white pine (*P. strobus*)

PLANT TYPE:
Coniferous tree

ORIGINS:
Japan (*Pinus parviflora*); Eastern North America (*P. strobus*)

HARDINESS:
USDA zone 5 (*Pinus parviflora*); zone 3 (*P. strobus*)

SUN:
Full sun

WATER:
Consistent soil moisture with good drainage

ULTIMATE SIZE:
40 feet (12 m) tall by 16–26 feet (5–8 m) wide for *Pinus parviflora*; 50–80 feet (15–24 m) tall by 20–36 feet (6–11 m) wide for *P. strobus* (dwarf cultivars are available)

BLOOM:
May

POLLINATION:
Wind pollinated (*Pinus parviflora*); cross-pollination is recommended (*P. strobus*)

PRUNING:
Do structural pruning in late winter, limit current season's growth by pruning needle candles in early summer

Pineapple Guava

SPECIES:
Acca sellowiana (syn. *Feijoa sellowiana*)

A.K.A.:
Feijoa, guavasteen

PLANT TYPE:
Evergreen shrub

ORIGINS:
South America

HARDINESS:
USDA zone 7–8

SUN:
Part to full sun

WATER:
Consistent soil moisture with good drainage

ULTIMATE SIZE:
5–6 feet (1.5–1.8 m) in colder climates

BLOOM:
July

POLLINATION:
Most require cross-pollination

PRUNING:
Light pruning in late winter

This attractive evergreen shrub has been around coastal British Columbia for a long time, hailing back to the tropical garden design trend in the 1990s. It is currently enjoying resurgence as an edible plant, as both the exotic-looking flowers (which taste like cotton candy) and egg-shaped green fruits are delicious. The main issue with this species is hardiness. It is often rated as zone 8, but I have seen it thrive in many zone-7 gardens with some shelter from cold winds; it also doesn't tolerate poor soil drainage in winter. Another important aspect of this plant is that it appears to be deer-resistant.

These are very showy shrubs with thick pink and white flowers accented by prominent bright red stamens and glossy green foliage with a silvery-white reverse. They can be trained as an informal hedge and I have even seen a few local shrubs pruned into an attractive standard form. Ripening is an issue in colder climates, which is why a warm, sheltered site (where it will come into flower earlier) is important and given that the fruit ripens so late, I know a few gardeners growing these under cover to try to extend the season.

As mentioned earlier, most clones or cultivars of pineapple guava will need cross-pollination to set the fruit, which is usually cut in half and eaten with a spoon. This can be a little problematic in areas with a limited supply of these shrubs, and even I have only been able to get my hands on several species clones and 'Mammoth', an early-ripening cultivar with large fruits. I expect NIKITA (compact growth habit, early ripening) and 'Coolidge' (large fruits) to come onto the market shortly, with the latter being described as reliably self-fertile.

ABOVE: Ripening pineapple guava fruit.
INSET: Pineapple guava flowers.

WHAT'S EDIBLE:
Flowers and fruits

HARVEST TIME:
July for flowers, November for fruits

TASTES LIKE:
Fruits are like pineapple with subtle mint, flowers taste of cotton candy

Plum

The first thing I always did as a kid who had to move every three years was to explore the forests and fields around my new home. My big find on that second day in Winnipeg was a wild plum tree (*Prunus americana*) full of fruit, sitting on a bank of the Red River—I filled my mouth and pockets, and fell in love with the bounty of plums.

For sheer production and ease of care, I think the egg-shaped European plums are a good choice. When picked a little early they have a nice tartness for fresh eating, or you can let them ripen to full sweetness for making fruit leather or homemade plum brandy. Some of my favourite cultivars include 'Early Italian' (purple skin), 'Yellow Egg', 'Green Gage' and 'Victoria' (red blush), all fairly common. Equally productive, but better for cooking or preserves, is the damson plum (*P. insititia*), which has small rounded purplish-blue fruits and is self-fertile. Another species with similar-shaped fruits is the mirabelle plum (*P. domestica* subsp. *syriaca*), whose yellow fruits are delicious for fresh eating but often ripen all at once.

The large rounded plums you buy in the store are Japanese (*P. salicina*), with 'Santa Rosa' being reliably self-fertile; other delicious varieties include 'Shiro' (yellow) and 'Black Amber'. While not always easy to find, the plum-apricot hybrids have unique flavours and are available as PLUOT (75 percent plum, 25 percent apricot), 'Plumcot' (50 percent plum, 50 percent apricot) and APRIUM (25 percent plum, 75 percent apricot).

WHAT'S EDIBLE:
Fruits

HARVEST TIME:
Mid to late summer

TASTES LIKE:
Sweet to tart, often with a juicy peach texture

OPPOSITE: The prolific mirabelle plum.
LEFT: 'Santa Rosa' Japanese plum.

SPECIES:
Prunus domestica; *P. salicina*

A.K.A.:
European plum (*Prunus domestica*); Japanese plum (*P. salicina*)

PLANT TYPE:
Deciduous tree

ORIGINS:
Europe to West Asia (probably garden origin) for *Prunus domestica*; China (*P. salicina*)

HARDINESS:
USDA zone 5 (*Prunus domestica*); zone 5–6 (depending on cultivar) for *P. salicina*

SUN:
Full sun

WATER:
Consistent soil moisture with good drainage

ULTIMATE SIZE:
12–20 feet (3.7–6 m) high and wide (depending on rootstock)

BLOOM:
Early spring

POLLINATION:
Prunus domestica is self-fertile, but crops better with cross-pollination; *P. salicina* includes both self-fertile cultivars and those that require cross-pollination

PRUNING:
Early spring for structural pruning, summer pruning to restrict growth

LEFT: 'Czar' European plum. RIGHT: 'Methley' Japanese plum.

Plum cultivars

Both European and Japanese plums are highly productive, with the only problem being what to do with all the leftover fruit when you grow weary of eating it fresh. There are numerous tasty solutions—from making plum-smoothie popsicles to fruit leather to delicious brandy or even barbecue sauce—with the only limitation being imagination.

The following list includes cultivar name, description of fruit and uses:

EUROPEAN PLUMS

'Blufre' (syn. 'Blue Free'): Large blue freestone with yellow flesh

'Czar': An old cultivar with reddish-purple skin at peak, best for cooking

'Mount Royal': Rounded form, dark blue skin with yellow flesh

'Stanley': Medium-sized dark blue freestone with yellow flesh

'Valor': Medium-sized semi-freestone with dark purple skin

JAPANESE PLUMS

'Beauty': Bright red over yellow skin with amber flesh

'Burbank': Medium-sized dark red freestone

'Early Golden': Golden freestone with a slight red blush

'Methley': Medium-sized purple plum with a red blush

'Redheart': Round deep red fruit with reddish-purple flesh

'Stanley' European plum.

Pomegranate

I consider pomegranates in Canada a work in progress, meaning I know of a lot of coastal gardeners who are successfully overwintering these to the point of flowering, but that's where the success seems to grind to a halt. The problem is that while hardier cultivars are available, this species still needs long hot summers for fruit to form and ripen—although some growers are working with cold frames to extend the growing season. My point here is that as long as there are Canadian gardeners out there in zone denial, there is always the potential for a sport or mutation to arise that meets the needs of our cooler summers.

The cultivars I see being trialled right now include FAVORITE, a Russian cultivar with vivid orange blooms and flavourful fruit borne on young plants. 'Wonderful' is another common variety that features large red fruits, (up to 4 inches/10 cm) and has a USDA hardiness rating of zone 8. 'Granada' is a sport of 'Wonderful' with improved hardiness and deeper red blossoms and fruits, while ANGEL RED features reddish-orange flowers and large flavourful fruits with soft seeds.

For the skeptics out there, I suggest growing the dwarf pomegranate *Punica granatum* var. *nana*, as it is readily available and does produce small fruits in Canada. These are ideal for container culture and I have one growing in a pot by my west-facing front door. The brilliant orange flowers smother the plant in midsummer but the fruit usually doesn't begin to set until late summer, ripening in early winter. Admittedly, there are few seeds to enjoy in these tiny thick-skinned fruits. This cultivar can be grown as a houseplant but is deciduous when kept outdoors.

SPECIES:
Punica granatum

A.K.A.:
Pomegranate

PLANT TYPE:
Deciduous shrub

ORIGIN:
Eastern Mediterranean to Himalayas

HARDINESS:
USDA zone 7

SUN:
Full sun

WATER:
Average, increase during bloom and fruiting

ULTIMATE SIZE:
5–6 feet (1.5–1.8 m) high by 4–5 feet (1.2–1.5 m) wide

BLOOM:
July to September

POLLINATION:
Self-fertile

PRUNING:
Structural pruning in late winter

ABOVE: 'Granada' pomegranate in bloom. INSET: Harvested dwarf pomegranate fruits.

WHAT'S EDIBLE:
Aril around the seed

HARVEST TIME:
Late fall to early winter

TASTES LIKE:
Sour cherry with tayberry

Prickly Pear Cactus

ABOVE: Whipple cholla fruits.
OPPOSITE: Beavertail cactus in flower.

Growing cactus in Canada may seem a bit absurd to some, but we are situated at the northern range of a few species—from *Opuntia fragilis* in the dry interior of British Columbia to plains prickly pear (*O. polyacantha*, edible fruit) across the southern Prairies to *O. humifusa* (edible pads and fruit) in southwestern Ontario.

The edible pads or nopales are delicious once steamed and sliced, with a mild asparagus flavour; they are traditionally scrambled with eggs, added to tacos or served as a vegetable side dish. You do have to remove the spines and fine hairs (or glochids), but this is easily done using a vegetable peeler and rinsing with cold water afterwards. The edible prickly pear fruit, known as "tuna" in Spanish, comes from many species and it can be skinned (again, watch out for thorns) and eaten fresh, but expect many hard little seeds. It is often processed into delicious jellies. *O. ficus-indica*, or Barbary fig (hardy to zone 8), with its strawberry-coloured flesh, is most common for fruit production. *O. engelmannii* (zone 7) and several species of *Cylindropuntia* also produce edible fruits with varying degrees of palatability.

Prickly pear cactus grows well in containers and can be overwintered in a cold frame with good air circulation or brought indoors as a houseplant.

WHAT'S EDIBLE:
Young pads, fruits (*Opuntia basilaris*); fruits (*Cylindropuntia whipplei*)

HARVEST TIME:
Harvest in late summer when fruits are fully coloured (red to purple, yellow to orange)

TASTES LIKE:
Young cooked pads taste like green bean or asparagus, fruits vary by species and can be sweet to tart with peach or tropical fruit flavours

SPECIES:
Opuntia basilaris; *Cylindropuntia whipplei*

A.K.A.:
Beavertail cactus (*Opuntia basilaris*); whipple cholla (*Cylindropuntia whipplei*)

PLANT TYPE:
Evergreen perennial

ORIGINS:
Southern United States to Northern Mexico

HARDINESS:
USDA zone 6 (*Opuntia basilaris*); zone 5 (*Cylindropuntia whipplei*)

SUN:
Full sun

WATER:
Low moisture with sharp drainage, drought resistant

ULTIMATE SIZE:
12–24 inches (30–60 cm) high by 30–48 inches (76–120 cm) wide for *Opuntia basilaris*; 3–4 feet (90–120 cm) tall by 4–5 feet (120–150 cm) wide for *Cylindropuntia whipplei* (smaller outside its natural range)

BLOOM:
Mid-spring to early summer (*Opuntia basilaris*); late spring to early summer (*Cylindropuntia whipplei*)

POLLINATION:
Includes both self-fertile species and those that require cross-pollination

PRUNING:
Pruning is not usually required, shape after the new growth has matured

Quince

I love this fruit not only because it is the base of my very favourite jelly but also due to its being virtually theft-proof. The thieving in question is courtesy of your typical marauding animals—such as raccoons and, of course, those of the human persuasion. While both usually pass quince by for more tasty spoils, one quince tree at the nursery where I work was not so fortunate and has provided me with a very fond memory. A trucker from the business next door jumped the ditch to help himself to a handful of what I'm sure he thought were delicious golden pears. But both he and his teeth soon found out in no uncertain terms that while the beautiful yellow quince fruit he had absconded with looked like pears and smelt wonderfully enticing at the perfect peak of ripeness, they are hard as rocks and virtually inedible when raw.

Quince is an ancient fruit dating back to biblical times, when its name translated as "golden apple," which has led some to speculate that this was the true fruit of temptation in the Garden of Eden. In modern times, this deciduous tree really does deserve a place in our gardens, as it is self-fertile, reasonably compact and resistant to disease, deer and bears. Plus, it is very attractive with pale pink to white flowers, rounded pubescent foliage and an eye-catching silvery reverse. Once processed, the fruit makes a delicious reddish-pink jelly and is also quite tasty when sliced up and cooked with pork.

While it was once a popular North American fruit that later fell out of fashion, interest in this tree is resurging with the arrival of Eastern European immigrants who love it dearly—so it is getting a little easier to find. Some popular cultivars include 'Orange' (large-sized fruits), 'Champion' (juicy flesh), 'Pineapple' (a Luther Burbank selection with a slight pineapple flavour) and 'Le Borgeot' (syn. 'Le Bourgeault'), a variety known for heavy production.

SPECIES:
Cydonia oblonga

A.K.A.:
Fruiting quince

PLANT TYPE:
Deciduous tree

ORIGIN:
Southwest Asia

HARDINESS:
USDA zone 5

SUN:
Part to full sun

WATER:
Consistent soil moisture with good drainage

ULTIMATE SIZE:
12–15 feet (3.7–4.6 m) high and wide

BLOOM:
Mid to late spring

POLLINATION:
Self-fertile

PRUNING:
Prune out crowded branches in late winter

OPPOSITE, TOP: Fruiting quince in bloom.
INSET: Ripening 'Le Borgeot' quince fruits.

WHAT'S EDIBLE:
Pear-shaped to rounded fruits, after cooking

HARVEST TIME:
Autumn

TASTES LIKE:
Tart crabapple and pear

Raisin Bush

ABOVE: BRANDYWINE raisin bush berries.
OPPOSITE: Dried berries on a raisin bush.

I'll be the first to admit that I chose this deciduous shrub more for its aesthetics than its edible potential. As the common name implies, raisin bush has berry clusters that are often left on the plant to dry for eating in late autumn. They really do look just like raisins, but have a fruitier prune flavour and each has a large seed, so processing is impractical—basically you are left with nibbling dried berries off the bush.

Now that I have fully disclosed the edible limitations of raisin bush, let me extoll the landscape potential. While this tall species can be difficult to find, the two most common cultivars 'Winterthur' and BRANDYWINE ('Bulk') are much more compact in nature, averaging 6 feet (1.8 m) high and wide. 'Winterthur' has deep maroon autumn foliage and more fruit (when cross-pollinated), while BRANDYWINE is reliably self-fertile with intensely coloured berries. Expect large clusters of fragrant creamy-white flowers in spring, followed by a dazzling display of berries as they mature from pale pink to deep pink with blue to finally a dark purplish-blue just as the foliage shifts to burgundy-red in the fall. The fruits are much loved by songbirds and if any are left to dry on the bush you will get raisins.

There is a northern raisin bush, known as *Viburnum cassinoides* (or *V. nudum* var. *cassinoides*), native from Ontario to Newfoundland and virtually identical to *V. nudum*, except at zone 3 it is much hardier. For those of you who must have fruit for jam or jellies, try nannyberry (*V. lentago*), which is also zone-3 hardy and grows wild in southeastern Canada.

WHAT'S EDIBLE:
Dried raisin-like berries

HARVEST TIME:
Late autumn for dried fruits

TASTES LIKE:
Raisin to prune, occasionally with a slightly bitter aftertaste

SPECIES:
Viburnum nudum

A.K.A.:
Possumhaw, smooth witherod

PLANT TYPE:
Deciduous shrub

ORIGIN:
Eastern United States

HARDINESS:
USDA zone 5

SUN:
Part to full sun

WATER:
Consistent soil moisture, tolerates quite moist soils

ULTIMATE SIZE:
5–12 feet (1.5–3.7 m) high and wide

BLOOM:
May to June

POLLINATION:
Better yields with cross-pollination, some cultivars are self-fertile

PRUNING:
Thin and shape after bloom to preserve flowers and fruit production

Raspberry

I can still remember the first time my two eldest daughters visited their great-grandparents' farm just outside of Winnipeg. It wasn't the huge red barn or old tractors that really impressed them, but rather the long rows of raspberries—taller than their young heads, with fruit as far as the eye could see—that they could pick and eat as much as they wanted!

Raspberries certainly aren't an exotic fruit and have been around so long that most of us take them for granted, and yet for sheer production, fresh taste and ease of care they are hard to beat. There are basically two fruiting types: summer-bearing, producing one large crop all at once in early to midsummer, and ever-bearing, producing smaller crops from late summer into autumn. The latter will also produce a secondary crop of smaller berries the next summer. Most people prune out the spent canes of summer-bearing types immediately after fruiting, and I prefer cutting the ever-bearing canes down entirely in late winter, as the secondary crop is usually inferior.

I have two favourite cultivars, 'Tulameen', a summer-bearing type with huge berries and great autumn colour, and the ever-bearing 'Fall Gold', which despite being yellow has a true raspberry flavour. A dwarf (2–3 feet/60–90 cm tall) thornless cultivar that works well in large containers or smaller gardens is RASPBERRY SHORTCAKE ('NR7'). Another newer thornless type is the ever-bearing 'Joan J' with large tasty berries. 'Autumn Bliss', an RHS Award of Garden Merit winner, and 'Heritage' are the most common ever-bearing types found at the local garden centre, while 'Boyne' is good for cold hardiness and 'Meeker' for processing due to its large summer crop.

ABOVE: 'Tulameen' raspberry autumn tones.
OPPOSITE: Ever-bearing 'Fall Gold' raspberries.

WHAT'S EDIBLE:
Berries

HARVEST TIME:
Summer-bearing, early to midsummer (*Rubus idaeus* var. *idaeus*); ever-bearing, late summer to fall (*R. idaeus* var. *strigosus*)

TASTES LIKE:
Tart and sweet, raspberry

SPECIES:
Rubus idaeus var. *idaeus*; *R. idaeus* var. *strigosus*

A.K.A.:
European red raspberry (*Rubus idaeus* var. *idaeus*); American red raspberry (*R. idaeus* var. *strigosus*)

PLANT TYPE:
Deciduous woody perennial

ORIGINS:
Europe, Northern Asia (*Rubus idaeus* var. *idaeus*); North America (*R. idaeus* var. *strigosus*)

HARDINESS:
USDA zone 3–4 (depending on cultivar)

SUN:
Part to full sun

WATER:
Consistent soil moisture with good drainage

ULTIMATE SIZE:
3–5 feet (90–150 cm) tall by 2+ feet (60+ cm) (spreads by underground rhizomes)

BLOOM:
Summer-bearing, spring (*Rubus idaeus* var. *idaeus*); ever-bearing, midsummer to frost (*R. idaeus* var. *strigosus*)

POLLINATION:
Self-fertile

PRUNING:
Cut out old canes after fruiting

Redbud

Few of us realize that these highly attractive shade trees are an excellent food source, as the impressive flower display followed by often equally beautiful heart-shaped leaves of glossy purple, translucent gold or even marbled white ('Floating Clouds') leads most of us to believe that they are strictly ornamentals. The best part is that the flowers taste as good as they look, provided you are willing to tamper with the display—thankfully, blooms are abundant on mature trees.

These blooms emerge just before the leaves, with those of the species being a rosy purple, although many other colours are available, including white ('Alba'), fuchsia ('Appalachian Red'), lavender ('Hearts of Gold'), pink ('Ace of Hearts') and salmon in bud ('Pauline Lily'). They can be eaten raw in salads or baked into muffins, and I like to make homemade fritters or pancakes with them. The young seed pods are also edible and can be used much like snow peas, but these are best eaten in moderation after being lightly cooked and served with butter.

The ornamental uses of this species are numerous, as many different tree forms are available, including weeping ('Ruby Falls'), zig-zag branching ('Covey') and dwarf ('Little Woody'). But where redbuds really excel is in the foliage department, with one of my favourites being 'Forest Pansy', with glossy deep purple spring foliage. Other foliar options include peachy orange (THE RISING SUN), white variegated ('Silver Cloud') and golden yellow ('Hearts of Gold'). This species tolerates full sun in coastal gardens but in hotter locations would probably prefer partial shade in order to avoid scorch. For those interested in the edible aspects of redbud, consider looking at the European species *Cercis siliquastrum* or Judas tree, whose flowers and young seed pods are also quite tasty.

SPECIES:
Cercis canadensis

A.K.A.:
Eastern redbud

PLANT TYPE:
Deciduous tree

ORIGIN:
Eastern North America

HARDINESS:
USDA zone 6

SUN:
Part shade to full sun

WATER:
Consistent soil moisture with good drainage

ULTIMATE SIZE:
20–30 feet (6–9 m) high and wide

BLOOM:
Early spring before leaves

POLLINATION:
Self-fertile

PRUNING:
Mature trees, just after flowering

ABOVE: 'Appalachian Red' redbud in bloom.
INSET: 'Forest Pansy' redbud foliage.

WHAT'S EDIBLE:
Flowers and young seed pods

HARVEST TIME:
Early spring to early summer

TASTES LIKE:
Flowers are like nutty sweet pea, seed pods taste of slightly sour snow pea

Rose

SPECIES: *Rosa rugosa*; *R. moyesii*

A.K.A.: Rugosa rose, sea tomato (*Rosa rugosa*); Mandarin rose (*R. moyesii*)

PLANT TYPE: Deciduous shrub

ORIGINS: East Russia, China, Korea, Japan (*Rosa rugosa*); Western China (*R. moyesii*)

HARDINESS: USDA zone 2 (*Rosa rugosa*); zone 4 (*R. moyesii*)

SUN: Part to full sun

WATER: Average moisture, drought tolerant once established (*Rosa rugosa*); consistent soil moisture with good drainage (*R. moyesii*)

ULTIMATE SIZE: 3–6 feet (0.9–1.8 m) high and wide for *Rosa rugosa*; 13 feet (4 m) tall by 8 feet (2.5 m) wide for *R. moyesii*

BLOOM: Late spring to midsummer, with repeat blooms into late summer (*Rosa rugosa*); late spring to early summer (*R. moyesii*)

POLLINATION: Most are self-fertile

PRUNING: Head back or remove deadwood in late spring

WHAT'S EDIBLE:
Flower petals and hips

HARVEST TIME:
Flowers in bloom, hips when they turn red or reddish orange

TASTES LIKE:
Tart floral flavour

OPPOSITE: Rugosa rose hips.
ABOVE: Mandarin rose bloom.

Thirty-five years of professional gardening means a lot of pruning, deadheading, spraying and mulching, at least as far as hybrid tea or floribunda roses are concerned. It makes me wish there were roses out there that didn't need all this fuss and bother to flower . . . and the good news is that there are—rugosa roses! Let's go through the want list: fragrance, flower colour variation, repeat bloom, disease resistance, drought tolerance, cold hardiness and low maintenance—and you can say yes to all of these with this versatile species.

Both the rugosa rose's flower petals and hips are edible, with blossoms used in salads and cold drinks, and candied in desserts, while hips (which are high in vitamin C) make great tea or delicious jelly. Some of my favourite rugosa cultivars include 'Hansa' (double violet red, fragrant), 'Purple Pavement' (purplish pink, repeat bloomer), 'Frau Dagmar Hastrup' (silvery pink, clove scented), 'Scabrosa' (purplish crimson, large hips) and 'Blanc Double de Coubert' (semi-double white, repeat bloomer). There is also a Russian variety called JUBILEE, favoured for its very large red hips.

Rosa moyesii, or Mandarin rose, is equally disease resistant and can be grown as a large shrub or short climber. It bears white to pink or terracotta-red blooms, followed by huge bottle-shaped hips—these are quite flavourful and can be used much like the rugosa fruits. 'Geranium' (scarlet blooms) and 'Nevada' (white hybrid) are the most common cultivars and both are RHS Award of Garden Merit winners.

Rubus

WHAT'S EDIBLE:
Berries

HARVEST TIME:
Late spring to early summer (*Rubus spectabilis*); midsummer (*R. phoenicolasius*)

TASTES LIKE:
Mild raspberry (*Rubus spectabilis*); tangy raspberry with a hint of strawberry (*R. phoenicolasius*)

SPECIES:
Rubus spectabilis; *R. phoenicolasius*

A.K.A.:
Salmonberry (*Rubus spectabilis*); Japanese wineberry (*R. phoenicolasius*)

PLANT TYPE:
Deciduous shrub (*Rubus spectabilis*); deciduous woody perennial (*R. phoenicolasius*)

ORIGINS:
West Coast of North America (*Rubus spectabilis*); Japan, Korea and China (*R. phoenicolasius*)

HARDINESS:
USDA zone 5

SUN:
Open shade to full sun (*Rubus spectabilis*); part to full sun (*R. phoenicolasius*)

WATER:
Evenly moist to seasonably wet (*Rubus spectabilis*); evenly moist with good drainage (*R. phoenicolasius*)

ULTIMATE SIZE:
6–10 feet (1.8–3 m) tall by 5–8 feet (1.5–2.5 m) wide for *Rubus spectabilis*; 7 feet (2 m) tall and wide for *R. phoenicolasius*

BLOOM:
Early to mid-spring (*Rubus spectabilis*); late spring (*R. phoenicolasius*)

POLLINATION:
Self-fertile

PRUNING:
Thin and remove old wood after fruiting (*Rubus spectabilis*); cut back fruiting stems after picking (*R. phoenicolasius*)

OPPOSITE: Japanese wineberry fruit cluster.
ABOVE: Salmonberry in bloom.

These are two plants that we don't normally consider for fruit production, although both yield delicious berries. Salmonberry is a West Coast native commonly found on the forest's edge producing bright magenta-pink early-spring flowers that are highly sought after by rufous hummingbirds. These are followed by delicious red to golden raspberry-like fruits, which are one of the first wild berries to ripen and were highly prized by First Nations communities for fresh eating. Salmonberry is a large thicket-forming deciduous shrub that may only be appropriate in stream-side or open forest sites where other edible plants may not be practical.

Unfortunately, you will want to avoid the very beautiful cultivar 'Olympic Double', as the fruiting is usually sparse or of poor quality. Another native species to side-step is thimbleberry (*Rubus parviflorus*), as the tasty-looking red berries are quite bland in flavour.

Japanese wineberry, on the other hand, produces terminal clusters of delicious orange to red fruits that have a nice tang and sophisticated berry flavour. This species is considered an invasive plant in many states but is also used extensively for berry breeding, so whether or not you grow it is a judgement call. It can be cultivated much like a summer-bearing raspberry, although it is a bit lanky or vine-like. Simply prune out older canes after fruiting (or in fall) and leave any new ones to produce fruit the following year. These delicious berries are highly prized for fresh eating (although some find them seedy), wine-making, baking or processing into preserves.

Saffron

I'll be the first to admit that growing saffron in Canada is seriously impractical permaculture, as it takes about 150 flowers to produce just 1 ounce (30g) of this valuable spice. Then there's the problem with where I live, coastal British Columbia, as this crocus often doesn't bloom well in wet or cool climates, and with saffron it is all about the flowers. Still, I like the fact that I am growing a spice that was once cultivated by the ancient Greeks, Romans and Phoenicians, and I can find a microclimate in my garden to accommodate it, such as under my west-facing eave near the house foundation where the soil is very sandy and well drained. In any case, wherever you live, you will need to find a planting space with equally sharp drainage and sun at the time of flowering. Despite its challenges, saffron is reasonably hardy at zone 5 and readily available at most garden centres.

Saffron is a true crocus that blooms in October with purple flowers that are equipped with abnormally long red stigmas, exactly three per flower. You can harvest the stigmas by gently removing and drying them, as fresh saffron is tasteless and needs to be stored for about a month before use. The thin grass-like leaves emerge just before the flowers and are held throughout winter, dying back in spring and becoming completely dormant by summer.

There are a few pests to look out for—slugs seem to home right in on the flowers, rabbits will nibble on the tops, and mice and voles have been known to eat the bulbs. Saffron crocus is a triploid and as such is sterile, so propagation is done by the bulb or corm offsets that are produced annually.

SPECIES:
Crocus sativus

A.K.A.:
Saffron crocus

PLANT TYPE:
Bulbous perennial

ORIGIN:
Greece

HARDINESS:
USDA zone 5

SUN:
Full sun

WATER:
Consistent soil moisture with very sharp drainage

ULTIMATE SIZE:
4–8 inches (10–20 cm) tall

BLOOM:
October

POLLINATION:
Not required

PRUNING:
Removal of stigmas and dormant leaves

OPPOSITE, TOP: Saffron crocus in flower.
INSET: Saffron crocus bulbs.

WHAT'S EDIBLE:
Three red stigmas

HARVEST TIME:
October

TASTES LIKE:
Subtle floral with honey

Sage

Few things are as vibrant and lively as a mature sage bush in full bloom, as the spires of lavender-blue flowers seem alive with every kind of pollinator—including bumblebees, hoverflies, honeybees and butterflies. It is almost like Mother Nature has erected a giant flashing neon sign overhead!

Aesthetically, *Salvia officinalis* also has a lot going for it, including numerous variegated and purple-leaf forms that integrate well into most ornamental landscapes, particularly in combination with English lavender, *Coreopsis verticillata* 'Zagreb' and taller sedums. As an herb, it provides important antiseptic properties that many of us find in delicious sage honey, and the Thanksgiving turkey just wouldn't be the same without a few fresh leaves in the stuffing. This drought-tolerant subshrub has many readily available cultivars, including 'Aurea' (gold-edged foliage), 'Purpurascens' (purple-tinted leaves) and 'Tricolor' (green with cream edge, pink to purple highlights), with the best culinary varieties being 'Berggarten' or 'Grower's Friend'.

Russian sage is no slouch with regard to attracting pollinators, but what few gardeners realize is that this attractive perennial has tasty edible flowers with a peppery sage flavour. Again, this is an ideal plant to integrate into mixed borders, as it blends well with ornamental grasses. A classic pairing is achieved when combined with *Rudbeckia fulgida* 'Goldsturm'. Dwarf forms are also available ('Little Spire'). A few fresh flowers added to a salad or frozen in ice cubes will definitely add a little spice to your summer meals.

WHAT'S EDIBLE:
Leaves and flowers (*Salvia officinalis*); flowers (*Perovskia atriplicifolia*)

HARVEST TIME:
Flowers in bloom, harvest leaves during the growing season

TASTES LIKE:
Savoury pepper herbal flavour (*Salvia officinalis*); peppery sage flavour (*Perovskia atriplicifolia*)

OPPOSITE: 'Little Spire' Russian sage blooms.
LEFT: 'Purpurascens' common sage.

SPECIES:
Salvia officinalis; *Perovskia atriplicifolia*

A.K.A.:
Common sage, culinary sage (*Salvia officinalis*); Russian sage (*Perovskia atriplicifolia*)

PLANT TYPE:
Evergreen subshrub (*Salvia officinalis*); woody perennial (*Perovskia atriplicifolia*)

ORIGINS:
Mediterranean, North Africa (*Salvia officinalis*); Southwest and Central Asia (*Perovskia atriplicifolia*)

HARDINESS:
USDA zone 6 (*Salvia officinalis*); zone 5 (*Perovskia atriplicifolia*)

SUN:
Full sun

WATER:
Low to average, drought tolerant once established

ULTIMATE SIZE:
30 inches (76 cm) tall by 40 inches (100 cm) wide for *Salvia officinalis*; 48 inches (120 cm) tall by 24–40 inches (60–100 cm) wide for *Perovskia atriplicifolia*

BLOOM:
Early to midsummer (*Salvia officinalis*); July to October (*Perovskia atriplicifolia*)

POLLINATION:
Pollination not required

PRUNING:
Remove deadwood in early spring, shape after flowering (*Salvia officinalis*); cut back to main stems in early spring (*Perovskia atriplicifolia*)

Sansho

This is *the* tree for foodies—particularly those fond of Japanese cuisine, as almost every part of it is central to their cultural dishes. I have friends who grow sansho commercially (on a small scale) for the fresh leaves and flowers, which are highly sought after by local sushi restaurants looking to achieve that authentic flavour.

The good news is that this is an easy-to-grow, relatively small deciduous tree—so small, in fact, that *Zanthoxylum piperitum* is a popular bonsai specimen, making container culture definitely within the realm of possibility. This is a dioecious species, meaning that there are separate male and female plants, and they are often sold immature and unsexed—if berries are in the plans, try to find a self-fertile female. This large spiny shrub (there is a commercially grown thornless variety called *Asakura sansho*) or small tree has fine compound foliage that emerges a bright green and shifts to a golden yellow in fall.

The young leaves are an essential ingredient in miso soup and are ground into a paste or pesto used to dress salads. The yellowish-green flowers are borne from mid to late spring, with the male blooms traditionally eaten as hana-sansho. Green berries are picked in summer and blanched and salted (to be cooked with fish), while the mature fruits harvested in autumn are dried, ground and used in shichimi spice. Szechuan pepper (*Z. simulans*) is a closely related species with spiky knobs on the mature trunk that make it look like a medieval weapon—its dried berries are one of the ingredients of five-spice powder.

WHAT'S EDIBLE:
Leaves, flowers, berry hulls and seeds

HARVEST TIME:
Leaves when young, flowers in bloom, green berries in summer, ripe fruits in autumn

TASTES LIKE:
Peppery citrus with a hint of cilantro

OPPOSITE: Sansho in flower.
ABOVE: Sansho berries.

SPECIES:
Zanthoxylum piperitum

A.K.A.:
Japanese pepper tree, prickly ash

PLANT TYPE:
Deciduous shrub or small tree

ORIGINS:
China, Japan, Korea, Taiwan

HARDINESS:
USDA zone 6

SUN:
Part to full sun

WATER:
Consistent soil moisture with good drainage

ULTIMATE SIZE:
7½–10 feet (2.3–3 m) high and wide

BLOOM:
Mid to late spring

POLLINATION:
Dioecious, male and female required, self-fertile females available

PRUNING:
Lightly prune for form in late winter

Saskatoon Berry

Saskatoon berries and I have a history that dates back to my childhood, when I lived on an isolated military base in the middle of Saskatchewan. There was little there but a radar station on the top of a hill (diligently watching for Russian aircraft during the Cold War), our homes at the bottom and a scrubby forest full of Saskatoon berries between the two. Summer brought the hope of Saskatoon berry pie, and my mother never had to ask me more than once to go picking for her, as few desserts have ever tasted as good.

Prairie gardeners can take pride in the superior flavour of their homegrown berries, as those I've sampled from coastal locales rarely rival their unique taste. That said, all Canadians can enjoy the gorgeous display of pure-white flowers that much resemble tiny star magnolia blooms. Equally beautiful are the autumn hues of yellow, orange and red that vary with the season and sun exposure. These multi-stem bushes can grow to the size of small trees, although regular pruning (particularly juvenile plants) can keep them to a reasonable picking height. The blue fruit clusters resemble blueberries but are much more flavourful, as evidenced by the appetites of wild birds who know a good thing when they taste it.

Named cultivars are readily available, with 'Smokey' (sweetest flavour), 'Thiessen' (largest berry, heavy production), 'Honeywood' (tangy sweet flavour) and 'Northline' (uniform growth habit) being the most common. Besides their superb flavour, Saskatoon berries are high in both antioxidants and calcium. A few related species worth considering include downy serviceberry (*Amelanchier arborea*), juneberry (*A. canadensis*) and apple serviceberry (*A.* × *grandiflora*), all of which feature attractive flowers, edible fruit and spectacular autumn foliage.

SPECIES:
Amelanchier alnifolia

A.K.A.:
Serviceberry, shadbush

PLANT TYPE:
Deciduous shrub

ORIGIN:
North America

HARDINESS:
USDA zone 2

SUN:
Part to full sun

WATER:
Consistent soil moisture with good drainage

ULTIMATE SIZE:
7–23 feet (2–7 m) tall by 5–10 feet (1.5–3 m) wide

BLOOM:
Early spring

POLLINATION:
Self-fertile

PRUNING:
Remove old wood in early spring

ABOVE: Saskatoon berry flowers.
INSET: Ripening Saskatoon berries.

WHAT'S EDIBLE:
Berries

HARVEST TIME:
Early to midsummer

TASTES LIKE:
Wild blueberry with cherry

Sea Buckthorn

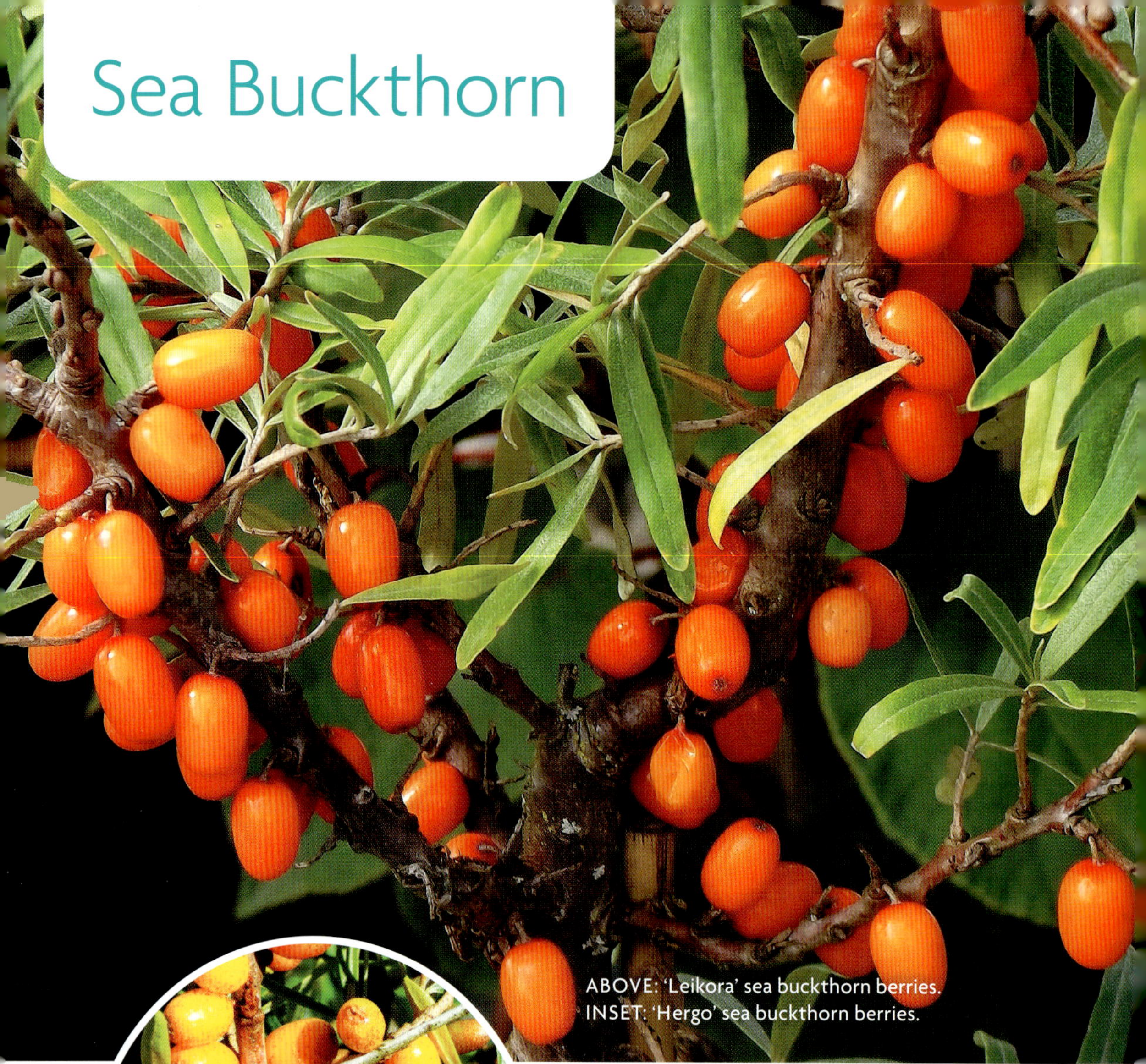

ABOVE: 'Leikora' sea buckthorn berries.
INSET: 'Hergo' sea buckthorn berries.

WHAT'S EDIBLE:
Berries

HARVEST TIME:
Late summer

TASTES LIKE:
Tart citrus

While North Americans are virtually oblivious to this crop, it is highly regarded in Eastern Europe and Russia, where most of the cultivars originate. Sea buckthorn is a spiny deciduous shrub with thin silvery-green foliage and a very unruly growth habit. As the common name implies, it is often found in the wild, growing in sandy soils near the ocean, making it quite tolerant of sea-salt exposure. It is a dioecious species, meaning male and female flowers are found on separate shrubs, with the female berries often being higher in vitamin C than lemons. In fact, a beverage made from sea buckthorn was used in East Germany during the Cold War as a healthy replacement for orange juice.

This shrub requires a full-sun exposure and regular pruning to aid light penetration because if lower branches are shaded they cease to produce or die off altogether. This species fixes its own nitrogen and is wind pollinated, with the flowers emerging just before the leaves unfurl. The male and female plants (a 1 to 6 ratio is fine) will need to be no more than 10 feet (3 m) apart at maturity to ensure pollination and good fruit set.

While harvesting can be difficult due to the bush's thorny nature, many gardeners simply prune out fruit-laden branches and freeze them, after which the berries readily fall off and can be processed into delicious sauces, jellies, jams, tea and cold beverages. Some of the better female cultivars include TITAN (larger berries that are easier to harvest), 'Leikora' (orange berries with intense flavour), ASKOLA (deep orange berries, high vitamin C), 'Hergo' (yellow to light orange juicy berries) and BAIKAL (bright orange fruits, compact growth habit).

SPECIES:
Hippophae rhamnoides

A.K.A.:
Seaberry

PLANT TYPE:
Deciduous shrub

ORIGINS:
Europe, Asia

HARDINESS:
USDA zone 3

SUN:
Full sun

WATER:
Consistent soil moisture with good drainage

ULTIMATE SIZE:
7½–12 feet (2.3–3.7 m) high and wide

BLOOM:
Spring

POLLINATION:
Male and female plants required, wind pollinated

PRUNING:
Prune in late winter to improve light penetration

Shipova

You would think that a rare intergeneric hybrid (a cross of European pear and whitebeam or *Sorbus aria*) more than 400 years old would find some place in a demonstration garden, but such is not the case for the very enigmatic shipova. Thankfully, I found a supplier on Denman Island: Tree Eater Nursery is a permaculture-based nursery run by Peter Janes and Magdalene Joly, who grow many rare food-bearing trees and were kind enough to share their experiences with growing shipova.

Let's start with the fruit itself—much resembling a squat Asian pear, with yellow skin and a nice red blush, it has a very dense texture and floral pear flavour. Peter and Magdalene enjoy the fruit fresh and dried (very sweet), and it can also be canned like any other pear.

Maturity can take a while (7 to 8 years on mountain ash rootstock) but there is a dwarf form (grafted onto *Aronia* rootstock) that is supposed to reach a maximum height of 8 feet (2.5 m) and comes into bearing 2 to 3 years earlier. The white flowers open in April on Denman Island, late enough to not be bothered by frosts, and the downy-haired green leaves take on a silvery hue. Zone-3 hardiness makes this a viable option for even prairie gardeners, with fruit generally ripening from mid to late summer. The only disease of concern is fire blight, but this can be avoided by limiting excessive pruning and fertilization, which promote the new growth that is susceptible to this bacterium.

WHAT'S EDIBLE:
Fruits

HARVEST TIME:
Mid-August to late summer

TASTES LIKE:
Aromatic European pear but with a denser, chewier texture

OPPOSITE: Shipova in flower. ABOVE: Ripening shipova fruit. *Both photos courtesy of Tree Eater Nursery*

SPECIES:
× *Sorbopyrus auricularis*

A.K.A.:
Bollwiller pear

PLANT TYPE:
Deciduous tree

ORIGIN:
Garden origin in France, around 1610

HARDINESS:
USDA zone 3

SUN:
Part to full sun

WATER:
Consistent soil moisture with good drainage

ULTIMATE SIZE:
15–20 feet (4.6–6 m) tall by 15 feet (4.6 m) wide (depending on rootstock)

BLOOM:
April to late spring

POLLINATION:
Partially self-fertile but can be cross-pollinated with a European pear or mountain ash that blooms at the same time

PRUNING:
Requires little pruning as it has a naturally open growth habit with a pyramidal form

Sour Cherry

ABOVE: 'Romeo' sour cherry in bloom. OPPOSITE: 'Montmorency' sour cherry.

SPECIES:
Prunus cerasus

A.K.A.:
Morello cherry, tart cherry

PLANT TYPE:
Deciduous tree

ORIGINS:
Natural hybrid occurring in Eastern Europe or the Middle East

HARDINESS:
USDA zone 4, with some cultivars being hardier

SUN:
Full sun

WATER:
Consistent soil moisture with good drainage

ULTIMATE SIZE:
12–20 feet (3.7–6 m) high and wide, smaller cultivars and hybrids exist

BLOOM:
Spring

POLLINATION:
Generally self-fertile

PRUNING:
Thin in late winter

WHAT'S EDIBLE:
Red fruits

HARVEST TIME:
Early to midsummer

TASTES LIKE:
Tart but intense cherry

As far as fresh eating is concerned, sour cherries are an acquired taste; however those accustomed to their flavour often prefer them over sweet cherries. While this smaller fruit used to be grown exclusively for processing into pie filling, juices or even that awful cough syrup flavouring, the arrival of Eastern European immigrants to Canada changed the focus to fresh eating.

Standard varieties in the past included 'Montmorency' (very productive, medium-sized fruit), 'Meteor' (large bright red fruit), 'North Star' and 'Schatten Morello' (dark burgundy fruit), but these were not always hardy in parts of the Prairies and northern gardens. Then came 'Evans', an old cultivar rediscovered in an orchard near Edmonton, Alberta—it is zone-3 hardy, naturally compact and quite productive, but some find the fruit a little too sour tasting.

The next generation of dwarf sour cherries, known as *Prunus × kerrasis*, came from the University of Saskatchewan and involved crosses of Mongolian cherry (*P. fruticosa*) and *P. cerasus*. The first release was 'Carmine Jewel' in 1999, which was followed by the Romance Series. These are self-fertile cultivars that are compact (averaging 8 feet/2.5 m tall) and have fruit with a high brix (Bx) or sugar content, with the exception of 'Valentine', which was intended for processing or pies. The other four, including 'Crimson Passion' (22 Bx), 'Juliet' (20 Bx), 'Romeo' (22 Bx) and 'Cupid' (19 Bx), can all be eaten fresh. Their zone-3 hardiness and dwarf nature make them ideal candidates for growing in pots, and I have had a containerized 'Romeo' for several years now—it is about 4 feet (1.2 m) tall (with little pruning), absolutely stunning in bloom and very productive.

Sumac

ABOVE: Staghorn sumac fall colour.
OPPOSITE: Staghorn sumac fruit.

While sumac has a reputation for being a thuggish plant, much in part due to a suckering growth habit, that same aggressive nature makes it indispensable for erosion control on slopes or river banks. Granted, sumac can be a bit overwhelming in urban applications, but with a little planning can be contained or collared, much like running bamboo. So why would one go to all this bother for a large deciduous shrub often relegated to abandoned farms and rural parks?

The reason is that sumac has a lot to offer the modern landscape—with its groves of suckering stems looking much like a miniature forest—and is useful for screening unwanted views or dividing larger properties. Both *Rhus glabra* and *R. typhina* have spectacular autumn tones of scarlet, bright orange and yellow, and this is nicely contrasted by the burgundy-red velvety fruit clusters held on female plants. Which brings us to the edible benefits of these two species. Sumac lemonade looks and tastes just like pink lemonade (when sweetened) and this refreshing beverage is easily made by harvesting ripened fruit and lightly squeezing the broken-up clusters in water. Start by using 4 large ripened cones for every quart or litre of cool water, breaking them apart by hand, adding to the water and squeezing to release flavour. Let sit for 2 to 4 hours and then strain, using cheesecloth. The resulting pale yellow to pinkish beverage can be refrigerated and sweetened to taste.

Getting back to the ornamental aspects of these species, there are several cultivars worth considering. *R.* × *pulvinata* 'Red Autumn Lace' is a *glabra* × *typhina* hybrid that features fiery autumn tones, while *R. typhina* 'Dissecta' bears elegant finely cut foliage and TIGER EYES ('Bailtiger') produces new bright chartreuse growth and is slow to spread.

WHAT'S EDIBLE:
Fruit clusters on female plants

HARVEST TIME:
Mid-August to October

TASTES LIKE:
Lemon

SPECIES:
Rhus glabra; *R. typhina*

A.K.A.:
Smooth sumac (*Rhus glabra*); staghorn sumac (*R. typhina*)

PLANT TYPE:
Deciduous suckering shrub

ORIGINS:
North America and Northern Mexico (*Rhus glabra*); Eastern North America (*R. typhina*)

HARDINESS:
USDA zone 3

SUN:
Part to full sun

WATER:
Average moisture, drought tolerant once established

ULTIMATE SIZE:
7½–15 feet (2.3–4.6 m) high and wide for *Rhus glabra*; 16 feet (5 m) tall by 20 feet (6 m) wide for *R. typhina*

BLOOM:
Summer

POLLINATION:
Male and female plants are required

PRUNING:
Remove dead branches in late spring

Sweet Cherry

ABOVE: 'Rainier' sweet cherry fruits.
INSET: 'Glacier' sweet cherry fruits.

WHAT'S EDIBLE:
Fleshy drupes or fruits

HARVEST TIME:
Midsummer

TASTES LIKE:
Sweet true cherry

When I was a kid, we spent our summer vacations at my grandmother's Okanagan home. She had a small cherry orchard and we always seemed to arrive just as the fruit was ripening on the trees. Our tradition was for me to climb them and gorge on cherries while she reminded me about what happens when you eat too much fruit all at once. I never listened—and she was always right. That garden is long gone now, but the memories of it come alive every time I eat a cherry.

Since those days, there have been changes with regard to this delectable fruit, with a trend away from the larger cultivars (often occupying whole backyards) that required cross-pollination (a.k.a. the neighbour's tree) to more compact, self-fertile varieties that fit well into modern urban gardens. This was accomplished through new dwarfing rootstocks and breeding, meaning old-fashioned varieties such as 'Van', 'Bing', 'Lambert' and 'Sam' are not as popular as they once were for home gardeners.

The rootstock in question is GISELA (of which there are several), with GISELA 5 creating a tree 50 percent the size of one grown on standard mazzard rootstock. 'Lapins' is the most popular of the newer cultivars—often referred to as a self-fertile 'Bing'; it is late maturing, split resistant and produces large juicy fruits. Several other good choices include 'Glacier' (large dark fruits), SWEETHEART (red fruits, productive), 'Compact Stella' (dwarf), SANDRA ROSE (juicy fruits) and SKEENA (large fruits). Of course, I would be remiss not to mention the popular yellow (with a red blush) cherry 'Rainier', often found on multi-graft trees, and a new self-fertile version called STARDUST has been released by the Summerland Research and Development Centre.

SPECIES:
Prunus avium

A.K.A.:
Bird cherry

PLANT TYPE:
Deciduous tree

ORIGINS:
Europe, Southwest Asia, North Africa

HARDINESS:
USDA zone 5

SUN:
Full sun

WATER:
Consistent soil moisture with good drainage

ULTIMATE SIZE:
15–30 feet (4.6–9 m) high and wide depending on rootstock, genetic dwarfs are also available

BLOOM:
Mid-spring

POLLINATION:
Some cultivars are self-fertile while others require cross-pollination

PRUNING:
Prune late winter to early spring to thin crown and remove old wood

Sweet Woodruff

While sweet woodruff might seem like an unusual edible to include in this book, it has been used for culinary and medicinal purposes since the Middle Ages. Of all its edible uses, none is as famous as its inclusion in May wine (Maiwein), a traditional German infusion often served on May Day.

May wine is easy to make and you can start by steeping ½ cup (120 mL) dried organically grown sweet woodruff leaves in a bottle of Riesling wine for 1 to 2 hours (some let it sit overnight for a stronger flavour). After infusion, the leaves are strained out and another bottle of white sparkling wine or champagne is added, along with a few sweet woodruff flowers and ½ cup (120 mL) fresh chopped strawberries, preferably wild (*Fragaria vesca*). Stir and serve right away for an unusual herbal cocktail that will remind some people of sangria.

Herbal teas made from the leaves of this semi-evergreen perennial are no longer recommended, as large quantities can cause adverse reactions, such as dizziness. As far as the plant proper is concerned, I think sweet woodruff is unfairly branded an invasive rather than the tough ground cover it really is. While it is true that it readily spreads, it also grows extremely well in difficult locations, such as beneath trees and in the deepest shade, and if not pampered with too much water and fertilizer, generally stays at a 4-inch (10-cm) height. This makes it easy to combine with slightly taller woodland perennials, such as bleeding heart, hellebore, hosta and bishop's hat (*Epimedium*). As an added bonus, sweet woodruff's star-shaped leaves and fragrant white flowers are deer resistant.

SPECIES:
Galium odoratum (syn. *Asperula odorata*)

A.K.A.:
Sweetscented bedstraw

PLANT TYPE:
Herbaceous perennial

ORIGINS:
Europe, North Africa

HARDINESS:
USDA zone 4

SUN:
Shade to partial sun

WATER:
Consistent soil moisture

ULTIMATE SIZE:
4–8 inches (10–20 cm) high with an indefinite spread

BLOOM:
Late spring into summer

POLLINATION:
Not required

PRUNING:
Cut back in spring for fresh growth

ABOVE: Sweet woodruff in flower.
INSET: Sweet woodruff May wine.

WHAT'S EDIBLE:
Leaves and flowers

HARVEST TIME:
Late spring

TASTES LIKE:
Herbal, fresh-cut hay with honey

Violet

ABOVE: MIRacle 'Classy Pink' violet.
OPPOSITE: Sweet violet in bloom.

The thing I love about violets is that they always taste as good as they smell, especially the old-fashioned *Viola odorata*. It also makes a durable ground cover for open shade if you can tolerate its sprawling nature. That said, this species keeps a fairly low profile and combines well with taller shade-tolerant perennials, such as variegated Solomon's seal and Lenten roses (*Helleborus × hybridus*).

Both the leaves and flowers are edible, with the latter making the most beautiful garnish for baking when candied. These are easily produced by picking fresh flowers and painting them with egg white using a small artist's brush, then coating both sides of each flower with a fine berry sugar and allowing them to dry on wax paper. There are any number of cultivars to choose from, including tried-and-true ones such as 'Rosea' (pink), 'White Czar' and 'Queen Charlotte' (highly scented), although the newer MIRacle Series of 'Intense Blue', 'Classy Pink' and 'Bride White' are just as floriferous and fragrant as the older ones.

Horned violet (*V. cornuta*) is sometimes sold as the perennial pansy and comes in myriad shades with small flowers that add a lot of colour and a bit of flavour (mild pea) to fresh salads and wraps—just be sure the violets you use are organically grown, as most are produced as bedding plants, not edibles. Last but not least, *V.* × 'Etain' is an English hybrid with large lemon-yellow blooms edged in lavender, making it an absolutely elegant flower for edible decor.

WHAT'S EDIBLE:
Flowers and young leaves

HARVEST TIME:
When in bloom

TASTES LIKE:
Sweet floral (*Viola odorata*); mild pea (*V. cornuta*)

SPECIES:
Viola odorata; *V. cornuta*

A.K.A.:
English violet, sweet violet (*Viola odorata*); horned violet (*V. cornuta*)

PLANT TYPE:
Herbaceous perennial

ORIGINS:
West and South Europe (*Viola odorata*); Spain (*V. cornuta*)

HARDINESS:
USDA zone 5

SUN:
Shade to full sun (*Viola odorata*); part to full sun (*V. cornuta*)

WATER:
Consistent soil moisture with good drainage

ULTIMATE SIZE:
6–8 inches (15–20 cm) high by 12+ inches (30+ cm) wide for *Viola odorata*; 6 inches (15 cm) high by 12–16 inches (30–40 cm) wide for *V. cornuta*

BLOOM:
Late winter to mid-spring for *Viola odorata*; best display from March to June for *V. cornuta* (bolts in the heat and blooms sporadically from late summer through winter)

POLLINATION:
Not required

PRUNING:
Deadhead to prolong flowering, cut back after the plant bolts

Wasabi

ABOVE: Wasabi in flower.
INSET: Wasabi root.

WHAT'S EDIBLE:
Leaves, stems, flowers, rhizomes

HARVEST TIME:
Harvest leaves and flowers on immature plants, rhizomes in late spring to early summer

TASTES LIKE:
Hot horseradish

Wasabi is an evergreen perennial in the brassica family, meaning it is related to cabbage, broccoli and horseradish (*Armoracia rusticana*, which often takes its place as the spicy green condiment you get with your sushi). It has only been readily available to the public as a garden plant in the last few years, and in the wild grows naturally on shaded wet stream banks with the protection of the forest canopy. This makes it ideal for those wet, shady parts of our gardens where little else grows, let alone anything edible.

Wasabi also takes well to container culture, although you will have to be diligent with the watering, and a compost-based soil medium is a must, as it is a heavy feeder. This portability also enables gardeners in colder climates to overwinter their wasabi indoors or in a cool greenhouse. The rhizomes are traditionally harvested from late spring to early summer after 2 to 3 years, at which time they are usually about 6–8 inches (15–20 cm) long and 1 inch (2.5 cm) in diameter. The offsets that surround the main rhizome are also replanted at this time as your next crop. I have had my plant for about two years now so haven't yet harvested the rhizome, although I did cook a batch of delicious wasabi leaves fried in tempura and served with a light soy sauce.

Adding sulphur in the form of organic gypsum to the soil will make the flavour of your wasabi more pungent. Sun exposure is critical with this plant, as too much will result in scorched leaf margins or overall wilt, with open shade being the best exposure. And protect your plant from slugs and snails, as these pests love wasabi and can make its large leaves look like Swiss cheese in no time.

SPECIES:
Wasabia japonica (syn. *Eutrema japonica*)

A.K.A.:
Japanese horseradish

PLANT TYPE:
Evergreen perennial

ORIGINS:
China, Japan, Korea

HARDINESS:
USDA zone 8

SUN:
Shade to open shade

WATER:
Moist to wet soil at all times

ULTIMATE SIZE:
18–24 inches (46–60 cm) tall and wide

BLOOM:
Early spring

POLLINATION:
Pollination not required

PRUNING:
Remove damaged leaves any time

Wild Strawberry

SPECIES:
Fragaria vesca

A.K.A.:
Alpine strawberry, fraise des bois

PLANT TYPE:
Evergreen perennial

ORIGIN:
Northern Hemisphere

HARDINESS:
USDA zone 4

SUN:
Part to full sun

WATER:
Consistent soil moisture with good drainage

ULTIMATE SIZE:
6–8 inches (15–20 cm) tall by 12 inches (30 cm) wide

BLOOM:
May to August

POLLINATION:
Most are self-fertile

PRUNING:
Remove old leaves at the end of growing season

Wild strawberries in the form of a few 'Golden Alexandria' plants have been a family favourite for quite some time in my household and I regularly raid the trio of plants in a pot on my back patio for berries, usually for topping my morning oatmeal. The fruits are much smaller (about ⅗ inch/1.5 cm) than those most people are used to, but the intense strawberry-bubblegum flavour really entices the taste buds. Recent immigrants from Europe are behind the resurgence of this diminutive fruit and it can be difficult to keep plants in stock at the nursery I manage at times, as demand often outstrips supply.

While most of the cultivated varieties are runner-less, this is not the case in the wild. That said, it makes the domesticated forms easier to integrate into the garden when you know you can count on a mature plant size, although some self-seeding should be expected.

Fragaria vesca is ever-bearing, with tiny white flowers borne just above the foliage line for most of the growing season. Among the numerous cultivars that can be grown from seed are 'White Soul' (white berries, faint pineapple flavour), 'Ruegen' (larger red berries), 'Mignonette' (red berries, intense flavour), 'Yellow Wonder' (yellowish-white berries, non-attractive to birds), 'Baron Solemacher' (red berries with good flavour), 'Weise Solemacher' (white berries) and 'Alexandria' (large red berries).

For a little variation in foliage colour, try 'Variegata' (creamy-white margins) or the aforementioned 'Golden Alexandria' (bright chartreuse foliage). These are also showing some promise as permanent indoor plants, provided they have a bright window for sunlight (or artificial grow lights) and are hand-pollinated with a Q-tip or fine camel-hair paintbrush to produce fruit.

Cultivated Strawberries (Fragaria × ananassa)

'Albion': Very large dark red with excellent flavour, day-neutral

'Honeoye': Heavy producer with tasty bright red berries, June bearing

'Ozark Beauty': Consistent producer with sweet red berries, ever-bearing

'Seascape': Firm and delicious with good flavour, day-neutral

'Totem': Large and firm with outstanding flavour, June bearing

WHAT'S EDIBLE:
Berries

HARVEST TIME:
Early summer into autumn

TASTES LIKE:
Intense strawberry and bubblegum

OPPOSITE, TOP: 'Golden Alexandria' wild strawberry fruit. INSET: 'Yellow Wonder' wild strawberry fruit.

Wintergreen

ABOVE: 'Peppermint Pearl' wintergreen berries. OPPOSITE: Wintergreen berries and bronzed foliage.

SPECIES:
Gaultheria procumbens

A.K.A.:
Checkerberry, teaberry

PLANT TYPE:
Evergreen subshrub

ORIGIN:
Eastern North America

HARDINESS:
USDA zone 3

SUN:
Open shade to part sun

WATER:
Consistent soil moisture with sharp drainage

ULTIMATE SIZE:
3–6 inches (7.5–15 cm) tall by 12–18 inches (30–46 cm) wide

BLOOM:
Midsummer

POLLINATION:
Self-fertile

PRUNING:
None required except removing dieback

WHAT'S EDIBLE:
Leaves and berries in small quantities

HARVEST TIME:
Berries in late autumn into winter, leaves at any time of the year

TASTES LIKE:
Bubblegum and menthol

Wintergreen is the quintessential plant of Christmas and this evergreen subshrub can be found at almost any garden centre in the months leading up to the big day. The large red berries (up to ⅓ inch/9 mm) are perfect for holiday season and persist from late fall until well into January and beyond, which is why this plant is so popular in winter planters. The colder weather also shifts the already attractive glossy green foliage to a burgundy red, adding yet more colour to the dull winter season.

This plant is also my tried-and-true method for getting kids to behave at the nursery I manage—if I see a child acting up or fighting with their siblings, I ask if they would like to see a bubblegum plant. When I tear off a leaf to let them smell it for themselves, without fail, they instantly have a newfound respect for the garden centre. Wintergreen oil is traditionally used to flavour candy, chewing gum and toothpaste. A refreshing tea can be made from brewing fresh leaves (or allowing them to steep in water over a few days) but is not recommended for pregnant or nursing mothers or small children. But for the rest of us, up to a couple of fresh berries make a delicious snack and are a pleasant reminder of the bubblegum enjoyed in our youth.

Wintergreen the ornamental plant is an RHS Award of Garden Merit winner, and there is a white-berried cultivar available too, called 'Peppermint Pearl'. Midsummer brings a showy display of large white heather bells, and this plant is a great companion to other acid-loving shrubs, such as azaleas, mountain laurel and rhododendrons. Good drainage is a necessity, as it will quickly rot away in wet soils.

Wisteria

Here's an unexpected edible that many of us already have in our yards. The blooms of both Japanese and Chinese wisteria add panache, crisp texture and a sweet-pea flavour to salads or fresh spring rolls, and can even be candied and used to decorate cakes, although they should be eaten in moderation.

If you don't know what species you have, one way to tell is by the direction in which it twines; *Wisteria sinensis* (Chinese) grows counter-clockwise, while *W. floribunda* (Japanese) twines in the opposite direction. Another distinction is that Chinese wisteria blooms before the leaves, while Japanese has flowers and foliage at the same time and often bears longer racemes. If you're not getting flowers, you are probably being too nice to your plant or it's in too shady a spot or you are pruning improperly. Avoid high-nitrogen fertilizers, as these promote foliage and not flowers, and make sure the vine is getting full sun. Remember, too, that it blooms on last year's buds, so if you are pruning all the side branches back to the main vine stalk, you are cutting off the flowers. Lastly, for those newly planting this vigorous vine, it needs careful placement in order to avoid creating the need for excessive pruning in future. Both these species require some room to sprawl and a sturdy arbour or pergola support, as lumber less robust than 2×2 will be crushed when the wisteria twines around it and gains girth—so forget those flimsy lathe trellises.

Easy-to-find Japanese wisteria cultivars include 'Alba' (white racemes up to 24 inches/60 cm), 'Violacea Plena' (double dark violet blooms), 'Rosea' (pale rose-pink trusses up to 24 inches/60 cm) and 'Caroline' (bluish-purple flowers). For Chinese wisteria, either 'Amethyst' (violet blue) or 'Prolific' (lilac blue, heavy flowering) are readily available and RHS Award of Garden Merit winners.

SPECIES:
Wisteria floribunda; *W. sinensis*

A.K.A.:
Japanese wisteria (*Wisteria floribunda*); Chinese wisteria (*W. sinensis*)

PLANT TYPE:
Deciduous vine

ORIGINS:
Japan (*Wisteria floribunda*); China (*W. sinensis*)

HARDINESS:
USDA zone 5

SUN:
Full sun for best flower display

WATER:
Consistent soil moisture with good drainage

ULTIMATE SIZE:
13–30+ feet (4–9+ m) tall

BLOOM:
Late spring

POLLINATION:
Not required

PRUNING:
Cut back new shoots to 5–6 leaves in summer and when dormant, prune these again to 2–3 buds and do any structural pruning

OPPOSITE, TOP: Double-flowering 'Violacea Plena' Japanese wisteria. INSET: 'Pink Ice' Japanese wisteria in bloom.

WHAT'S EDIBLE:
Flowers

HARVEST TIME:
When in bloom

TASTES LIKE:
Young pea with floral undertones

Yuzu

ABOVE: Yuzu tree in West Vancouver.
OPPOSITE: Ripening yuzu fruits.

I had been hearing rumours about hardy lemons for years, and when Ray Mattei of Tropic to Tropic Plants told me he knew of an established tree in Vancouver, I had to go see it for myself. I made my way to the west-end garden of UBC professor Michael Bostock, whose interest in exotic plants was evident by the tree ferns I walked by en route to his backyard. His yuzu tree is about 8 feet (2.5 m) tall and was planted back in 2009 as a one-year-old graft. With the first few fruits showing up in 2013, average annual yields are now between 100 to 200 of the rounded, warty-skinned fruits about 3 inches (7.5 cm) in size and ripening from green to yellow.

Michael has trained his tree to a small standard with two forks and has noticed it exhibits *alternance*, a French term referring to biennial cropping, with one side producing one year and the other the next. The tree is reliably evergreen down to 14F (−10C) but sheds old leaves in November. It has some thorns, and the leaves much resemble kaffir-lime foliage.

Fruits ripen quite late, turning yellow by late October, and are highly sought after by local chefs who use the tasty zest in many drinks and dishes. Expect a lot of seeds and only a quarter of the juice you would get from an average lemon, but the tart flavour lends itself to Japanese cuisine and jams or marmalades. And there is another related hardy citrus entering the market; called *Sudachi ichandrin*, it has fruits that look like tangerines and a reportedly better flavour than yuzu. Both can be container grown where not hardy.

WHAT'S EDIBLE:
Yellow fruits

HARVEST TIME:
Late October to November

TASTES LIKE:
Tart lemon-lime to grapefruit, with a hint of Mandarin orange

SPECIES:
C. ichangensis × *C. reticulata* var. *austera* (syn. *C. junos*)

A.K.A.:
Hardy lemon, yuzu ichandrin

PLANT TYPE:
Evergreen tree or large shrub

ORIGIN:
East Asia

HARDINESS:
USDA zone 7

SUN:
Part to full sun

WATER:
Consistent soil moisture (particularly while fruit is forming) with good drainage

ULTIMATE SIZE:
5–10 feet (1.5–3 m) high and wide

BLOOM:
Early May

POLLINATION:
Self-fertile, with some growers recommending hand-pollination

PRUNING:
Prune to increase light penetration before flowering in spring

Zingiber

Those of you cursed with a shaded garden can breathe a sigh of relief, as both these tasty species love their partial shade. In my opinion, Japanese ginger, or mioga in particular, should be much more widely planted, as this herbaceous perennial comes in many variegated forms that really brighten up those dark corners in the landscape.

The most common of these is 'Dancing Crane' with bold white inset streaking and a reputation for actually being hardier than the species—I can certainly vouch for its strong vigour in the garden. Two other variegated cultivars include 'Silver Arrow' (emerges gold with leaves maturing to streaks of cream, grey and green) and 'White Feather' (a reverse variegated form of 'Dancing Crane'). Clumps can get quite large over time, which is opportune, because edible harvests include the young shoots (blanch before eating) and immature flower buds. Both of these have a subtle ginger flavour and are tasty when finely shredded raw in soups, salads or as a garnish on steamed rice, or cooked as tempura.

Growing your own true ginger (*Zingiber officinale*) has become something of a trend lately, with a few gardeners claiming to overwinter it in zone 8. While starter plants are becoming popular, you can sprout your own from a piece of organic (not treated with growth inhibitors) ginger root that has a green eye bud. When container grown, these can be brought in for winter and treated much like a houseplant. Given Canada's shorter growing season, it is best to plant in early spring (under cover) and harvest as late as possible, digging up the entire plant just as the leaves begin to fade.

WHAT'S EDIBLE:

Young leaves and shoots, flowers and flower buds (*Zingiber mioga*); rhizomes (*Z. officinale*)

HARVEST TIME:

Spring for shoots and young leaves, late summer for flower buds (*Zingiber mioga*); harvest in fall when the leaves start to die back (*Z. officinale*)

TASTES LIKE:

Mild ginger (*Zingiber mioga*); true spicy ginger (*Z. officinale*)

OPPOSITE: Japanese ginger in bloom.
ABOVE: 'Dancing Crane' Japanese ginger.

SPECIES:
Zingiber mioga; *Z. officinale*

A.K.A.:
Japanese ginger, mioga (*Zingiber mioga*); ginger root, true ginger (*Z. officinale*)

PLANT TYPE:
Herbaceous perennial (*Zingiber mioga*); tender perennial (*Z. officinale*)

ORIGINS:
China, Japan, Korea (*Zingiber mioga*); Indian subcontinent (*Z. officinale*)

HARDINESS:
USDA zone 6 (*Zingiber mioga*); zone 9 (*Z. officinale*)

SUN:
Partial shade

WATER:
Consistent soil moisture with good drainage

ULTIMATE SIZE:
36–48 inches (90–120 cm) tall by 18–40+ inches (46–100+ cm) wide for *Zingiber mioga* (continues to spread over time); 18–40 inches (46–100 cm) tall by 18–24 inches (46–60 cm) wide for *Z. officinale* (grows larger in warmer climates)

BLOOM:
Late summer to early autumn (*Zingiber mioga*); grown as an annual, rarely blooms (*Z. officinale*)

POLLINATION:
Not required for *Zingiber mioga*; not required for *Z. officinale*, usually sterile

PRUNING:
Cut back dormant stems in fall (*Zingiber mioga*); none required (*Z. officinale*)

Growing Edibles

BEFORE YOU EAT

Common sense dictates that you exercise caution whenever consuming a fruit or vegetable you haven't encountered before. *And caution is particularly important for people with severe allergies, those who take medications (which may interact with the natural chemicals found in some foods), those with compromised immune systems, pregnant or nursing women and young children.* Ultimately, we are all personally responsible for what we put in our mouths, and it's better to be safe than sorry.

Respect Limits: It is best to limit your initial intake to gauge any potential allergic reactions. And always heed any warnings to keep consumption to a small amount, as too much of a good thing can cause harm.

To Cook or Not to Cook: Following preparation or cooking instructions is equally vital, as some foods (such as the fiddleheads *Matteuccia struthiopteris*) are toxic in a raw state.

Know What Parts are Edible: Just because the flowers or berries of a particular plant are edible, never assume that this means other parts of it can also be eaten—in many instances, as in the case of rhubarb's toxic leaves, some portions of an "edible plant" can be poisonous.

Proper Identification is Essential: Similarly, because one plant is edible, don't assume lookalike plants are okay for eating. For example, while the flowers of one jasmine (*Jasminum officinale*) are edible, the blooms of all jasmines are not—in this case, Carolina jasmine or *Gelsemium sempervirens* is quite toxic. This makes proper identification and exacting research with regard to the plant you eat absolutely critical—and always rely on the botanical epithet rather than common names (which are unreliable and may apply to several different species).

Choose Organic: When purchasing seeds or plants for immediate consumption, try to buy those that have been organically

OPPOSITE, CLOCKWISE FROM TOP LEFT: Pot marigold and borage; a winter planter with lingonberry; 'African Blue' basil; dwarf pineapple; purple appleberry.

Painted lady butterfly on echinacea.

grown (usually indicated by sign or label). As many seeds have chemical coatings, and commercially grown plants are routinely sprayed with fungicides and pesticides that leave residuals, they may not be safe to eat. Your other option here is to simply grow out non-organically produced plants (with the exception of those treated with the very persistent neonicotinoids) for four to six weeks before consumption to allow residual chemicals time to break down and/or be washed off by rain or irrigation.

POLLINATION IS KEY

While pollination is critical to fruit production, many home gardeners are blissfully unaware of this requirement when they take their fruit trees home, concentrating instead on choosing a particular variety. Nurseries can be equally complicit in this ignorance, focusing on the sale instead of informing potential buyers about the pollination needs.

To better understand the intricacies of pollination, ask yourself a few simple questions before purchasing a fruit tree:

1. What transfers the pollen—wind, insects or bees?
2. Is this particular cultivar self-fertile?
3. Or does it need a cross-pollinator?
4. Is this species dioecious, with separate male and female plants?

Hoverfly on aster.

5. Or is it monoecious (with both male staminate and female carpellate flowers found on the same plant)?

Wind-pollinated fruits can be either monoecious or dioecious, with fertilization occurring when the pollen from the male catkins drifts on the wind to the female flowers. If the trees are dioecious, male and female trees must be in close proximity (about 6 feet/1.8 m apart at maturity) to each other. Dioecious vines, such as kiwi, should also be trained on the same arbour or support system so pollinating insects have access to both male and female flowers to facilitate fruit production.

If your tree is insect pollinated, a lack of these pollinators in urban environments or due to inclement weather can lead to poor pollination. In this case, it becomes imperative to your fruit production to attract pollinators to your garden.

Self-fertile species or cultivars that have perfect flowers or male and female blooms on the same tree can pollinate themselves, although even these trees will benefit from cross-pollination, which results in larger fruits and more abundant crops.

Fruits that require cross-pollination are either weakly self-fertile or require the pollen from a different cultivar of the same species that blooms at the same time to set fruit. An exception here is triploid apples, such as 'Gravenstein' and 'Jonagold', which effectively have sterile pollen and cannot pollinate other apples.

ATTRACTING POLLINATORS

Your garden may be filled with healthy berries and fruit trees, but unless there are pollinators present, expect little to no production. The reason being that about a third of domesticated food crops and 90 percent of wild plants depend on insect pollination for fruit or seed production.

The diversity of insect pollinators goes well beyond the domestic honeybee (*Apis mellifera*), currently suffering from colony collapse disorder on a worldwide scale. Lesser-known pollinators include bumblebees, butterflies, wasps, hoverflies, solitary bees, flies (including that pesky housefly), moths and even some beetles. Many of these insects are also on the decline, due to habitat loss from urban development, light pollution affecting nocturnal insects, domestic and agricultural pesticide use and climate change. To encourage them into your garden:

A foraging wild rabbit.

- Recognize pollinators as friends, not foes, and limit pesticide use (even organic) when plants are in bloom.
- Instead of developing every square foot of your landscape, consider dedicating a fallow plot to plants that attract and support natural pollinators (and many seed companies are now offering flower blends that will do just that).
- If you have no room for a dedicated space for pollinators, integrate perennials that attract them into your existing garden—a few good choices are aster, bee balm, echinacea, gaillardia, helenium, lavender, liatris, lupine, milkweed and sea holly (*Eryngium*).
- To attract pollinators of every stripe, plant trees and shrubs such as California lilac (*Ceanothus*), Oregon grape (*Mahonia*), sourwood (*Oxydendrum*), black locust (*Robinia*) and all members of the *Prunus* family (both wild and domestic).
- Hang a mason-bee nest to cultivate these native solitary stingless bees that pollinate up to two hundred times more efficiently than your average honeybee. They will overwinter in cocoons and wake up in early spring to do their work as ideal urban pollinators.

In order to enjoy the fruits of our labours, we need to find ways to attract a diversity of insect pollinators and ensure that they too can thrive in our modern world.

DEALING WITH FRENEMIES

Most of us have a love-hate relationship with wildlife. On one hand, it is lovely to see deer and birds inhabiting our gardens. On the other, if they start eating our fruits and vegetables, that tender sentimental feeling evaporates into an unequivocal *how dare you!* So here are a few strategic compromises:

Bears: As bears are always looking for food, remove such temptations as bird feeders, garbage cans, compost, pet food and uncleaned barbecues. When it comes to young fruit trees, they will simply push them over or break branches to enjoy edibles at ground level, so your best bet is an 8-foot (2.5-m) heavy chain-link fence fortified with a low-voltage electric system.

Birds: Garden netting is probably your most effective barrier, but it needs to be properly draped over the plant or tree and secured to the ground; otherwise birds may get in, and many die in the process of trying to free themselves. Shiny Mylar streamers and plastic owls moved on a regular basis will deter most birds except crows; in this case, hanging some crow decoys upside down in a tree should do the trick.

Deer: A barrier of an 8-foot (2.5-m) high fence or 5-foot (1.5-m) double fence set 3–5 feet (0.9–1.5 m) apart (which messes with a deer's depth perception) is your best solution, although low-voltage electric systems also work well. Homemade deterrents of human hair or scented soap bars hung in mesh bags have limited effectiveness, while commercial repellents utilizing blood products or predator urine work well if replenished after rainfall.

Rabbits: Along with the presence of a dog, creating a fence out of 3-foot (0.9-m) chicken wire buried 6 inches (15 cm) below ground will keep rabbits at bay. Good-quality ultrasonic units also work, as does any blood-based repellent, such as Plantskydd, as rabbits are deathly afraid of this smell.

Raccoons: These rascals like to moisten food before consumption, so removing any water features will help. Fences (unless electrified) won't work, as raccoons are adept climbers. They also quickly accustom themselves to motion-activated sprinklers. Clear plastic deli containers, such as those used for baked goods, can be snapped around ripening grape clusters as a temporary protective measure.

Squirrels: While few barriers deter these ninjas of the natural world, dogs will keep them above ground level. Repellents using cayenne pepper or paprika will work for a short period of time but, if things get out of hand, I suggest you use a live trap with peanut butter on the trigger plate. Keep a careful eye on the trap to ensure you don't leave a squirrel trapped without food or water, and relocate those you catch immediately.

Black-tailed deer.

A DELICATE BALANCE

Until we stop thinking of this planet as *our* world and the place we occupy as *my garden*, we are not going to grasp the fact that we are just a single member of the 8.7 million species that belong here. Whether you believe nature is the result of millions of years of evolution or that life was created, most can agree that *we* (animals, plants, bacteria, etc.) all have a place and purpose in this biosphere.

Gardeners have been some of the worst offenders in terms of urban environmental damage, and I include myself. Most of this destruction has been quite subtle and includes:

- Stripping riparian zones alongside streams to create domesticated gardens
- Removing native plants that feed local wildlife
- Planting or dumping invasive species so that they take over wild areas
- Using too many chemicals to ensure lawns are lush and weed-free
- Spraying pesticides to control other superficial problems

And it all adds up to a long-term environmental disaster. These actions focused on aesthetic vanity have devastating side-effects for wildlife. Removing native plants like salmonberry (*Rubus spectabilis*) can leave bears without much-needed natural forage, adding invasive species such as *Lamium galeobdolon* or *L. maculatum* (usually from discarded hanging baskets) can lead to a forest understory being choked out, and pesticides like Diazinon are toxic to bees, birds, fish and amphibians. What's required is recognition of how we have been self-centred regarding the impacts of our past gardening practices—we need a new forward-looking attitude that considers the well-being of *all of us*.

It really doesn't take much effort to accommodate nature. This can be as simple as planting pollinator-friendly plants, leaving seed heads on dormant perennials for winter birds to forage on and using less of the lawn fertilizer that is fouling our waterways with its nitrate and phosphate run-off. In the end, it will be many small changes from all of us that will save this world.

Cultural Problems

Cultural problems are those issues that fall outside the purview of pests and diseases—with some of the most common being quirky fruiting habits of certain cultivars or species, weather conditions affecting development, unsuitable pH, mechanical damage and inadequate drainage. By way of example:

- 'Italian' prune plums commonly shed overly abundant immature fruits they don't have the natural energy to ripen in a process called "June drop." And Asian pears need annual fruit thinning to prevent limb breakage and to be able to produce reasonably sized pears.
- Biennial cropping is another quirk of nature, with apples such as 'Bramley's Seedling' prone to producing heavy crops one year and little to none the next—regular thinning of juvenile fruits will help to rectify this problem.
- Extreme weather conditions, such as excessive rain, leave plants much more susceptible to fungal infections (such as peach leaf curl or apple scab) and can lower yields due to a lack of pollinators. Conversely, drought may cause leaf wilt or marginal scorch, and can lead to stress conditions that attract insect pests.
- Acid-loving or ericaceous fruits, such as highbush blueberry (*Vaccinium corymbosum*), can often appear chlorotic or yellowed when the pH rises too high. This can be a result of lime being added to an adjacent lawn, top dressing with mushroom manure (which is often alkaline) or irrigating with city water treated with calcium carbonate. While it is always recommended that you choose plants based on the conditions you have, temporary disorders such as this are easily remedied with a soil acidifier such as aluminum sulphate or elemental sulphur.
- Mechanical damage, usually from weed trimmers, is all too common, and once a tree or shrub is girdled or had the bark removed around its base, you can expect a slow but sure demise. Instead, anticipate and prevent this sort of injury by providing trees and shrubs with a protective plastic collar or planting them away from lawn areas.

Iron chlorosis in highbush blueberry.

- Last but not least is drainage. Wet soils with poor aeration can lead to root rot, weak anchoring and the eventual demise of many trees. Your options are to install a costly drainage system or create large raised beds, keeping in mind that the perched root system may be affected by windthrow once the tree has grown and is bearing a load of fruit. Conversely, sandy or sharply drained soils with little or no summer irrigation may also result in premature fruit drop, as adequate moisture is essential for developing fruits.

MANAGING PESTS AND DISEASES

Pests and diseases are a normal part of growing edible plants, and all gardens are affected by them. Once you accept that fact, you can learn to live with superficial damage or minor infestations that don't affect production. Your best defence against pests and diseases is to choose species or cultivars that thrive in your region or climate zone, and to select newer varieties resistant to common problems such as apple scab. And to adopt the "right plant for the right place" philosophy—as optimal growing conditions mean increased resistance to pests and diseases. Good soil nutrition will also go a long way to keeping your plant healthy.

When the inevitable problem does ensue, I utilize integrated pest management (IPM), which always starts by positively identifying the source of the problem, and this can be misleading at times. Take currant blister aphid (*Cryptomyzus ribis*), for instance. The first symptom gardeners notice is usually distorted reddish-purple foliage. This looks to be fungal in nature; however, a fungicide would do nothing to resolve this problem. In fact, the plants can still produce just fine with this minor infestation and, once you

Apple scab can be brought on by extreme weather.

understand its life cycle, you learn that one of the best controls is a dormant application of horticultural oil to smother overwintering eggs.

There are many control options in the IPM system, including:

- Physical—sticky barriers or traps
- Cultural—removing alternate host plants
- Biological—parasitic insects
- Low-impact pesticides or fungicides—such as insecticidal soap and sulphur

Whatever is decided upon, the emphasis should always be on balancing effective results with impact on the environment.

Whether we like it or not, those days of using pesticides and fungicides for every minor blemish are over, as most municipalities have bylaws that strictly regulate or ban their use and, for the most part, domestic pesticides (those designed for use by home gardeners) are being deregulated across Canada.

THE ORGANIC ARSENAL

While the term "organic" is usually defined as being "sourced from nature," more importantly, it has become the antithesis of all things synthetic or chemical. With many of us trying to break from the latter when it comes to pest control, we are also speculating that some of our organic options seem to be less effective than products we formerly used—but this is perception more than reality. Organic measures may take a little more time to work than synthetic options, but can be just as effective in the long run.

Diatomaceous Earth: An organic-arsenal favourite is diatomaceous earth, essentially finely ground fossils that scratch the exoskeleton of insects and cause them to dehydrate and die. Often used to control ants, it should be applied where they travel and, as

Lures can be used to trap apple-maggot flies.

it dissipates quickly with rainfall or irrigation, replenished as needed.

Lures or Pheromone Traps: A good example is a red sphere covered in sticky paste and baited with pheromones to lure apple-maggot flies to the viscous surface before they lay their eggs in the fruits. Minor limitations with this system are that you often need multiple traps (unless you are only using it as a monitoring device) and they require regular cleaning.

Organic Slug Bait: While organic slug baits, made from iron phosphate or ferric sodium EDTA, may take longer to kill slugs and snails than those discontinued metaldehyde baits, pests do stop eating after ingesting them. While it may have been more fast-acting, the old product was extremely toxic to cats and dogs. (That said, ferric sodium EDTA has been linked to some dog poisonings and earthworm kills too, so be careful where you place it.)

Natural Predators: Ladybugs are a good example of a natural predator, sold to control aphid infestations. The limitation here is that while ladybugs are voracious eaters, they tend to look elsewhere for more food once the aphids are gobbled up.

Pesticides: While pesticides are often the most contentious substances gardeners utilize, the organic products I use the most are horticultural oil for scale, mealy bugs and mites, and Trounce (aphids, whiteflies, caterpillars), a dual-action pesticide that combines insecticidal soap and pyrethrin. Both pesticides are effective but also non-selective (meaning they kill all insects, even beneficial ones), and pyrethrin is quite toxic to fish, so do not use near bodies of water.

While many organic options may not be perfect, and some still have environmental impacts, they are clearly a step up ecologically from our past attempts at pest control.

COMPOST AND FERTILIZER

Compost or fertilizer, which is better?

In my opinion, this is an easy choice. Compost not only feeds the plants, it enhances soil microbes, improves drainage (over time) and increases moisture retention. Adding too much commercial fertilizer, on the other hand, will result in an excess of salts that can potentially harm both plants and soil microbes.

Home Composting: Do this using alternate layers of browns (carbon sources like leaves, hay, sawdust or small twigs—but not walnut foliage) with greens (nitrogen sources like vegetable scraps, coffee grounds, grass clippings, fresh weeds) and top with thin layers of soil or manure. Pay close attention to the carbon to nitrogen ratio, which should be around 30 (carbon) to 1 (nitrogen). Add too many browns and your garden waste will take too long to decompose; too many greens and you will have slimy or smelly compost. Lightly moisten each layer as it is laid. Manage your compost in side-by-side three-bin systems—with the first used for fresh layering, the second for turning partially decomposed material into compost and the third for curing or storing finished compost.

Worm Composting: Another option for making good use of household green waste is worm composting, using a three-tier bin kept in a cool garage or storage area with a year-round temperature range of 59–77F (15–25C). This system requires red wiggler worms (*Eisenia fetida*), kept in moistened bedding of shredded newspaper (no colour ink) or leaves and regularly fed kitchen scraps such as vegetable and fruit peels, crushed egg shells and coffee grounds. This food waste is digested by the red wigglers, which provide nourishing castings in exchange. Add finished compost directly to your garden soil or make plant-boosting compost tea: steep 4 cups (1 L) finished compost in 5 gallons (23 L) dechlorinated water with 1 tablespoon (15 mL) organic molasses; allow to sit for 24 hours and strain. If your worm composter has leachate (liquid run-off), dilute 1 part leachate to 10 parts water and use to fertilize non-edible plants.

Fertilizers: As far as this third and last choice is concerned, I prefer organic

Gypsum intensifies the flavour of garlic.

sourced. Many are suitable for vegans, who choose to avoid such animal products as bone, blood or feather meal. Good choices include cottonseed, alfalfa and kelp meal for nitrogen; rock phosphate for phosphorus; greensand for iron and potassium; and glacial rock dust for calcium and magnesium. Fertilizers can intensify flavours, with many gardeners adding gypsum (calcium sulphate) to soil when planting garlic, as the sulphur content increases its spiciness.

CONTAINER CULTURE

Growing fruits in pots or containers dates to the ancient Egyptians and is now for most of us in the modern world a matter of necessity. With the new norm being townhouses, minuscule urban lots, or condominiums with balconies or patios as the only available outdoor space, container culture is the sole gardening option available to many of us. My wife and I are included in that number, with our backyard patio being home to a genetic dwarf nectarine ('Golden Prolific'), a couple of columnar apples ('Golden' and 'Scarlet Sentinel'), a 'Romeo' cherry hybrid (*Prunus* × *kerrasis*) and 'Petite Negra' fig. Our 'Scarlet Sentinel' apple tree has lived in a container for not quite a decade now and with just a single repotting has grown to 6 feet (180 cm) tall by 2 feet (60 cm) wide and is quite productive. Here are a few tips we've learned along the way:

- Success depends on choosing the right cultivars (and rootstock), using an appropriately sized container with good drainage (including rocks or gravel at the bottom), planting with a well-drained organic soil medium, and fertilizing and watering regularly. While neither a standard peat-based container mix nor straight topsoil (which is too heavy) are suitable mediums by themselves, a half-and-half blend of the two can be used for contained fruit, although I prefer the Sea Soil Container Gardening Mix, which is certified organic.
- Container fruits with their drain holes flush to the surface they are placed on need to be raised slightly, using pot feet, tile or cedar lathe, to avoid freezing over during colder weather. As the roots of fruits in containers are more exposed to freeze-thaw cycles, larger pots (minimum 15–20 US gallon or 57–76 L for mature specimens) and hardier cultivars, such as the Romance Series of cherries (zone 3), should be considered.
- Consistent summer watering (micro-irrigation with a timer works well) and some fertilization after its first season of growing in the compost blend are equally essential to fruit production. I use an Osmocote or slow-release fertilizer for macronutrients, along with some glacial rock dust to replace depleted minerals.
- Beyond genetic or hybrid dwarfs, some standard fruits can be grown in containers if they are grafted onto a dwarfing rootstock such as M9 for apples or GISELA 5 for cherries, with an example being 'Compact Stella'.

SPACE-SAVING ESPALIERS

As you get to be an older and wiser gardener, you begin to realize that the most valuable assets of any landscape are available sunlight and room to grow. You need six to eight hours of summer sunlight for most fruits to be productive, and yet one only has to plant a few trees for that sun exposure to be noticeably diminished by the multiple crowns.

One way to avoid this scenario is to utilize espalier pruning to train your fruit trees to inhabit a lower, flat plane on the edge of the garden, leaving plenty of light exposure for adjacent plants. The three most common forms include the tiered horizontal cordon, the fan or palmette and the candelabra, somewhat similar to the newer upright fruiting offshoots (UFO) fruit-training system that employs a single horizontal trunk (which is low to the ground) and renewable fruiting branches that grow upright—this is becoming common in cherry production. Points to note are:

- Espaliers should be grafted onto a dwarfing rootstock and require some sort of support system, such as a south- or west-facing wall or fence, usually with galvanized support wires to tie onto.
- While multi-graft and single-variety espaliers can be purchased, these are almost always three-tier horizontal cordons. With single varieties, be sure there is a cross-pollinator nearby, or in the same front or backyard as the fruit tree (because while people often assume that all three-tier espaliers are multi-grafts of different cultivars, many are in fact single varieties that require cross-pollination).
- Vigorous-growing fruits such as cherries, plums and peaches are best grown as fan espaliers, as this form accommodates their upright growth habit.
- Apples and pears tolerate the tiered horizontal cordon system, provided you diligently remove water sprouts and head back upright shoots (do not allow the shoots from one tier to cross over another) to promote the development of fruit spurs closer to the supporting branch.
- With multi-grafts, you get the required cross-pollination but will also notice the different growth rates between the varieties, so more vigorous ones might require extra pruning initially.
- With the restriction of upright growth, the tree will need room for lateral branching, with the minimum required width per espalier tree being 8 feet (2.5 m).

PROPAGATION

Simple propagation is entirely within the grasp of all gardeners and can be an effective means of building food production. The types of propagation I am referring to include saving and planting seeds, dividing perennials, taking stem and root cuttings, and layering.

Saving Seeds: Let's start with seeds. Very importantly, remember that hybrid plants often don't pass their desirable genetic traits (fruit flavour, growth habit) through their seed, and that it usually reverts to one of the parents' attributes. To save seeds, grow open-pollinated plants (many of which are heirlooms) or species, such as asparagus pea (*Lotus tetragonolobus*), as these produce true to species, unlike hybrids. Once collected, seeds need to be properly air-dried and stored away from moisture and light until planting time.

Dividing Plants: Edible herbaceous perennials, like hosta and monarda, are easily divided in early spring or autumn—but be sure to use the outer, more vigorous portion of the root ball for replanting. My go-to method of dividing is to choose a cool or overcast day and use a sharp spade to dig out the entire clump, gauging the size of the root ball by the drip line. Once dug, you can utilize the spade to cut large outer divisions or for finer-textured perennials, try an old serrated bread knife. Trim any ragged roots at this time and replant right away, being sure to replenish the soil of the existing hole with some compost.

Propagating Stem and Root Cuttings: Cultivated varieties or cultivars can be vegetatively propagated by stem cuttings to retain the desirable characteristics. This works well for such plants as blueberry, kiwi and rosemary. Stem cuttings (2–6 inches/5–15 cm long) are generally taken from hardened new wood, with the cut just below the bottom node and lower leaves stripped off. The base of the cutting is lightly dipped in rooting hormone or gel and poked into a tray of sterile seed mix with bottom heat and topped with a plastic dome to maintain humidity. Keep them in bright indirect light, and you should have rooted cuttings in a matter of weeks. Basal or root cuttings are a popular way of propagating suckering plants, such as raspberry and sumac; generally taken in early spring, they tend to establish very quickly.

Tip Layering: This way of propagating plants like blackberries is also very simple—just dig a 4-inch (10-cm) hole to bury the growing tip of a current season's cane. It will eventually grow upwards again and produce roots where it bends, at which time it can be severed and planted separately.

A SIMPLE GRAFT

Grafting is a specialized skill and not one most gardeners would normally attempt. However, there are times when a simple graft can be utilized as a means of salvaging an unproductive tree or creating your own multi-graft where space is limited.

By way of example, quite often we are reliant on cross-pollination from a neighbour's plants and if these are removed, a once prolific fruit tree is suddenly barren. One solution is to graft a different cultivar (that is compatible and blooms at the same time) of the same species to act as the cross-pollinator, thus saving you the expense of replacing your existing tree. Raymond Barker of the Silverhill Apple Orchard in Mission, British Columbia, was kind enough to demonstrate his simplified whip-and-tongue grafting technique. Taught to him by his grandfather, it has a 95 percent success rate. See the illustrations on the opposite page.

Tools and Timing: Raymond does his grafting from February to early April. The tools he uses are a basic grafting knife with a flat blade and some grafting rubbers that are ⅕ × 6 inches (0.5 × 15 cm) long, although thick elastic bands can also be used.

Step 1: Begin by firmly holding the branch being grafted onto the tree and making an upward cut between two nodes. Your branch should have a diameter of ⅓ inch or between 0.8 and 0.9 cm.

Step 2: The angle of the cut should be about 1 inch (2.5 cm) long on both the scion wood and grafting candidate—if too long or short, it should be recut immediately.

Step 3: Cut the scion wood the same way, leaving only three buds above the graft union and removing any tip or terminal buds—it should also have a diameter of ⅓ inch, or between 0.8 and 0.9 cm.

Step 4: Align the scion and grafting cut on the tree, making sure the angled pieces line up on the outside edges—the cambiums (layer of cells just below the bark) must line up on at least one side.

Step 5: Hold the graft together by winding the grafting rubber from the bottom up, being careful to create tension and overlapping in order to exclude any air. Tie a knot

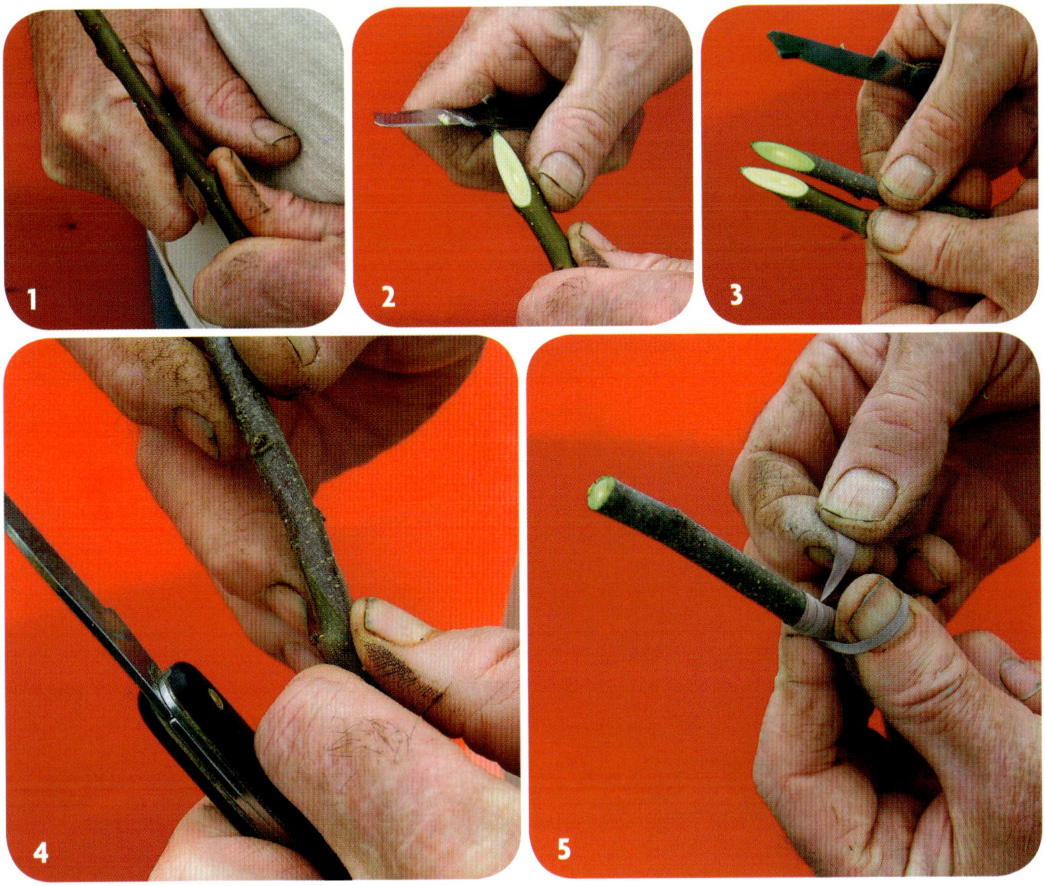

The steps for a simple graft. See opposite page for more detail.

on top by using the thumb to support a loop—if tied properly, grafting wax should not be necessary.

PRUNING BASICS

While I am not going to be able to explain the entirety of pruning fruits within the confines of this chapter, I can certainly leave you with some valuable tips.

- The first thing you need to understand is when and on what your berries, vines and trees produce fruit—be it one- or two-year wood, fruit spurs, or buds produced on last season's growth, such as with grapes. To show how important this is, I had a perplexed gardener at one of my pruning seminars who claimed his 10-year-old apple tree never flowered or produced fruit. When I enquired about his pruning practices, he told me he diligently removed the "little stubs" every autumn—in other words, he pruned out the spurs that produce fruit before he could identify them as flower buds. The lesson is to learn as much as you can about the flowering and fruiting cycle of your plants before you prune.

- Once you have fruit, you also need to remember that thinning is an important part of the pruning process for many trees, such as apples, Asian pears and peaches. An overloaded juvenile plant will only result in branch breakage and mature specimens not thinned will bear small fruits.
- Your pruning basics include the removal of dead or diseased limbs and crossing branches, followed by trimming for structural form and overall tree shape—which means knowing the best form for the relevant species and its fruit production.
- The tools you use should be of a good quality and, even more importantly, kept sharpened, as a dull tool crushes wood and damages with every cut.
- Where diseases such as bacterial canker of *Prunus* (cherry, plum, peach) are present, all pruning tools should be disinfected between trees, using either a rubbing alcohol, Lysol or 10-percent bleach solution to scrub the blades. It is equally important to summer prune or remove wood with bacterial canker during dry weather, in order to limit the spread of infection.
- Generally, dormant (winter) pruning (which stimulates growth) is structural, while summer pruning is used to slow growth and remove excessive vegetation shading the developing fruit. I don't like fall pruning, as there are too many fungal spores during this time of wet weather, and wound closure is very slow.

An apple fruit spur.

BUY A CHEAP GARDEN TOOL . . . KILL A CORAL REEF

As gardeners, most of us are somewhat environmentally aware, switching to low-impact pesticides, composting organic waste instead of throwing it into the garbage and limiting fertilizer to necessity—but when it comes to buying pruners or shovels, we often go the cheap route. The popular belief that using inexpensive tools will save money in the long run is totally false, as future generations will be forced to pay the price for this disposable buying habit.

Every time a tool is forged—be it well-designed or of a poorer quality:

Diving in Belize made me more aware than ever of the environmental destruction that is made worse when we buy cheap gardening tools and other disposable products.

- Energy is expended
- Natural resources are dug out of the ground and refined
- Packaging is created
- Fossil fuels are spent on shipping, much of it long distance

All this contributes to greenhouse gases and the acceleration of global warming.

And nowhere are the impacts more visible than in our oceans. It wasn't until I dived the pristine waters off the coast of Belize that I realized most of the coral formations I had previously seen off the coast of Florida and Hawaii, and throughout the Great Barrier Reef, were mere skeletal remains of their once glorious selves. Like terrestrial ghost towns, they were virtually uninhabited. If we bumped into this level of environmental devastation on land during our day-to-day life, I can tell you that no reminders would be needed.

Buying a good-quality tool will definitely cost you more initially, but it can and should last a lifetime—or longer. Take my trusty hand pruners or secateurs as an example. I have used and abused them (as wire cutters and a light hammer) for these past 18 years, but when properly maintained and sharpened, they still cut as cleanly as the first day I bought them . . . and every part is replaceable! So, remember that at the edge of every garden is an ocean, and the well-being of every creature in it—from the tiniest coral polyp to the massive whale shark—depends on the decisions you and I, and gardeners everywhere, make.

IDENTIFYING MICROCLIMATES

"Microclimate" can be loosely defined as the weather conditions of a relatively small area unique from its environs. Put in lay terms, this likely means you can grow plants your neighbours can't!

There are many factors that determine microclimate, and they differ in every garden—these include:

- Slope
- Soil type
- Drainage
- Wind exposure

Male fuzzy kiwi flowers.

- Humidity
- Precipitation
- Snow cover
- Sun exposure
- Surrounding structures

With careful observation and plant selection, microclimates can make it possible to grow edibles not normally found in your area.

One of the best examples I've come across is a kiwi (*Actinidia deliciosa*) orchard, 7½ acres (3 ha) in size, thriving in the middle of the Fraser Valley where "experts" declared it wouldn't be viable due to hardiness. George Petkov searched for that perfect location and found it in rural Abbotsford, where well-drained fertile soils combined with a gentle southeastern slope that allows cold air and frosts to sweep downhill out of harm's way. Now British Columbia's largest commercial kiwi operation, Petkov's orchard is currently producing more than 150 thousand pounds, or 70 metric tons, a year.

In fact, most of the marginally hardy fruits described in this book can be successful with careful planting based on a thorough examination of the local microclimate—and if conditions aren't ideal, you can always bend the rules. I know of several growers who raise figs (*Ficus carica*) in unheated cold frames, as these structures often trap enough heat in autumn to artificially extend the growing season and allow the second or main crop to ripen. Left outdoors, this second crop would fail in the cool fall weather.

When considering microclimates, there are a couple key points to remember. Firstly, urban areas usually have higher ambient air temperatures, due to warmth radiating from surrounding buildings and off surfaces such as concrete or asphalt, which absorb sunlight by day and release heat in the evening. And, secondly, landscapes at the bottom of a slope can be subject to poor soil drainage and cool air that travels downhill, creating a potential frost pocket or dead zone.

Design Essentials

EDIBLE GROUND COVERS

If you are dedicated to the concept of permaculture, the idea of filling all those voids between your fruit trees and berries becomes a true obsession. As some of these areas are shaded or difficult to cultivate due to root competition or on the edge of a retaining wall with full-sun exposure and sharp drainage, there are challenges to this. For success, plan for ground covers from the outset of the design process, so that they have time to establish before the roots of adjacent trees and shrubs begin to compete for water and nutrients. Secondly, take the "right plant for the right place" concept seriously.

Ground Covers for Shade: We'll begin by discussing shade-tolerant ground covers. Mock strawberry (*Duchesnea indica*, also known as *Potentilla indica*), thrives in open shade and much resembles wild strawberry in foliage and fruit, although the flowers are yellow. The red berries are bland but edible, while young leaves can be tossed into a salad or dried for tea; there is also an attractive form with creamy-white leaf margins known as 'Variegata' or 'Harlequin'. The native subshrub bunchberry (*Cornus canadensis*) is another shade-tolerant ground cover, with tiny white dogwood bracts and edible red berries that can be eaten fresh (mild apple flavour) or added to other fruits to make delicious jelly.

Ground Covers for Well-drained Sun Exposures: This gives us a lot more choice, including many sedums (*Sedum acre*, *S. album*, *S. spathulifolium*, *S. spurium*) with edible young leaves (pick before flowering) that add a little crunch to salads, or even trailing bellflower (*Campanula poscharskyana*) with slightly sweet foliage and flowers. The evergreen ground cover bearberry (*Arctostaphylos uva-ursi*) has edible red fruits that are bittersweet and mealy when raw but make delicious jelly when cooked. Lawn substitutes are also in high demand, with Roman chamomile (*Chamaemelum nobile*), golden oregano (*Origanum vulgare* 'Aureum') and numerous thymes (*Thymus praecox*, *T. serpyllum*, *T. herba-barona*) all working well and providing leaves for herbal use or flowers for tea. Creeping raspberry (*Rubus pentalobus*) rounds out our list of lawn

Bearberry fruits are excellent for jelly-making.

replacements, with scalloped evergreen foliage and tasty pale orange berries.

VINES WITH FOOD VALUE

The vertical element of any landscape design is essential, as it affords us shade, privacy and, with a little planning, another dimension to grow our edibles. While a number of vines, such as kiwi, grapes and jasmine, have already been discussed, I would like to introduce a few unusual species, along with some very ordinary vines you may not have realized were edible.

Common Vines with Edible Properties: Already growing in many gardens, Japanese honeysuckle (*Lonicera japonica*) provides nectar-rich flowers for fragrant tea. Meanwhile, the edible purple, blue and turquoise fruit of the familiar porcelain berry vine (*Ampelopsis brevipedunculata*) makes a stunning garnish and is safe to eat, although not particularly tasty.

Rare Vines with Delicious Elements: The purple appleberry (*Billardiera longiflora*), with Australian origins and zone-7 hardiness, has specific cultural needs, preferring a sunny sheltered site with cool roots (mulch with compost) and evenly moist well-drained soil, rewarding you with purplish-blue berries that taste like stewed apple (but don't eat the seeds). Two other unusual vines are five-flavour berry (*Schisandra chinensis*) and sausage vine (*Holboellia coriacea*), related to akebia and dead man's fingers. While the latter is a bit tender (zone 7), it is worth growing for purplish-pink pods of edible jelly. Five-flavour berry is much hardier at zone 4, with red fruits that resemble currant clusters and provide all the taste sensations—salty, sweet, sour, spicy and bitter! These are produced on fertilized female vines or the self-fertile 'Eastern Prince' and used for juices and teas. Those in colder zones can also consider groundnut (*Apios americana*)—this native of Ontario, Quebec and New Brunswick is a zone 3–hardy herbaceous vine that dies back to the ground for winter. It produces purplish-pink flowers and edible potato-like tubers with a nutty flavour that works well in soups and stews.

PERENNIALS FOR THE PLATE

Most gardeners have an appreciation for herbaceous perennials, given their long seasons of bloom, reliable year-to-year performance and the ability of these plants to blend into almost any landscape design. What some of us don't realize is that we are harbouring edibles in those perennial borders—beautiful flowers and foliage that will look just as good on our plates as they do in the garden.

LEFT: English thyme and common chives. RIGHT: Tall garden phlox with nasturtium.

Anise Hyssop: For a unique taste, try the mildly licorice-flavoured edible leaves and flowers of *Agastache foeniculum*, a member of the mint family.

Bellflower: Easy-to-find species that feature tasty blooms and delicious young leaves are clustered bellflower (*Campanula glomerata*), spotted bellflower (*C. punctata*) and giant bellflower (*C. latifolia*) with bold spires of purplish blue, pink or white.

Carnations or Pinks: Equally taste-tempting are *Dianthus caryophyllus* and *D. plumarius*, with edible flower petals (cut the bitter base off) that range in flavour from floral to spicy clove.

Daylily: The flower petals of *Hemerocallis* have a crunchy sweetness that are delicious when fresh, although you might want to cut the bitter base off, and the buds can be pickled or deep-fried tempura-style for a delicious asparagus–sweet pea flavour. You may want to choose later-blooming cultivars to avoid hemerocallis gall midge; this pest lays eggs in the buds of early-flowering varieties, with the emerging larvae developing inside the distorted bud (which should be removed and destroyed, not thrown into the compost).

Hollyhock: *Alcea rosea* offers a similar colour range to primrose, but with larger blooms. Although quite bland tasting, they make a very impressive garnish with their glossy petals.

Electric Daisy

Anyone who knows me personally will understand why I had to include electric daisy in this book, as this is a plant with a wry sense of humour, like mine. This tender annual is attractive enough, with bronze-green leaves and rounded yellow flowers with red pupils that look like a bunch of alien eyes staring back at you—but, more importantly, this is the Pop Rocks of the plant world.

Both the flowers (eaten whole) and the young leaves when chewed will cause a sensation in your mouth that feels like the sort of jolt of electricity that you get when you touch your tongue to a 9-volt battery (don't ask me how I know this). It starts with a subtle herbal citrus or pineapple flavour, then tingling, followed by excess salivation and a slightly altered sense of taste—which is why the flowers and foliage are popular additions to cocktails at parties, as half the fun is just watching the reactions as guests dare each other to try them out.

The most animated response I have witnessed was from one of my herb suppliers who has a very keen palate. His cynicism was cured in about 30 seconds after tasting electric daisy, and it took another 15 minutes of wiping his tongue before he was able to swear off the plant altogether for the rest of his life. Others seem to take the sensations in stride, but chewing a whole flower definitely produces the strongest effects. For those of you looking for a less potent introduction to electric daisy, just add small amounts of fresh finely chopped leaves to salads, sorbets or stews. This species can be grown from seed and thrives in containers.

Phlox: The tall garden phlox (*Phlox paniculata*) has been an ornamental mainstay for decades now. The flowers have a mild spicy or peppery flavour best enjoyed fresh—just don't confuse this one with other phlox species, which I do not eat.

Primrose: *Primula vulgaris* is another one of those standard perennials we may not realize has edible flowers; they can be crystallized with egg whites and berry sugar (much like violet blooms) for lovely cake decorations.

APPETIZING ANNUAL FLOWERS

Not only do summer flowers delight the eye, many please the palate with their sweet to spicy or slightly bitter flavours. Just be sure they are pesticide free, as most are grown for ornamental use.

Annual Herbs: The blooms of annual herbs present another culinary front, with the flowers of dillweed (*Anethum graveolens*) having a stronger flavour than its leaves, and pineapple sage (*Salvia elegans*) blooms making the perfect fruit-salad garnish. Basil's blossoms (*Ocimum basilicum*) should also not be forgotten—often milder-tasting than leaves, they are a beautiful touch when sprinkled over pasta dishes.

Marigolds: While most marigolds have edible flowers (such as the tiny petals of the fern-leaved *Tagetes tenuifolia* which have a pleasant lemon or citrus flavour), those of your typical French (*T. patula*) and African (*T. erecta*) types are a bit too pungent for most people's tastes. Another marigold worth looking for is *T. lucida*, commonly known as Mexican or Spanish tarragon because the leaves taste like French tarragon (*Artemisia dracunculus*) and are often brewed with the flowers into an anise-flavoured tea. The pot marigold (*Calendula officinalis*) is not closely related, but bears a striking resemblance with orange and yellow blooms. The petals have a peppery taste with a slight bitterness and are generally sprinkled over soups and salads, although they can also be used to colour broths and butters.

True Blues: Vibrant blues really pop as a garnish: cucumber-flavoured borage blossoms (*Borago officinalis*) are ideal for adding to cool summer drinks or freezing in ice cubes for a unique presentation. And the petals of annual cornflower (*Centaurea cyanus*) or bachelor's buttons have a spicy clove flavour that enlivens any salad and is an ingredient in Lady Grey tea.

ORNAMENTAL HERBS

Few things are as satisfying in life as a plant that looks as good as it tastes, which is why ornamental herbs are an essential part of any edible landscape.

Angelica: If you are looking for a bold plant with some architectural interest, try old-fashioned *Angelica archangelica*, which grows up to 6 feet (1.8 m) tall; its aromatic lacy white umbels, stems, leaves and seeds all have culinary value.

Basil: My two favourites are 'African Blue' (*Ocimum kilimandscharicum* × *basilicum* 'Dark Opal'), whose purple-tinted leaves have a high camphor content but make a great pesto when used sparingly, and the variegated 'Pesto Perpetuo' (*O.* × *citriodorum*), which is a superb edible garnish.

English Thyme: *Thymus vulgaris* is a kitchen staple and quite striking when in bloom, and those flowers are also edible. The variegated 'Silver Posie' is my culinary thyme of choice, with white leaf margins that stand out in any garden.

Fennel: As much as I love the anise-licorice flavour of bronze fennel (*Foeniculum vulgare* 'Purpureum'), along with its form—tall feathery stalks and yellow umbels that look majestic in the background of a mixed perennial border—it is a rampant self-seeder, so remove blooms as they fade.

LEFT: 'Black Pearl' pepper. RIGHT: Purple sprouting broccoli.

Or harvest the tasty seeds before they fall to the ground and toss into baking or steep into delicious tea.

Chives: Both garlic (*Allium tuberosum*) and common chives (*A. schoenoprasum*) look great in bloom and have edible white or pink flowers that are tasty in any salad.

Japanese Wild Parsley: One less common herb with ornamental flare is the purple mitsuba (*Cryptotaenia japonica* f. *atropurpurea*), or Japanese wild parsley, with bronzy-purple foliage, tiny light pink flowers and a distinct celery-parsley flavour, although the green-leaf version is considered more savoury.

Rosemary: Gardeners are often drawn to the beauty of gold-leaved *Rosmarinus officinalis* 'Golden Rain' or 'Wilma's Gold', as the foliage provides the perfect foil for flowers that are the colour of faded denim and delicious to eat. These are much less hardy than their green counterparts, though, and should be overwintered in sheltered containers.

THE BEAUTIFUL VEGETABLES

As gardeners shift from a dedicated plot system to full integration of edibles throughout the landscape, the definition of a vegetable garden is changing. Increasingly, vegetables with ornamental appeal are creeping into our landscapes.

Asparagus: *Asparagus officinalis* is particularly attractive in its fern-like foliage stage and makes an elegant backdrop to flowering perennials or shorter ornamental shrubs, although it will take a few years to bulk up.

Eggplant: Not only does *Solanum melongena* have eye-catching violet to white flowers, the glossy white to purple fruits (some of which are striped) look as good as they taste.

Endive: *Cichorium endivia* has a beautiful frilled growth habit, with frisée-type 'Zidane' giving ornamental kale a run for its money as far as attractiveness is concerned.

Peas and Beans: Purple-podded *Pisum sativum* 'Shiraz' or 'Purple Mist' show well when growing through a fence or scrambling over the base of an arbour, and this same colour scheme can be found in such beans as 'Royal Burgundy' (bush), 'Dragon Tongue' (striped) and 'Purple Peacock' (pole).

Peppers: For me, few vegetables are as attractive as the many specialty peppers (*Capsicum annuum*) currently on the market—'Black Pearl' being one of my favourites, with jet-black foliage and spicy round peppers that shift from ebony to bright red as they ripen. A close second is the variegated 'Fish', an heirloom variety used in seafood recipes, and 'Loco', an RHS Award of Garden Merit chili pepper with purple fruits that ripen to red.

Purple Sprouting Broccoli: For winter colour, *Brassica oleracea* var. *italica* will brighten dull days with shoots that can be harvested from late fall through early spring, depending on variety.

Swiss Chard: With multicoloured stems of red, orange, pink and yellow, *Beta vulgaris* will look right at home with your summer flowers and also works well as a container-garden centrepiece.

CANADIAN EDIBLE NATIVE PLANTS

Indigenous species have an important role to play in the edible landscape, particularly if you live next to a greenbelt or riparian zone where planting might be restricted by covenant. Native plants are already adapted to local climatic conditions and many provide food for wildlife—and for you. All that's needed is a close examination of the local microclimate with regard to sun exposure, soil type, drainage and existing species to determine what native plants will succeed where.

Blueberry: A number of wild blueberries work well in varying situations, including the extremely cold-hardy *Vaccinium myrtilloides* (zone 2), moisture-tolerant bog blueberry (*V. uliginosum*), compact bilberry (*V. caespitosum*) and, among the most flavourful, mountain huckleberry (*V. membranaceum*).

Juniper: Found across Canada, common juniper (*Juniperus communis*) does well in full sun with adequate soil drainage. It offers berries that when dried make an excellent spice, one that is always added to my family's Thanksgiving turkey marinade.

Labrador Tea: For sites with wet soils or poor drainage, choose *Rhododendron groenlandicum* (formerly *Ledum groenlandicum*), which grows across Canada and features attractive white flowers, along with leaves used to make a refreshing tea—although you do not want

LEFT: Labrador tea in flower. RIGHT: Common juniper berries.

to brew them for too long, due to toxicity concerns.

Miner's Lettuce: *Claytonia perfoliata* is a self-seeding annual often found in moist sandy loam soils and, as the common name implies, was used by early prospectors who ate the sweet-tasting succulent leaves and stems both raw and cooked.

Nodding Onion: If you are dealing with well-drained soils with full sun, *Allium cernuum* might be the plant for you. This herbaceous perennial is zone-3 hardy, native from British Columbia to Ontario and features showy purplish-pink blooms that attract both hummingbirds and butterflies. The flowers, leaves and bulbs are all edible and were used extensively by First Nations communities—expect a strong onion flavour that sweetens and mellows with cooking.

Soapberry: Another unusual classic Canadian edible worth looking for is *Shepherdia canadensis*. Its fruits were added to water, whipped and mixed with other berries by First Nations communities to make a frothy "ice cream" dessert.

CROPS WITH FALL COLOUR

There is no reason why an edible landscape can't have a little seasonal interest, and for me there is no better choice than fall colour.

LEFT: 'Brant' grape foliage. RIGHT: Striking fall Japanese angelica leaves.

Clove Currant: *Ribes odoratum* provides rich autumn colour with its attractive mahogany-red foliage. Like all the plants mentioned below, it requires a place in the garden with six to eight hours of summer sun in order to provide the best fall display.

Grape: Few vines match the vibrant fall colours of *Vitis* 'Brant', often sold as an ornamental although it bears black grapes that can be used for jelly or wine. Expect a vigorous growth habit (up to 30 feet/9 m high) and autumn tones of reddish burgundy (often with yellow veining) from this RHS Award of Garden Merit winner.

Highbush Blueberry: The best place to start for fall colour is with easy-to-grow *Vaccinium corymbosum*. Optimal cultivars for autumn foliage tones and excellent berry producers are 'Bluecrop' (deep red), 'Chandler' (maroon to orange), 'Duke' (yellow to orange), 'Jersey' (brilliant orange to red) or 'Reka' (red to burgundy). Gardeners with less space or restricted to containers can try the compact *V. angustifolium* (reddish bronze), 'Top Hat' (orange to red) or BLUEBERRY GLAZE (deep red to dark burgundy).

Highbush Cranberry: Few shrubs catch the eye in fall as well as *Viburnum opulus* and *V. trilobum*. Not only does the foliage shift to a blazing scarlet or burgundy, the translucent red berries are often still dangling in terminal clusters.

Japanese Angelica Tree: While *Aralia elata* may be a little hard to control with its suckering nature, come fall this grove of pinnate foliage fires up into layered autumn tones of deep burgundy, red, gold and green—making for an almost three-dimensional display. (See Tasty Tempura on pages 261–62 for how to eat its buds.)

Saskatoon Berry: This one and its close relatives provide gardeners in colder regions with reliable autumn foliage, with *Amelanchier alnifolia* STANDING OVATION (red

LEFT: Shiitake mushrooms growing on a sawdust block. RIGHT: Mountain papaya is perfect for growing indoors.

to orange), *A. canadensis* RAINBOW PILLAR (brilliant yellow, orange and red), and *A.* × *grandiflora* 'Autumn Brilliance' (reddish orange) or 'Ballerina' (deep red and orange) being readily available across the country.

THE GREAT INDOORS

For any enthusiastic gardener, it's a sad day when you realize you have run out of planting space, with every possible nook and cranny occupied. To all of you who are horticulturally downtrodden, I say look to the great indoors—because houseplants bring a whole new facet to the edible garden:

Curry Leaf: The tender spice *Murraya koenigii* is used like bay leaves in Asian cooking, and can be grown as an indoor houseplant in a warm room with as much light as possible.

Dwarf Pineapple: One of my favourite indoor plants is *Ananas nanus*, and while it is often overlooked as an edible because there is very little fruit left after coring and peeling, its flavour is superb. The scent of the ripening pineapple emanates so strongly that this one should be kept in the middle of the dining table, where it can stir up some healthy appetites.

Mountain Papaya: Another tropical fruit that is ideal for growing indoors is the mountain papaya or babaco (*Vasconcellea* × *heilbornii*), which hails from Ecuador and crops well with cooler temperatures, tolerating partial shade such as the bright indirect light found indoors. It grows well in large pots (15 US gallon/57 L at maturity), with exotic leaves atop a sturdy stem that produces yellow ribbed 8–10 inch/20–25 cm fruits with a pineapple-kiwi flavour, and is best kept in temperatures that don't fall below 32F (0C) in winter.

Mushrooms: Mushroom kits are another relatively unexplored edible option for indoor culture and you can grow the expensive species, such as shiitake, blue oyster, reishi or lion's mane. Most are based on a substrate block made of sawdust (often red alder) and enriched with wheat bran that is inoculated with spawn and bagged. These blocks are refrigerated for a short time (to simulate fall temperatures), kept watered and left to grow in a ventilated low-light area. You can expect two to three crops, after which the block is depleted.

Orchids: The fact that some orchids are edible shouldn't surprise us, as vanilla flavouring is sourced from the cured pods of a member of this family, *Vanilla planifolia*. *Dendrobium* is the primary source of edible orchid flowers, with *Dendrobium chrysotoxum* blooms being popular for tea and the flowers of *D. phalaenopsis* (now *Vappodes phalaenopsis*) used as a cake and salad garnish.

DUO-PURPOSE PLANTERS

Whoever said you can't have your cake and eat it too certainly never thought of combining edible and ornamental plants in a container to create a space-saving duo-purpose planter. The only concern here is that everyone—especially children—with access to the pot should know the difference between what is safe to eat, along with what specific parts of the plant are edible, and the strictly ornamental features.

This pot grouping includes dwarf pomegranate and golden bay laurel.

Where I live on the mild West Coast, many gardeners have a tradition of revamping their front-door planters for winter. Some of my seasonal top-sellers are lingonberry (*Vaccinium vitis-idaea*) and wintergreen (*Gaultheria procumbens*), with their cheery red berries, and mountain pepper or *Tasmannia lanceolata* (formerly *Drimys lanceolata*), an evergreen shrub with glossy green leaves and contrasting red stems. All have culinary value, with the lingonberry and wintergreen both providing edible berries while the mountain pepper's leaves and fruits are dried as spice or as a pepper substitute. The latter is rather tender at zone-8 hardiness and will need to be grown in a container to be sheltered for winter in even the mildest parts of Canada.

Pot clusters that include some edibles are another option, and I have a grouping on the west side of my townhouse that gets rather hot with the full-sun exposure and brick siding behind it. For this location, I chose heat-loving plants, such as dwarf pomegranate (*Punica granatum* 'Nana') and golden bay laurel (*Laurus nobilis* 'Aurea'), to complement a lemon cypress that is surrounded by ornamental, non-edible yellow-flowering bidens and some gold-leaved sweet potato vine that might produce an edible tuber or two. It really is the best of both worlds when flowers and food can share a space, and it might even make the dedicated vegetable garden obsolete in your landscape.

Of course, there are many other edibles with aesthetic qualities readily available at most garden centres, including such vegetables as frilled mustards and red-leaved lettuces, and small fruits like the alpine strawberry 'Golden Alexandria' or pink-flowered *Fragaria* × *ananassa* 'Toscana', which also produces juicy red berries. Herbs round out my garden designs, with my top three being variegated lemon thyme (*Thymus* × *citriodorus* 'Variegata'), 'Red Rubin' basil (*Ocimum basilicum*) and *Salvia officinalis* 'Icterina'—all of which should be available in small pots at your nursery.

Cinderella pumpkin is popular with young gardeners.

GROWING FOOD WITH CHILDREN

For my three daughters, having a gardener for a father hasn't always been the easiest of experiences, as I have often worked long hours as a landscaper and come home late feeling quite tired. Then there were the many weekends I would drag them to botanical gardens or parks for research and yet they rarely complained, as they always found a flower, fruit, bird or turtle (thanks, VanDusen Botanical Garden) that fascinated them.

Even when we lived in an apartment, I would bring home a few pruned banana or palm leaves and watch my girls play jungle for hours on end. It is this connection to nature that allows children to grow up with a healthy respect for the environment that will last for a lifetime. I know this because my own love for nature came from my

Lexi and Rhys enjoy some quality time in the garden.

grandmother's garden. While that garden may have long since ceased to exist, the sense of curiosity and nurture it inspired continues to be an integral part of who I am to this day.

A recent visit to a small organic market garden reminded me of this, when I saw my friend Zdena Novy spend time in the vegetable patch with her grandchildren, Lexi and Rhys. They have their own growing beds and head-to-toe gardening attire, so getting dirty is not a problem. Lexi and Rhys help their grandparents with soil preparation, planting, harvesting and even chopping the compost—essentially learning the whole cycle of life and, most importantly, enjoying every minute of it.

When I encounter rambunctious kids at the nursery where I work, I only have to get their attention by introducing them to chocolate mint (*Mentha* × *piperita* 'Chocolate') or lemon balm (*Melissa officinalis*), in addition to that wintergreen "bubblegum plant" *Gaultheria procumbens*, before they settle down and I see a little light turn on in their eyes. Children need access to the natural world and, while parks and green spaces provide that experience to some degree, having their own garden space where they can choose to grow Cinderella pumpkins ('Rouge Vif d'Etampes') or wild strawberries (*Fragaria vesca*)—watching them flower and fruit right before their eyes—is when they become our future gardeners.

The Food Guide

NUTS AND SEEDS

I would like to start off with a cautionary tale about gathering nuts—in particular, those of the *Ginkgo biloba* tree. The reason you don't see ginkgo nuts very often is that male clones are being used exclusively as street trees, and not just to spare us from the female's fruit litter but, as I would find out in the worst possible way, also from the smell. I made a trip to the only place I know of where both a male and female tree are planted, the Riverview Arboretum in British Columbia, and began enthusiastically gathering the plum-like yellow fruits . . . it was only after a few minutes that I noticed, wafting up from the basket, a pungent cat-urine aroma, which is what my hands smelled like for a good week afterwards. The inner white-shelled nuts are not smelly once processed, and are actually sweetly resinous, but best consumed in moderation (10 or fewer per day) by chopping a few to add to chicken dishes.

Here are other trees for new seed and nut adventures:

Beech: Nuts from the European species (*Fagus sylvatica*) used to be pressed for cooking oil in times of shortages, such as during World War II, but contain more fagin (a mild natural toxin) than our native American beech, *F. grandifolia*, which is a better choice for that reason. Beechnuts can be eaten fresh, roasted, made into nut butter (after the skin is removed), or even used as a substitute for pecans in pie recipes. A few other nuts to consider include English walnut (*Juglans regia*), heartnut (*J. ailantifolia*) and buartnut, a butternut × heartnut cross.

Monkey Puzzle: Like *Ginkgo*, you need both male and female plants for harvests of seeds from the wind-pollinated monkey puzzle tree (*Araucaria araucana*). First introduced to Britain by botanist Archibald Menzies, who pocketed a few seeds from a dessert plate at a banquet hosted by the governor of Chile in 1795, these seeds are good fresh or roasted

OPPOSITE, CLOCKWISE FROM TOP LEFT: Dwarf pomegranate flowers; male hazelnut catkins; jujube fruits (*photo courtesy nataistock/iStock/Thinkstock*); pawpaw leaves; a linden tree (*photo courtesy IreneuszB/iStock/Thinkstock*); 'Beauty of Moscow' lilac.

LEFT: *Ginkgo biloba* fruits are unpleasantly pungent but the nuts inside are tasty. RIGHT: 'Flamingo' Chinese mahogany shoots are in high demand.

and remind me of hazelnut, while others claim they are reminiscent of pine nut.

Oak: Acorns can be eaten or made into a meal or flour by pulverizing the shelled nuts, pressing out the excess moisture, dehydrating and then grinding to a finer consistency in a grain mill. The best species for large and less bitter (lower tannin) nuts are white oak (*Quercus alba*), burr oak (*Q. macrocarpa*) and Oregon oak (*Q. garryana*).

EDIBLE SHOOTS AND SEED PODS

Edible shoots and seed pods are unexpected edibles, or those parts of the plant that we don't traditionally consider eating, and yet they can be surprisingly delicious.

Chinese Mahogany: Edible shoots, or the new growth of some shrubs and trees, are a potential food source, with *Toona sinensis* or Chinese mahogany being one most of us have not discovered yet. This Asian native is a suckering deciduous tree that is zone-6 hardy and often has red-tinged new growth. The savoury new shoots are highly sought after and often cooked with egg or bean curd, or dried as tea. The cultivar you are most likely to find is 'Flamingo', which has bright pink new growth that shifts to creamy yellow and matures green.

Japanese Raisin Tree: On my list of plant parts we don't usually consider for eating is the seed stalk or peduncle of the Japanese raisin tree or *Hovenia dulcis*. While the seeds themselves are not edible, the swollen stalks turn a reddish brown and have a sweet pear to raisin flavour; they are ready to harvest when they fall to the ground.

Nasturtium: While many of us use the leaves and flowers of nasturtium (*Tropaeolum majus*) in salads for their unique peppery-watercress taste, the seed pods are also edible and known in some circles as "poor man's capers." The trick is to pick them young (before they colour) to pickle with a little bay leaf or tarragon, after which they are ready to spice up your pasta dishes or salads.

Radish: Here's a vegetable most gardeners are familiar with—the common radish. While most of us are accustomed to eating the roots, when left to bolt, this plant produces young seed pods that have a delicious zest and crispness that can be enjoyed raw in salads or added to stir-fries. Try the heirloom variety (dating back to the 1860s) 'Rat's Tail', grown specifically for larger seed pods that are delicious when pickled.

Redbud: Both the eastern redbud (*Cercis canadensis*) and Judas tree (*C. siliquastrum*) provide seed pods that look and taste like snow peas; they need to be picked young and lightly cooked for best flavour.

Red orach produces striking salad greens.

EAT YOUR (COLOURFUL) GREENS

Somehow it is never quite enough for us to have delicious food with a sumptuous aroma—it has to look good too! And nothing enhances the plate better than a beautiful edible leaf that is any shade other than boring green. Just a few such dashes of colour make any salad more enticing, and in the edible landscape they offer much-needed contrast when grown as a border plant.

Arugula 'Dragon's Tongue': With oak-shaped leaves and reddish-purple veining, *Eruca sativa* is a beautiful pizza topping, adding spice without bitterness.

Burgundy Beet Leaves: The juvenile purplish-red foliage of 'Bull's Blood' beet (*Beta vulgaris*) is ever so slightly sweet; and if the leaves aren't harvested, it produces tasty roots with attractive concentric rings.

Colourful Kale: I would be remiss if I didn't mention trendy kale, with its well-known health benefits and impressive foliage colour range. Choose 'Redbor' (burgundy red), 'Scarlet' (frilled reddish purple), 'Blue Curled Scotch' (greenish blue) or 'Rainbow Lacinato' (turns from green and purple to purplish red in winter).

Mighty Mustards: Leafy vegetables of a different hue just seem to garner more attention because we expect them to taste better, and the mustards (*Brassica* spp.) never

LEFT: 'Red Frills' mustard greens make a great addition to sandwiches and salads. RIGHT: Tree spinach is delicious both raw and steamed.

disappoint. These are my middle daughter's favourite additions to sandwiches or salads, as Rochelle uses the wasabi-flavoured greens much the same way as we serve watercress (*Nasturtium officinale*). 'Red Frills' is her current favourite mustard, although there are many red- to purple-leaved cultivars, including 'Ruby Streaks', 'Osaka Purple' and 'Red Dragon'. These can be enjoyed as microgreens, although mature leaves are more pungent. While bolting can be a problem with summer heat, even the flowers are edible, so it's win-win whichever way this goes.

Red Orach: *Atriplex hortensis* 'Rubra' produces eye-catching fuchsia-pink foliage that tastes like lightly salted spinach and makes the salad bowl visually pop—there are also gold-leaved cultivars available.

Tree Spinach: *Chenopodium giganteum* is a tall annual quite common in Mexico and India, where the young pink-tinged leaves are used in salads or lightly steamed and eaten with a little butter.

WORLD CROPS

One of the best parts of living in a multicultural society is being exposed to foods and spices from around the world. And now, since we are happily appropriating their use, I consider them just as Canadian as maple syrup, and an essential part of the next generation of local cuisine. While

LEFT: Spiky chayote fruits. RIGHT: Hyacinth bean flowers.

some call it food fusion, I believe this is the natural evolution of the Western diet, which one can only hope will become more environmentally friendly as these choices become more readily available at local farms and in our own home gardens.

The following list includes common name, botanical name and description of edible portion:

Achocha: *Cyclanthera pedata*, young fruits eaten raw, older fruits cooked

Asparagus Pea: *Lotus tetragonolobus*, winged asparagus-flavoured pea

Bitter Melon: *Momordica charantia*, tangy-bitter squash, edible peel

Black Salsify: *Scorzonera hispanica*, European root crop

Chayote: *Sechium edule*, vine with spiky to smooth edible fruits

Chilean Wineberry: *Aristotelia chilensis*, edible black berries

Chinese Artichokes: *Stachys affinis*, edible white rhizomes

Cinnamon Vine: *Dioscorea polystachya*, nutty potato-like tubers

Cowpea: *Vigna unguiculata*, an African native plant grown for dried peas

Gobo or Burdock: *Arctium lappa*, oyster-flavoured roots

'Marguerite' sweet potato vine is a little-known but delicious edible.

Good King Henry: *Chenopodium bonus-henricus*, spinach-like pot herb

Hyacinth Bean: *Lablab purpureus*, flowers and beans edible when steamed

Jicama: *Pachyrhizus erosus*, yam bean produces small edible tubers

'Jing Orange' Okra: *Abelmoschus esculentus*, edible red to orange pods

Mayhaw: *Crataegus aestivalis*, edible hawthorn berries for jelly

Molokhia: *Corchorus olitorius*, annual Egyptian spinach

Mushroom Plant: *Rungia klossii*, leaves infuse a true mushroom flavour

Oca: *Oxalis tuberosa*, South American edible tubers of different colours

Sylvetta: *Diplotaxis eurocoides*, annual wild arugula for salads

Vietnamese Coriander: *Persicaria odorata*, edible leaves for salads and soups

INCIDENTAL EDIBLES

Free food is always a good thing, and what if you are composting or tossing out perfectly edible plants without knowing it? Here is a sampling of ornamentals that often go unrecognized as food:

Dahlia: This prolific bloomer is an incidental edible, with tubers that were once a staple of the ancient Aztec diet. The flavour can range from watery to wonderful depending on the cultivar, so I suggest you wait to plant until the new DELIDAHLIAS are available. Selected for eating by the Swiss breeder Lubera, the varieties include 'Black Jack' (asparagus and kohlrabi flavour), 'Buga München' (parsley), 'Kennedy' (fennel and celery) and 'Hoamatland' (black salsify). Once peeled, dahlia tubers can be mashed, boiled, steamed or roasted, just like potatoes.

Edible Canna: *Canna indica* var. *edulis* is another ancient edible of South America, with tubers roasted until sumptuously sweet. The peeled young shoots can also be thrown into a stir-fry as a tasty bamboo-shoot replacement.

Solomon's Seal: Shade gardeners will be thankful to add another edible to their pantry in the form of the new shoots or rhizomes of Solomon's seal—including the species *Polygonatum biflorum*, *P. commutatum*, *P. multiflorum* and *P. odoratum*. The young shoots are harvested in early spring, lightly cooked and eaten like asparagus. The starchy roots require boiling and drying multiple times, which hardly seems worth the bother. Just remember that the berries and seeds of all the species are poisonous.

Sweet Potato Vine: One of the best examples of an unrealized edible that I know of is the ornamental *Ipomoea batatas*, which is the same species as its vegetable cousin but primarily grown for brilliant foliage. When dug up in the fall, the tubers are often small and distorted (not like the huge one shown, which was from 'Marguerite') but can still be thinly sliced into medallions and deep-fried, rivalling any commercial French fry, especially with a little chipotle sauce.

Variegated Corn: Ornamental *Zea mays* var. *japonica*, often used much like a grass in dramatic container displays or as a centrepiece in large annual beds, produces small cobs of deep maroon seeds. Once cured, the seeds can be made into nearly hull-less popcorn; although smaller than traditional popcorn, they are delicious.

EAT YOUR ENEMIES

While there are a lot of ways to retaliate against pesky weeds—some gardeners pluck them whole and hang them on a clothesline to scorch in the sun, while others hack them to bits with a sharp hoe—I say the best vengeance is to eat them.

Daisy: An edible weed at hand is English daisy or *Bellis perennis*, whose tiny flowers invade our lawns. While they can be a little bitter, a few plucked petals lightly sprinkled on salads add a little bite without being overpowering.

Purslane is just one of many edible weeds.

Dandelion: *Taraxacum officinale* is a lawn weed that was actually brought to North America by early settlers as a medicinal plant, and which has been enjoyed as food by French Canadians for hundreds of years. I cook young dandelion leaves with bacon to serve with a poached egg on toast for a rustic eggs benedict much favoured by my family. The flowers are also edible, with a sweet, crunchy texture, and commonly used to make wine . . . but I will warn you that dandelion wine is a very acquired taste!

Purslane: My first experience with edible weeds came long before my professional gardening years, when I was just a young boy watching my East Indian neighbour carefully harvest *Portulaca oleracea* growing

LEFT: German chamomile makes a soothing herbal tea. RIGHT: 'Hillary's Sweet Lemon' is delicious in herbal tea and aids digestion.

in the gravel around her home. She saw my interest and invited me and my family over for lunch that day. The portulaca was served in a delicious curry with fresh naan bread and a yogurt dip to help those not used to the heat of the spice—and I was introduced to my now-favourite cuisine.

Stinging Nettle: Some 10 years later, I would be working on a 40-acre (16 ha) estate where I would help head gardener Wim Hunfeld carefully pick *Urtica dioica* for his family's supper. Once the plant is cooked, the sting is gone and replaced with a pleasant celery-mint flavour and plenty of vitamins.

Weeds to Grow or Get to Know: There are other common edible weeds out there, including chickweed (*Stellaria media*), pigweed (*Amaranthus retroflexus*), and sheep's sorrel (*Rumex acetosella*), but if you are unsure about identification, seed companies such as Richters and West Coast Seeds are now making these plants available so that you can grow them in your garden as a food crop.

HERBAL TEAS

Herbal teas are liquid comfort foods—and, with so many flavour choices available, you are bound to find a favourite you can grow in your garden.

Lemony: This is *the* flavour many of us enjoy in our teas, and it also aids digestion. For the Portuguese, there is none better than lemon verbena (*Aloysia citrodora*), although lemongrass (*Cymbopogon citratus*) and *Mentha* 'Hillary's Sweet Lemon' are tied for a close second.

Minty: While mint is the queen of herbal teas, there are so many selections that it can be hard to make a choice. Your best bets for hot teas include 'Moroccan', traditionally served with green tea, along

Drying green tea leaves.

with true peppermint (*Mentha × piperita*), the beautifully variegated 'Ginger' mint (*Mentha gracilis*), and the spicy 'Orange' and newer 'Strawberry' mint that work so well with chocolate.

Savoury: Teas like tomato-mint or spinach-chive, made from herbs and dehydrated vegetables, are trending, with parsley, sage (*Salvia officinalis*), cilantro and thyme all figuring prominently in this taste category.

Soothing: We also drink herbal teas for subtle medicinal purposes, such as calming—and perennial Roman chamomile (*Chamaemelum nobile*) and annual German chamomile (*Matricaria chamomilla*) are the most popular for this. Linden flower (*Tilia*) and lemon balm (*Melissa officinalis*) also have significant anti-anxiety qualities.

Sweet: Dried leaves from the natural sweetening herb *Stevia rebaudiana*, a tender plant from Brazil and Paraguay, are two hundred times sweeter than traditional white sugar but without the calories. While we can't overwinter this species outdoors in Canada, we can certainly grow it in summer and stockpile the foliage (dried leaves are sweeter than fresh) for year-round use as a tea sweetener.

To preserve tea herbs for drying, pick flowers as soon as they open, and cut leafy plants in late morning when the dew has dissipated, in order to prevent mildew. Your herb bundles should be free of blemishes from pests or disease. Hang upside down in a dark warm space with low humidity (not the kitchen). Air drying varies with moisture content and humidity.

HOW TO MAKE GREEN TEA

Whether you prefer Earl Grey, oolong or green tea, all are made from the leaves of just one plant, *Camellia sinensis*, although each variety may be flavoured or processed differently. There are as many techniques for processing and brewing fresh green tea as there are plants in your garden, so consider this simple method just one of many ways to procure that perfect cuppa.

1. **Harvesting:** Harvest your *Camellia sinensis* leaves when a new flush of growth occurs—usually spring through early summer and late summer to early autumn—with the first pick being the most flavourful. Some tea aficionados will only harvest the top two leaves and bud, although the young foliage immediately below this is fine too.
2. **Natural Drying:** Spread your tea leaves in a single layer over a mat (I use a woven reed mat, as it helps to absorb

moisture), a rack or any clean surface, and allow to wilt naturally for two to three hours, preferably in the shade. This helps reduce the water content in the leaves, and will make processing easier and improve flavour.

3. **Shaqing:** This brief heat treatment helps to stop further oxidization of the leaves, removing the organic grassy smell and enriching the flavour. This can be achieved by dry roasting in an open skillet or wok over a low heat for several minutes, stirring the leaves constantly so they don't get crispy. The idea is to remove an additional 30 to 40 percent of the remaining moisture, which also facilitates the hand rolling.
4. **Hand Rolling:** Using the palms of your hands, roll the heat-treated leaves when they are either hot or cold, although the latter preserves the green colour. This step helps to break down the leaves' structure and make them better for brewing or drying. Rolled leaves can be brewed immediately or preserved by placing on a baking sheet and drying in the oven for 20 minutes at 250F/121C. Allow to cool, and store in an airtight container.
5. **Brewing:** Your freshly processed green tea will not be as strong as commercial blends, so you may wish to use more leaves than is your normal habit. Also, sample your tea from time to time while it is steeping, as the flavours are complex and you don't want to miss that perfect balance of colour and taste!

SUMMER CORDIALS

While linden and elderflower cordials have already been mentioned, there are other blooms that can be used to make delicious summer beverages. Cordials are non-alcoholic drink concentrates—made from the leaves or flowers of edible plants—that are mixed with water or carbonated beverages to create refreshing drinks. The concentrates are generally made by adding flowers or leaves to a syrup base (equal parts water and sugar) and allowing the flavours to infuse the syrup, after which the base is strained and ready for use. Here are some other favourites for flavouring cordial:

Gorse: *Ulex europaeus* is found in British Columbia as an invasive plant. Its bright yellow blooms infuse a subtle coconut flavour to cordial, and it is also used to make a popular rustic wine. I'm not suggesting you plant this one, but if you have access to unsprayed gorse plants in a pristine area, using the flowers will help to prevent it from further self-seeding and spreading.

Milkweed: The strongly fragrant blossoms of *Asclepias syriaca* are nectar-rich and highly attractive to butterflies, and they make a delicious pink cordial that can be mixed with gin or Prosecco for a thirst-quenching summer cocktail.

Pineapple Sage: *Salvia elegans* not only brings its unique flavour, but the brilliant red blossoms also tint the cordial an eye-catching coral red, which dilutes to a beautiful pink.

Tea Herbs: Cordials can also be made from leaves and flowers of all herbs used to make hot teas, such as mint (*Mentha* spp.) and

LEFT: Golden pineapple sage in flower. RIGHT: Everything you need to make elderflower cordial.

lemon balm (*Melissa officinalis*), for delicious iced beverages in warm weather.

FRUIT AND HERB SYRUPS

Syrup is easy to make and a very versatile base to have around the kitchen. The potential uses are endless—drizzle it over vanilla ice cream, use it to flavour teas or lemonades, mix it with plain yogurt or cottage cheese, add it to carbonated water or cocktails, or treat it as a substitute for maple syrup on waffles or crepes—the end result is always delicious.

Fruit Syrup: A simple recipe of 1 part white sugar to 1 part water and 1½ parts fresh or frozen fruit (peeled and cut into small pieces where necessary) brought to a boil, and then simmered for 20 minutes and strained, will work for almost any fruit—with some of my favourites being blueberry, peach, rhubarb and blackberry.

Medicinal Syrup: Another possibility is a simple medicinal syrup, such as cough syrup made from the herb white horehound (*Marrubium vulgare*), easily produced by steeping about ½ cup (120 mL) fresh or ¼ cup (60 mL) dried leaves in 2 cups (475 mL) boiling water, straining and dissolving into an equal amount of honey. Some gardeners also add sage (*Salvia officinalis*) to increase the effectiveness of this natural cough syrup—keep this to about half the amount of horehound added and increase the water to 3 cups (710 mL) when making the base.

Herb-infused Honeys: These are another easy-to-prepare option and they are wonderful drizzled over pancakes or crepes, used in salad dressings or meat marinades, added to hot or cold teas for sweetening, or simply enjoyed on toast with butter. Herb-infused honeys are prepared by using 1–2 tablespoons (15–30 mL) dried herbs per 1 cup (250 mL) honey, preferably a light, mild-tasting type that doesn't overpower the herbal flavour. The dried herbs are simply added to the bottom of a mason jar, with the honey poured over top—allow to infuse for at least a week, after which it should be tested for flavour. Once the desired taste is acquired, the mixture can be strained through cheesecloth and stored in a cool, dark space. Some good herbal choices are lemon balm, chamomile, rosemary, thyme and lavender. These can be spiced up using vanilla bean (coarsely chopped), cardamom pods, star anise seeds, cinnamon sticks or freshly grated ginger.

SWEET AND SAVOURY JELLIES

Jellies are a way of preserving the tastes of nature, some of which you may not have considered before.

Haw Jelly: Hawthorn berries were a favourite of the "father of foragers," Euell Gibbons, who referred to his spread as "haw jelly." This is also known in England as hedgerow jelly, where one-seed hawthorn (*Crataegus monogyna*) is often found. Other species of hawthorn to consider are Washington (*C. phaenopyrum*) and English (*C. laevigata*, syn. *oxyacantha*), but keep in mind that the berry or haw seeds contain cyanide and must be removed before processing.

Rowan Jelly: Try this old-world Scandinavian food, made from mountain ash (*Sorbus aucuparia*). Traditionally served with game, such as venison, there is a slight bitterness to rowan jelly, even when prepared properly from berries that have been exposed to hard frosts on the tree or picked and put into the freezer (which sweetens them); combining the berries with crabapple or plum will make it more palatable.

Savoury Jelly: Savoury jellies, such as apple-thyme, hot pepper, redcurrant-rosemary or grapefruit-marjoram, are the perfect foil for those goat-cheese appetizers. Or use as a flavour-enhancing glaze when roasting meat.

It's fun to get creative with flavours, with mixes like elderberry with sumac or the little-known beautyberry (*Callicarpa americana*).

Or mix up a batch of apple butter—the epitome of comfort food in a jar. Choose tart apples, such as 'Gravenstein' or 'Granny Smith' (being sure to remove the seeds), for tangy spiciness and a smooth, thick texture best spooned onto toast.

If you are reluctant to use commercial pectin because it may contain GMO ingredients (such as corn-based dextrose), there are many fruits with naturally high pectin that you can cook with—including apples, currants, quince (*Cydonia*), plums, gooseberries, crabapples and blackberries.

HERB-INFUSED VINEGARS

Making herbal-infused vinegars is almost a rite of passage for novice gardeners, but just be sure you have a plan for how to use them. Besides working as delicious vinaigrettes for salads and sushi condiments, a splash of herbal vinegar will add zest to soup, chili, barbecue sauce and meat marinades. You can use most types beyond the traditional white—with red wine, sherry, malt, cider, champagne and rice vinegars all adding their own panache.

The best part of creating your own herbal vinegars is that the potential flavour combinations are endless, and producing

Red shiso gives vinegar a red tint.

your own signature blend is easily achieved with a little trial and error—with the resulting vintages making excellent gifts for your fellow gardeners.

For a basic recipe, use 1 cup (250 mL) loosely packed fresh herbs for every 2 cups (475 mL) vinegar; these should be fresh cut, washed clean and patted dry. Mix the herbs and vinegar in a glass bottle or jar, cover (avoiding metal lids) and store in a cool dark place for 2 to 6 weeks. Gently stir every few days and after 14 days taste weekly, allowing it to steep until you are satisfied with the flavour. Strain the finished herbal vinegar through cheesecloth to remove the infusing herbs and spices, and store in a dark space, as sun exposure will eventually cause clouding.

Some of the best herb combinations for infusing include:

- Lemon thyme and sage
- Tarragon and peeled garlic
- Pineapple sage and spearmint
- Dillweed and dried peppers
- And rosemary, various mints and salad burnet (*Sanguisorba minor*) all combine well with other herbs

There are also herbs that tint and flavour vinegar:

- Purple basil (reddish purple)
- Red shiso (burgundy red)
- Dillweed flowers (greenish yellow)
- Chive flowers (pink)
- Pineapple sage flowers (reddish)

Spices such as juniper berry (*Juniperus communis*), bay leaf, peppercorns or allspice can also be added at the infusing stage for extra flavour, but these should be kept whole and not ground, as the fine particles will eventually cloud the finished product.

TASTY TEMPURA

Tempura is a Japanese dish of seafood or vegetables deep-fried in batter. While most of us can agree that this may not be the healthiest way to prepare food, it is delicious.

Both sunflower buds and wasabi leaves make tasty tempura.

The best way to lighten the meal is to start with a simple batter that is applied ice cold (refrigerate until you are ready to use), while also keeping your oil at a consistent 350F (180C) for quick cooking. Longer cooking time will result in a heavy, greasy tempura, so don't fry too many items at once, as this quickly lowers the oil's temperature.

For a basic batter, blend 1 egg yolk with 1 cup (250 mL) cold sparkling water (which makes the batter lighter), after which you add ¼ cup (60 mL) cornstarch and ¾ cup (180 mL) rice flour. Mix using chopsticks, being careful not to overwork the batter, and refrigerate immediately. Then you are ready to choose from a nearly limitless array of delights to deep-fry. I suggest you start with squash blossoms stuffed with ricotta or soft goat cheese and spiced with a little fresh chopped parsley (flat leaf, of course) and marjoram. My daughter Nicole cooks these for me several times a year and it is a good way to make use of those early male flowers that show up before the female blooms.

Try these tempura treats:

Aralia: *Aralia elata* buds in tempura batter are gourmet fare, although you do have to pick these terminal buds in early spring before thorns begin to develop. The buds have a distinct asparagus flavour and are highly sought after in Korean and Japanese cuisine.

Dandelion: Leaves and flowers (be careful to choose pristine plants that have not been sprayed with pesticides) make a delicious tempura best eaten warm with a curry sauce or drizzled with honey.

Sunflower: Unopened sunflower buds are another good candidate, with a lovely artichoke flavour.

Wasabi: Try using wasabi foliage (*Wasabia japonica*) as a tempura vegetable. The smaller leaves cook to a perfect crisp, are ideal for dipping and retain a mild wasabi-horseradish taste.

Glossary

ANCIENT GARDEN ORIGIN: Bred or domesticated in ancient times with no official record

ANNUAL: A plant that completes its growing cycle within one year and then dies

ANTHERS: The pollen end of the stamen, or male flower organ

ARIL: The fleshy covering of some seeds, including pomegranate

AWARD OF GARDEN MERIT: A plant award based on performance, given by the Royal Horticultural Society (RHS)

BINE: A climbing plant that twines around a support

BLISTER RUST: A plant fungus, typically with blister-like spore bodies

BRACT: A specialized leaf that may appear like a flower petal

BRIX: A scale to determine the sugar content of fruit

BROADLEAF EVERGREEN: An evergreen plant with broad leaves instead of scales or needles

CAMBIUM: A layer of living plant tissue that is largely responsible for growth

CANDLE: The common name for the unopened new growth shoots of pines

CHLOROTIC: Pale foliage or yellowish appearance due to insufficient chlorophyll

CLONE: Plants that are genetically identical, often propagated vegetatively

COLUMNAR: Plants with a thin, upright growth habit, like a column

CORM: A swollen underground stem that acts as a bulb

CROSS-POLLINATION: The transfer of pollen from one plant to another, usually of the same species

CULTIVAR: A cultivated plant variety

DECIDUOUS: Trees or shrubs that shed their leaves seasonally, usually autumn

DIOECIOUS: Species with male and female structures on separate plants

DRUPE: A fruit with a fleshy outer portion that surrounds a pit or stone

FROND: A large divided leaf (with exceptions) typical of ferns

FERTILE FROND: Specialized fern leaves that support the spore structures

GARDEN ORIGIN: Originated from cultivation, as opposed to in the wild

GLOCHIDS: Hair-like spines found on some cactus

HAW: The fruit or pome of a hawthorn (*Crataegus*)

HERBACEOUS: Plants with no permanent woody structure above ground

HYBRID: A cross of two plant varieties or species

INDETERMINATE: Plant growth that is not restricted by genetic disposition

INTERGENERIC: A cross between two species from different genera

LEAFLET: Part of a compound leaf found on a plant

MARGINAL PLANT: Plant that naturally thrives in shallow water or bogs

MONOECIOUS: Having separate male and female flowers on the same plant

NECTAR: A sweet flower secretion that attracts pollinators

NODE: The place on the stem or branch where the leaf or bud is attached

PALMATE: A leaf form similar to an outstretched hand

PEDUNCLE: A plant stem that supports flowers or seeds

PERFECT FLOWER: A flower that possesses both male and female structures

PERMACULTURE: A system of agriculture based on using natural ecosystems

PH: A numeric scale (0 to 14) used to indicate acidity or alkalinity of soils

PINNATE: A compound leaf with leaflets on both sides of the stem

POLLEN: A powdery plant substance that contains male reproductive cells

POME: A fleshy fruit from the apple subtribe (Malinae) of the rose family

PSEUDOSTEM: A plant trunk or stem made from highly packed leaf sheaths

PUBESCENT: Plants having a covering of short hairs or down

PUP: The common name for a lateral shoot on banana plants

PYRIFORM: Shaped like the common pear

RACEME: A flower form with blooms borne on short stems along a common axis

REFLEXED: A flower structure or petal that flexes backwards

RHIZOMATOUS: A plant with modified underground stems that grow horizontally

RHS: Royal Horticultural Society, based in England

SCION: A detached piece of living plant material used for grafting

SELF-FERTILE: Capable of producing seeds or fruit without cross-pollination

SELF-SEEDING: Capable of reproducing by seed without human intervention

SEMI-EVERGREEN: Plants that retain some of their leaves during mild winter temperatures

SERRATED: A leaf form with a saw-tooth margin or edge

LEFT: Asparagus pea seeds. RIGHT: 'Galeux d'Eysines' pumpkin.

SPECIES: A two-word plant name that combines genus and a descriptive term

SPORT: A genetic mutation that differs from the rest of the plant

SPUR: A fruiting structure or spike that supports the flower

STAMEN: The entire male reproductive organ of a flower

STERILE FROND: A fern leaf without reproductive spores

STIGMA: The female reproductive organ of a flower, which sits on the style

SUBSHRUB: A short woody plant such as lavender and cranberry

TUBER: A fleshy underground growth of the stem or rhizome, like potato

WATER SPROUT: Sucker that arises above ground on bushes and trees

ZONE HARDINESS: Plant rating system determined by temperature tolerance or other conditions

Index

Page numbers in **bold** refer to photos

OPPOSITE, CLOCKWISE FROM TOP LEFT: 'Aureum' golden oregano; hummingbird on bee balm; hollyhock; an Abbotsford vineyard; honeybee on summer aster.

About the Author

Rochelle Lascelle photo

MIKE LASCELLE is a nursery manager and certified arborist, with a 35-year horticultural background that includes estate gardening, landscape construction and design. He has authored several books on plant selection and garden design, as well as articles for *Gardens West*, *Canadian Gardening*, *Coastal Grower* and *GardenWise*, and currently writes a biweekly garden column for the *Maple Ridge News*.